P9-DDX-435

Stories for the Heart

THE THIRD COLLECTION

Originally published as
Stories for a Kindred Heart

TORONTO PUBLIC LIBRARY
Sale of this book
supports literacy programs

Stories for the Heart

THE THIRD COLLECTION

*Over 100 Stories Celebrating
Friendship, Family, and Love*

COMPILED BY ALICE GRAY &
BARBARA BAUMGARDNER

Multnomah® Publishers *Sisters, Oregon*

STORIES FOR THE HEART, THE THIRD COLLECTION
published by Multnomah Publishers, Inc.
© 2000 by Alice Gray and Barbara Baumgardner
International Standard Book Number: 1-57673-773-X
Originally published as *Stories for a Kindred Heart*

Cover illustration by Georgie Mize
Background image by Photodisc

Scripture quotations are from:
The Holy Bible, New International Version (NIV)
© 1973, 1984 by International Bible Society,
used by permission of Zondervan Publishing House
Also quoted:
The Message © 1993 by Eugene H. Peterson
The Holy Bible, New King James Version (NKJV) © 1984 by Thomas Nelson, Inc.
The Living Bible (TLB) © 1971. Used by permission of Tyndale House Publishers, Inc.
All rights reserved.
The Holy Bible, King James Version (KJV)

Multnomah is a trademark of Multnomah Publishers, Inc.,
and is registered in the U.S. Patent and Trademark Office.
The colophon is a trademark of Multnomah Publishers, Inc.

Stories for the Heart is a trademark of Multnomah Publishers
and is registered in the U.S. Patent and Trademark Office.

Printed in the United States of America
ALL RIGHTS RESERVED
No part of this publication may be reproduced, stored in a retrieval system, or
transmitted, in any form or by any means—electronic, mechanical,
photocopying, recording, or otherwise—without prior written permission.
For information:
MULTNOMAH PUBLISHERS, INC.
POST OFFICE BOX 1720
SISTERS, OREGON 97759

Library of Congress Cataloging-in-Publication Data:

Stories for the heart: over 100 stories celebrating friends, family, and love / compiled by
Alice Gray and Barbara Baumgardner.
     p.cm.
  ISBN 1-57673-704-7 (pbk.)
  1.Christian life. I. Gray, Alice. 1939– II. Baumgardner, Barbara, 1931–
  BV4515.2.S835 2000
  242—dc21

                                                                    00–008678

01 02 03 04 05 06 — 11 10 9 8 7 6 5 4 3

There is no greater joy
than having hearts entwined with others
through time, laughter, and tears.

A Special Thank You to:

Doreen Button, Jennifer Gates,
Karen Jamison, Casandra Lindell, Teri Sharp.

Thank you for sharing your love of wonderful stories

and for your sweet friendship.

Our hearts are bound together by God's love.

Blessings,

Alice

My love and gratitude to those too-numerous-to-name

kindred friends who encouraged me, prayed for me,

and kept asking, "Is it a book yet?"

Finally, dear ones, it is. Let's go to lunch!

Hugs,

Barbara

CONTENTS

Encouragement

Friendship

Family

Memories

Because We Care

Encouragement

WHEN THE WINDS ARE STRONG

If your life is windy these days—
winds of change, winds of adversity,
or maybe the constant winds of demands and expectations
that leave you feeling, well…
windblown—take heart.
As my mother used to say,
"The roots grow deep when the winds are strong."

CHARLES R. SWINDOLL

THE GIFT

GARY SWANSON

FROM *FOCUS ON THE FAMILY* MAGAZINE

*T*he mother sat on the simulated-leather chair in the doctor's office, picking nervously at her fingernails. Wrinkles of worry lined her forehead as she watched 5-year-old Kenny sitting on the rug before her.

He is small for his age and a little too thin, she thought. His fine blond hair hung down smooth and straight to the top of his ears. White gauze bandages encircled his head, covering his eyes and pinning his ears back.

In his lap he bounced a beaten-up teddy bear. It was the pride of his life, yet one arm was gone and one eye was missing. Twice his mother had tried to throw the bear away, to replace it with a new one, but he had fussed so much she had relented. She tipped her head slightly to the side and smiled at him. It's really about all he has, she sighed to herself.

A nurse appeared in the doorway. "Kenny Ellis," she announced, and the young mother scooped up the boy and followed the nurse toward the examination room. The hallway smelled of rubbing alcohol and bandages. Children's crayon drawings lined the walls.

"The doctor will be with you in a moment," the nurse said with an efficient smile. "Please be seated."

The mother placed Kenny on the examination table. "Be careful, Honey, not to fall off."

"Am I up very high, Mother?"

"No dear, but be careful."

Kenny hugged his teddy bear tighter. "I don't want Grr-face to fall either."

The mother smiled. The smile twisted at the corners into a frown of concern. She brushed the hair out of the boy's face and caressed his cheek, soft as thistledown, with the back of her hand. As the office music drifted into a haunting version of "Silent Night," she remembered the accident for the thousandth time.

She had been cooking things on the back burners for years. But there it was, sitting right out in front, the water almost boiling for oatmeal.

The phone rang in the living room. It was another one of those "free offers" that cost so much. At the very moment she returned the phone to the table, Kenny screamed in the kitchen, the galvanizing cry of pain that frosts a mother's veins.

She winced again at the memory of it and brushed aside a warm tear slipping down her cheek. Six weeks they had waited for this day to come. "We'll be able to take the bandages off the week before Christmas," the doctor had said.

The door to the examination room swept open, and Dr. Harris came in. "Good morning, Mrs. Ellis," he said brightly. "How are you today?"

"Fine, thank you," she said. But she was too apprehensive for small talk.

Dr. Harris bent over the sink and washed his hands carefully. He was cautious with his patients but careless about himself. He could seldom find time to get a haircut, and his straight black hair hung a little long over his collar. His loosened tie allowed his collar to be open at the throat.

"Now then," he said, sitting down on a stool, "let's have a look."

Gently he snipped at the bandage with scissors and unwound it from Kenny's head. The bandage fell away, leaving two flat squares of gauze taped directly over Kenny's eyes. Dr. Harris lifted the edges of the tape slowly, trying not to hurt the boy's tender skin.

Kenny slowly opened his eyes, blinked several times as if the sudden light hurt. Then he looked at his mother and grinned. "Hi, Mom," he said.

Choking and speechless, the mother threw her arms around Kenny's neck. For several minutes she could say nothing as she hugged the boy and wept in thankfulness. Finally, she looked at Dr. Harris with tear-filled eyes. "I don't know how we'll ever be able to pay you," she said.

"We've been over all that before," the doctor interrupted with a wave of his hand. "I know how things are for you and Kenny. I'm glad I could help."

The mother dabbed at her eyes with a well-used handkerchief, stood up, and took Kenny's hand. But just as she turned toward the door, Kenny pulled away and stood for a long moment looking uncertainly at the doctor. Then he held his teddy bear up by its one arm to the doctor.

"Here," he said. "Take my Grr-face. He ought to be worth a lot of money."

Dr. Harris quietly took the broken bear in his two hands. "Thank you, Kenny. This will more than pay for my services."

The last few days before Christmas were especially good for Kenny and his mother. They sat together in the long evenings, watching the Christmas tree lights twinkle on and off. Bandages had covered Kenny's eyes for six weeks, so he seemed reluctant to close them in sleep. The fire dancing in the fireplace, the snowflakes sticking to his bedroom windows, the two small packages under the tree—all the lights and colors of the holiday fascinated him. And then, on Christmas Eve, Kenny's mother answered the doorbell. No one was there, but a large box was on the porch wrapped in shiny gold paper with a broad red ribbon and bow. A tag attached to the bow identified the box as intended for Kenny Ellis.

With a grin, Kenny tore the ribbon off the box, lifted the lid, and pulled out a teddy bear—his beloved Grr-face. Only now it had a new arm of brown corduroy and two new button eyes that glittered in the soft Christmas light. Kenny didn't seem to mind that the new arm did not match the other one. He just hugged his teddy bear and laughed.

Among the tissue in the box, the mother found a card. "Dear Kenny," it read. "I can sometimes help put boys and girls back together, but Mrs. Harris had to help me repair Grr-face. She's a better bear doctor than I am. Merry Christmas! Dr. Harris."

"Look, Mother," Kenny smiled, pointing to the button eyes. "Grr-face can see again—just like me!"

THE RED PURSE

LOUISE MOERI
FROM *VIRTUE* MAGAZINE

I know we are not supposed to judge people, but where Kennie Jablonsky was concerned, I found it impossible. I decided he was the wrong person in the wrong kind of work.

I'm a swing-shift nursing supervisor and it's my job to evaluate workers' performances at Homeland Convalescent Hospital.

Kennie Jablonsky was a new employee, tall and very strong, not bad looking with his blond hair cut to the collar and dark green eyes. After a few weeks' probation, I had to admit he was clean, punctual and reasonably efficient. But I just didn't like him.

Kennie Jablonsky looked like a hood. I knew the neighborhood he came from—a cesspool of gangs, drugs and violence. His language was street talk, his manner wry, his walk springy and controlled like a boxer's and his expression closed-off like the steel door on a bank vault. He seemed too large and carefully controlling of a powerful will to be able to fit into a highly specialized teamwork of a convalescent hospital.

The vast majority of our patients come to us in the final stages of terminal disease or with the most terminal of all diseases—old age. They come to us crippled, weakened, confused and defeated, no longer able to function out in the world. Many have lost the faculty of rational thought, a casualty of failing health and a world that often seems brutal and indifferent.

Mary B. was one of those. Attendants call her Mary B. because she was one of four Marys in the West Wing. At 94 years, Mary B. was frail as a cobweb. She outlived her husband and sisters, and if she had any children they had long since abandoned her. She was in almost constant motion as long as she was awake.

Mary B. had an obsession that someone had taken her purse. She searched for it all hours of the day and night. Unless tied to her bed or wheelchair, she would go through the door onto the street, into the men's wards, through the laundry room and into the kitchen, mindlessly searching and never giving up. When restrained, she wanted her wheelchair in the hallway, where she stopped everyone who came near.

"Can you lend me a comb?" she asked. "I've lost mine. It was in my red purse. My money is gone, too. Where is my purse? Where is my purse?"

Every day it was the same, until Mary B.'s queries became background noise, like the sound of hot carts loaded with trays rumbling down the halls, the hum of air conditioning or the static of the intercom.

We all knew Mary didn't have a purse. But on occasion someone would stop to listen to her out of kindness and concern, although we were furiously busy. Still, most of us maneuvered around her with, "Sure, Mary, if I see your purse I'll bring it back."

Most of us—but one.

The last thing I expected of Kennie Jablonsky was that he would listen to Mary B., but strangely, he always had a word for her.

What is he up to? I wondered, watching him. My first suspicion was that he might be working here to steal drugs. I thought I had spotted a potential troublemaker.

Every day as Mary B. stopped him to ask about her purse, and as Kennie promised to look for it, my suspicions grew. Finally I concluded that Kennie was planning something involving Mary. He's going to steal drugs, I told myself, and somehow hide them around Mary. Then some accomplice will come in and sneak them out of the hospital. I was so sure of all this that I set up more security systems around the drug dispensing department.

One afternoon, just before supper, I saw Kennie walking down the hall with a plastic grocery bag in his hand. It was heavy.

This is it, I told myself, scrambling from behind my desk. I started after him, but realized I needed more evidence. I halted behind a laundry cart, piled high with baskets.

It was tall enough to conceal me, but I still could see Kennie clearly as he strode down the hall toward Mary B. in her wheelchair.

He reached Mary and suddenly turned, looking over his shoulder. I dodged out of sight but I could still see him peering up and down the hall. It was clear he didn't want anyone to see what he was doing.

He raised the bag. I froze...until he pulled out a red purse.

Mary's thin old hands flew up to her face in a gesture of wonder and joy, then flew out hungrily. Like a starved child taking bread, Mary B. grabbed the red purse. She held it for a moment, just to see it, then pressed it to her breast, rocking it like a baby.

Kennie turned and glanced sharply all around. Satisfied no one was watching, he leaned over, unsnapped the flap, reached in and showed Mary a red comb, small coin purse and a pair of children's toy spectacles. Tears of joy were pouring down Mary's face. At least, I guessed they were. Tears streaked my face, too.

Kennie patted Mary lightly on the shoulder, crumpled the plastic grocery bag, threw it into the nearby waste can, then went about his work down the hall.

I walked back to my desk, sat down, reached into the bottom drawer and brought out my battered old Bible. Turning to the seventh chapter of Matthew, I asked the Lord to forgive me...

At the end of the shift, I stood near the door used by the aides coming to and leaving work. Kennie came bouncing down the hall carrying his coat and radio.

"Hi, Kennie," I said. "How's everything going? Do you think you'll like this job?"

Kennie looked surprised, then shrugged. "It's the best I'll ever get," he grunted.

"Nursing is a good career," I ventured. An idea was growing. "Uh, have you ever thought of going on to college for a registered nursing degree?"

Kennie snorted. "Are you kidding? I ain't got a chance for anything like that. The nurse's aide course was free or I wouldn't have *this* job."

I knew this was true. Kennie set down his radio and pulled on his coat. "Take a miracle for me to go to college," he said. "My old man's in San Quentin and my old lady does cocaine."

I clenched my teeth but still smiled. "Miracles do happen," I told him. "Would you go to college if I could find a way to help you with the money?"

Kennie stared at me. All at once the hood vanished and I caught a glimpse of what could be. "Yes!" was all he said. But it was enough.

"Good night, Kennie," I said as he reached for the door handle. "I'm sure something can be worked out."

I was sure, too, that in Room 306 of the West Wing, Mary B. was sleeping quietly, both her arms wrapped around a red purse.

ICE CREAM PARTY

ROCHELLE M. PENNINGTON

I stopped at Dairy Queen, purchased a sandwich, and sat down in the crowded dining room next to a family celebrating their son's basketball game over an ice-cream cake. Since the aisles were especially narrow, I soon felt like I was a part of the party.

"So, your team must have won this afternoon," I commented.

The little fellow smiled and wholeheartedly announced, "No, we lost 24 to 2!"

"Well, you must have made the only basket then," I said.

"No, I missed all of the eight shots I took, but three of them did hit the rim."

This child was elated. I was confused. They were celebrating because his team lost the game and because he had missed eight baskets! Seldom am I at a loss of words, but the only response I could muster up at that moment was a blank stare and a very large, insincere looking smile. Absolutely no clue.

After another mouthful of cake, and still grinning ear to ear, he added, "We're having a party because last week I missed nine shots and none of them even came anywhere near to the backboard. Dad says that all of my practicing this week really paid off. I'm making progress."

THE BUNNY AND
THE EGGHEADS

TED MENTEN

FROM *GENTLE CLOSINGS*

One of my groups of kids is bald from either chemo-therapy or radiation therapy. The children range in age from seven to 13. When they're alone they walk around without hats on— at least the boys do. The girls are embarrassed about losing their hair and tend to wear their hats.

Children adapt quickly and form tight circles from which outsiders are excluded. Although I'm an outsider who has all his hair, I'm not excluded from their games and their humor. In fact, I'm often the butt of their hairy jokes.

Among themselves the kids are called Eggheads. Of course I'm not supposed to know this because it's a secret and exclusive clan. Eggheads support and reassure one another as no outsider can. I consider it an honor even to be tolerated by them.

As Easter approached, the little girls were feeling some anxiety about wearing Easter hats. Bonnets were suggested but rejected as too babyish. None of them even considered wearing a wig. It was declared yucky.

As the time grew closer I decided on a plan that I thought they all would enjoy.

I checked around and found some water-base paint that could be

23

used safely on skin, and then rented the most awful rabbit costume I could find. It was a terrible fluorescent pink and very, very tacky. The Saturday before Easter, I arrived at the hospital dressed in the bunny suit and made my way to where the kids were waiting for me. When I came in they got hysterical and it took quite a while to get them settled down. Then the fun began.

One by one I decorated their heads in bright colors like Easter eggs—flowers and butterflies and stars and dots and stripes. The more garish the better. At first only the boys let me paint them, but eventually the girls took off their hats and I painted their heads with ribbons and flowers and tiny hearts. We laughed as each head was painted until everyone had a colorful dome. Then I took off my bunny head and revealed by own bald pate. Of course it was a fake, but it could be painted and all the kids got to draw something on it.

Later, when the nurse came in, she nearly had a heart attack. The doctors didn't find it at all funny but the kids loved it. The next week they voted me an honorary Egghead.

The Noble Art of Turning

The weathercock on the church spire,
though made of iron,
would soon be broken by the storm-wind
if it did not understand the noble art of turning
to every wind.

<small>HEINRICH HEINE</small>

MOLLY

BARBARA BAUMGARDNER
FROM *HUMANE SOCIETY OF CENTRAL OREGON* NEWSLETTER

*W*hen I take Molly for a walk, I frequently get way-laid by people who "once had a golden retriever." I call them *kindred hearts* because they don't seem to object as Molly leaves hair and drool all over their pant legs whenever I stop to chat. *Kindred hearts* are a lot more tolerant of things like shaggy, shedding, slobbering dogs—and of people, too, in general. Molly is learning to pick out those *kindred hearts* when we go visiting the nursing homes, assisted living centers and hospitals.

At 18 months old, I wasn't sure she would be able to calm down enough to be a "visiting dog" under the Humane Society program. She is a typical golden: affectionate but active, tail-wagging, always ready to play. Tom Davis described her well in his book, *Just Goldens,* when he said, "Goldens are imaginative, mellow, enemies of routine…quirky, fun-loving and full of surprises…you'd want a Golden to throw a party. A couple of hours into the festivities, it's the one wearing the lampshade."

That's Molly: the one wearing the lampshade.

She wasn't sure what her role was when we began to make our sched-uled visits. She'd wiggle and whop everyone around her with her tail; the tail that wags with such force it can hurt or it can clear the coffee table.

She thinks she is still a lap dog but we weren't visiting anyone healthy and big enough to hold her. However, like all goldens, she has that innate desire to please me. As I coached, she finally figured out that if she would sit, someone would pet her or better yet, hug her. And sometimes she would lay her head in a willing lap.

Recently on one of our visits, she performed like a pro. We were at a health care center, in the section where people need a lot of care. A woman, secured to a wheelchair, seemed so unaware that we nearly passed her by. Her hands were crippled and bent under; her head had fallen to one side, eyes closed. Molly paused and so did I.

The woman responded to my touch when I put my hand on her arm so I grasped a gnarled hand and touched it to Molly's soft fur. As her hand in mine stroked Molly's head, the woman opened her eyes and began to laugh. Soon she was alert, but giggling like a child as I continued to move her hand around the golden's body. Molly sat close, and soon put her head on the lap in the wheelchair. Then with her own strength, the woman managed to bend forward enough to push her arms around Molly's neck, her excited giggles catching the attention of the nurses close by. The woman couldn't speak, but she communicated her kindred heart: giving love through touch, in the same way Molly does.

My dog and I will return to visit the woman again. I think Molly finally understands that when she's on assignment, she must give up the lampshade and just be the light.

WE ALL NEED TO BE
LOOKED AFTER

MAX LUCADO

FROM *IN THE GRIP OF GRACE*

*G*ood, I'm glad you're sitting by me. Sometimes I throw up."

Not exactly what you like to hear from the airline passenger in the next seat. Before I had time to store my bag in the overhead compartment, I knew his name, age and itinerary. "I'm Billy Jack. I'm 14, and I'm going home to see my daddy."

I started to tell him my name, but he spoke first. "I need someone to look after me. I get confused a lot."

He told me about the special school he attended and the medication he took. "Can you remind me to take my pill in a few minutes?" Before we buckled up he stopped the airline attendant. "Don't forget about me," he told her. "I get confused."

Once we were airborne, Billy Jack ordered a soft drink and dipped his pretzels in it. He kept glancing at me as I drank and asked if he could drink what I didn't. He spilled some of his soda and apologized.

"No problem," I said, wiping it up.

When he started playing his Nintendo Game Boy, I tried to doze off. That's when he started making noises with his mouth, imitating a trumpet. "I can sound like the ocean, too," he bragged, swishing spit back and forth in his cheeks.

(Didn't sound like the ocean, but I didn't tell him.)

Billy Jack was a little boy in a big body. "Can clouds hit the ground?" he asked me. I started to answer, but he looked back out the window as if he'd never asked. Unashamed of his needs, he didn't let a flight attendant pass without a reminder: "Don't forget to look after me."

When they brought the food: "Don't forget to look after me."

When they brought more drinks: "Don't forget to look after me."

When any attendant passed, Billy Jack urged: "Don't forget to look after me."

I honestly can't think of one time Billy Jack didn't remind the crew that he needed attention. The rest of us didn't need it. We never asked for help. We were grown-ups. Sophisticated. Self-reliant. Seasoned travelers. Most of us didn't even listen to the emergency landing instructions. (Billy Jack asked me to explain them to him.)

An epistle to challenge the self-sufficient, the book of Romans was written for folks like us. Confession of need is admission of weakness, something we are slow to do. I think Billy Jack would have understood grace. It occurred to me that he was the safest person on the flight. Had the plane encountered trouble, he would have received primary assistance. The flight attendants would have bypassed me and gone to him. Why? He had placed himself in the care of someone stronger.

I ask, have you?

One thing's for sure: You cannot save yourself. God has sent His first-born Son to carry you home. Are you firmly in the grip of His grace? I pray that you are. I *earnestly* pray that you are.

One last thought. Billy Jack spent the final hour of the flight with his head on my shoulder, his hands folded between his knees. Just when I thought he was asleep, his head popped up and he said, "My dad is going to meet me at the airport. I can't wait to see him because he watches after me."

The apostle Paul would have liked Billy Jack.

LOVE LETTERS

BOB WELCH
FROM *WHERE ROOTS GROW DEEP*

*N*ear as anyone can tell, Sally's grandmother never touched a computer keyboard. She didn't particularly like talking on the phone. Instead, she communicated with her extended family through something far superior to anything high technology could offer, something better than even e-mail.

She reached out and touched us all with g-mail—Gram Mail.

Gram Youngberg, who died in the fall of 1997 at the age of 95, wrote letters. Thousands of letters spanning decades and decades, many of which my wife has saved. Part of Gram's legacy was how she lived her life, but part of it, too, was the words she left with us all—words that became an extension of the woman who penned them. Words that helped sustain and link the interdependent parts of her legacy tree.

They tell us of a simple, salt-of-the-earth woman who noticed the daily comings and goings of people with detailed enthusiasm. Like Emily, the young girl in *Our Town* who wonders if anyone but the "saints and poets" really notice the nuances of life around them, Gram, too, noticed the "clocks ticking, and Mama's sunflowers and new-ironed dresses and hot baths…" Mainly, she noticed her extended family and friends.

"Bud Payne," she wrote in one letter, "is still housebound with his severed knee ligament... Max Coffey plans on going to Haiti as a mechanic on the medical team the last of November... My, but Brad and Paul have grown!..."

The letters tell of someone for whom people were the utmost priority. She always wrote more about others than herself. She gloried in her family's victories, commiserated in our defeats. She welcomed in-laws into the family as if we were long-lost friends who, despite no blood links, belonged. She was always more amazed at the accomplishments of others than of her own, though she had many.

"Sally: We are so proud of you and Ann for doing your bit for others in Haiti..."

"Today, I've been painting the little wooden fire trucks, 11 of them, for needy children. Then sand them and paint again. Takes almost 20 minutes to do one."

The letters tell of someone who had a special heart for children.

"I'm enjoying my Sunday School class. I have eight 5 and 6-year-olds and they are nice little kids."

"Your boys' drawings are something. Ryan's cows are an active, happy bunch, and show such action."

The letters tell of someone who reveled in the bounty of God's earth, in weather and soil and seasons and sunsets. "I'm busy with Indian summer crops," she wrote. "I love this time of year. Freezing corn, drying prunes, and finishing up on canning. The apple crop—pears also—were nothing and the few on the trees were wormy and scaly. But there are peaches. And how we enjoyed them!"

In another letter: "Thermometer showed 20 degrees and white frost. Snow in the hills but not here—yet." And still another: "Have you been seeing the glorious sunsets: one last night—and then sunsets during the week. They are gorgeous to behold—to appreciate the handiwork of the Lord."

Her letters were full of recipes and news of chickens and cows and gophers and sewing and church potlucks and, of course, Pop. She always took time to ask about how your family was doing. She was fond of exclamation points and, for rare occasions (like when noting a granddaughter's husband was home from the service), used happy faces.

She seldom complained. Oh, a few letters included touching lines in the years after Pop died; she was lonely. But for the most part, she had an uncanny ability to see silver linings in the darkest of clouds, to accept that pain and loss were part of life, much as drought and hail were part of farming.

"Pop is tired," she once wrote, "but we can't complain."

From another letter, extolling the accomplishments of other family members: "Aren't we lucky."

Were Gram alive today, I know how she would respond to such glowing accounts of her life. She would react the same way she reacted after I told her what an inspiration she was and that I felt fortunate to be part of her family, even as an adjunct.

"Thanks for the complimentary letter, Bob, but to be honest, I'm very undeserving of such noble motives. For I'm doing what comes naturally. In my growing-up years, I learned to make do, to make use of what is on hand, so I do it."

Decades of letters. Letters whose stamps, in just the last 25 years, went from 8 cents to 32 cents. Letters that, for a while, after Gram broke her arm, were written left-handed. Letters first signed "Gram and Pop" then just "Gram," then finally stopped coming altogether—but only when she physically could no longer write.

Letters reminding us that, over the years, Gram really had two gardens: one with carrots and peas and tomatoes and corn. And one with a son and two daughters and grandchildren and great-grandchildren and nieces and nephews.

In addressing the church at Corinth, Paul writes, "You yourselves are our letter, written on our hearts, known and read by everybody." In a sense, Gram's life was one long love letter to her family and friends and God. A 95-year-long letter.

Nothing would make her prouder than to know that we had tucked that letter in our wallets and purses—better yet, hidden it in our hearts— and lived the same kind of other-oriented life she had lived. She would want us to look for the best in one another. To "make do" with what circumstances we've been given. And, of course, to stop and look at the sunrises and sunsets, for, as she wrote, "They are gorgeous to behold…the handiwork of the Lord."

Kind words are the music of the world.
They have power that seems to
be beyond natural causes,
as if they were some angel's song
that had lost its way and come to earth.

FREDERICK WILLIAM FABER

GOD DOESN'T MAKE NOBODIES

RUTH LEE
FROM *TOUCH 1* MAGAZINE

*I*t was the last day of an extremely beneficial Christian writers conference. Someone suggested we should gather that night in the prayer rooms of our dormitories for a time of sharing.

After the banquet was over, the ladies gathered in the second-floor chapel of my dormitory. In nightgowns and pajamas, we all seemed much alike. Someone suggested introductions, but I interrupted.

"Please," I said, "let's not just say our names. Share something about yourself."

By the time three people had responded, I knew I should have kept my mouth shut! One lady was a director of nursing, another taught English on the college level, and the lady next to her had just received her doctorate! There I sat, halfway around the room, and what was I?

Nobody. Oh yes, a wife, mother and grandmother, but nothing important.

After the introduction of two authors with published books, and other women with other claims to fame, it was my turn.

"My name is Ruth," I said, "and I feel so inferior I think I'll just go back to my room."

Everyone laughed, so I plowed ahead. "I guess you could call me a producer. In 30 years I've produced a well-adjusted respiratory therapist, a machinist and another happy homemaker. And I'm involved in the co-production of seven grandchildren."

I told them how full my life is. Full of checking on cows, helping fix fences, praying for rain and then praying it will stop raining. I told them of busy hours spent baby-sitting and contending with my household.

And then I told them how hungry I was. Hungry for the type of spiritual and emotional food I had received at this conference.

From the far corner of the room a quiet young girl spoke up. "Would you please turn so I can look at you?"

I did as she asked, and she continued to speak. "I want to remember your face when I write," she said. "I want to write for women just like you."

Suddenly I had no need for title or degree. I served a purpose. With her words, she had helped me realize what I should have known all along. God doesn't make nobodies. Everybody is somebody important to God.

Heart Friends

A friend will strengthen you with her prayers,
bless you with her love,
and encourage you with her heart.

AUTHOR UNKNOWN

OVERNIGHT GUEST

HARTLEY F. DAILEY
FROM *SUNSHINE* MAGAZINE

Greenbriar Valley lay almost hidden by the low-hanging clouds that spilled intermittent showers. As I plodded through the muddy barnyard preparing to do my afternoon chores, I glanced at the road that led past our place and wound on through the valley. There was a car parked at the side of the road a little way beyond the pasture corner.

The car was obviously in distress. Otherwise, no man so well-dressed would have been out in the pouring rain, tinkering with it. I watched him as I went about my chores. It was evident that the man was no mechanic—desperately plodding from the raised hood back to the car seat to try the starter, then back to the hood again.

When I finished my chores and closed the barn, it was almost dark. The car was still there. So I took a flashlight and walked down the road. The man was sort of startled and disturbed when I came up to him, but he seemed anxious enough for my help. It was a small car, the same make as my own but somewhat newer. It took only a few minutes for me to spot the trouble.

"It's your coil," I told him.

"But it couldn't be that!" he blurted. "I just had a new one, only about a month ago." He was a young fellow, hardly more than a boy—I should have guessed 21, at most. He sounded almost in tears.

"You see, mister," he almost sobbed, "I'm a long ways from home. It's raining. And I've just got to get it started. I just *got* to!"

"Well, it's like this," I said. "Coils are pretty touchy. Sometimes they'll last for years. Then again sometimes they'll go out in a matter of hours. Suppose I get a horse and pull the car up into the barn. Then we'll see what we can do for it. We'll try the coil from my car. If that works, I know a fellow down at the corner who'll sell you one."

I was right. With the coil from my car in place, the motor started right off, and it purred like a new one. "Nothing to it," I grinned. "We'll just go see Bill David down the road. He'll sell you a new coil, and you can be on your way. Just wait a minute while I tell my wife, Jane, where I'm going."

I thought he acted odd when we got down to David's store. He parked in the dark behind the store and wouldn't get out. "I'm wet and cold," he excused himself. "Here's 10 dollars. Would you mind very much going in and getting it for me?"

We had just finished changing the coil when my little daughter, Linda, came out to the barn. "Mother says supper's ready," she announced. Then turning to the strange young man, she said, "She says you're to come in and eat, too."

"Oh, but I couldn't," he protested. "I couldn't let you folks feed me. I've got to get going anyway. No, no, I just can't stay."

"Don't be ridiculous," I said. "After all, how long will it take you to eat? Besides, no one comes to Jane's house at mealtime and leaves without eating. You wouldn't want her to lie down in mud in front of your car, would you?"

Still protesting, he allowed himself to be led off to the house. But it seemed to me as if there was something more in his protests than just mere politeness.

He sat quietly enough while I said the blessing. But during the meal he seemed fidgety. He just barely picked at his food, which was almost an insult to Jane, who is one of the best cooks in the state and proud of it.

Once the meal was over, he got quickly to his feet, announcing that he must be on his way. But he had reckoned without Jane.

"Now, look here," She said, and she glanced at me for support. "It's still pouring rain out there. Your clothes are all wet, and you can't help being cold. I'll bet you're tired, too; you must have driven far today. Stay with us tonight. Tomorrow you can start out warm and dry and all rested."

I nodded slightly at her. It isn't always advisable to take in strangers that way. Unfortunately, there are many who cannot be trusted. But I liked this young man. I felt sure he would be all right.

He reluctantly agreed to stay the night. Jane made him go to bed and hung his clothes to dry by the fire. Next morning she pressed them and gave him a nice breakfast. This meal he ate with relish. It seemed he was more settled that morning, not so restless as he had been. He thanked us profusely before he left.

But when he started away, an odd thing happened. He had been headed down the valley toward the city the night before. But when he left, he headed back north, toward Roseville, the county seat. We wondered a great deal about that, but decided he had been confused and made a wrong turn.

Time went by, and we never heard from the young man. We had not expected to, really. The days flowed into months, and the months into years. The Depression ended and drifted into war. In time, the war ended, too. Linda grew up and established a home of her own. Things on the farm were quite different from those early days of struggle. Jane and I lived comfortably and quietly, surrounded by lovely Greenbriar Valley.

Just the other day I got a letter from Chicago. A personal letter, it was, on nice expensive stationery. "Now who in the world," I wondered, "can be writing me from Chicago?" I opened it and read:

Dear Mr. McDonald:

I don't suppose you remember the young man you helped, years ago, when his car broke down. It has been a long time, and I imagine you've helped many others. But I doubt if you have helped anyone else quite the way you helped me.

You see, I was running away that night. I had in my car a very large sum of money, which I had stolen from my employer. I want you to know, sir, that I had good Christian parents. But I had forgotten their teaching and had got in with the wrong crowd. I knew I had made a terrible mistake.

But you and your wife were so nice to me. That night in your home, I began to see where I was wrong. Before morning, I made a decision. Next day, I turned back. I went back to my employer and made a clean breast of it. I gave back all the money and threw myself on his mercy.

He could have prosecuted me and sent me to prison for many years. But he is a good man. He took me back in my old job, and I have never strayed again. I'm married now, with a lovely wife and two fine children. I have worked my way to a very good position with my company. I am not wealthy, but I am comfortably well off.

I could reward you handsomely for what you did for me that night. But I don't believe that is what you'd want. So I have established a fund to help others who have made the same mistake I did. In this way, I hope I may pay for what I have done.

God bless you, sir, and your good wife, who helped me more than you knew.

Robert Fane

I walked into the house, and handed the letter to Jane. As she read it, I could see the tears begin to fill her eyes. With the strangest look on her face, she laid the letter aside.

"For I was a Stranger, and ye took Me in," she quoted. "I was hungered, and ye fed Me; I was in prison, and ye visited Me."

UNTHANKED PEOPLE

STEVE GOODIER

When William Stidger taught at Boston University, he once reflected upon the great number of unthanked people in his life. Those who had helped nurture him, inspire him, or cared enough about him to leave a lasting impression.

One was a schoolteacher he'd not heard of in many years. But he remembered that she had gone out of her way to put a love of verse in him, and Will had loved poetry all his life. He wrote a letter of thanks to her.

The reply he received, written in the feeble scrawl of the aged, began, "My dear Willie." He was delighted. Now over fifty, bald, and a professor, he didn't think there was a person left in the world who would call him "Willie." Here is that letter:

> My dear Willie,
>
> I cannot tell you how much your note meant to me. I am in my eighties, living alone in a small room, cooking my own meals, lonely, and, like the last leaf of autumn, lingering behind. You will be interested to know that I taught school for fifty years and yours is the

first note of appreciation I ever received. It came on a blue-cold morning and it cheered me as nothing has in many years.

Not prone to cry easily, Will wept over that note. She was one of the great unthanked people from Will's past. You know them. We all do. The teacher who made a difference. That coach we'll never forget. The music instructor or Sunday school worker who helped us believe in ourselves. That scout leader that cared.

We all remember people who shaped our lives in various ways. People whose influence changed us. Will Stidger found a way to show his appreciation—he wrote them letters.

Kind words can be short and easy to speak
but their echoes are truly endless.

MOTHER TERESA

ANGELS ONCE
IN A WHILE

BARB IRWIN

In September 1960, I woke up one morning with six hungry babies and just seventy-five cents in my pocket. Their father was gone.

The boys ranged from three months to seven years; their sister was two. Their dad had never been much more than a presence they feared. Whenever they heard his tires crunch on the gravel driveway they would scramble to hide under their beds. He did manage to leave fifteen dollars a week to buy groceries. Now that he had decided to leave, there would be no more beatings, but no food either. If there were a welfare system in effect in southern Indiana at that time, I certainly knew nothing about it.

I scrubbed the kids until they looked brand new and then put on my best homemade dress. I loaded them into the rusty old '51 Chevy and drove off to find a job. The seven of us went to every factory, store, and restaurant in our small town. No luck. The kids stayed, crammed into the car, and tried to be quiet while I tried to convince whoever would listen that I was willing to learn or do anything. I had to have a job. Still no luck.

The last place we went to, just a few miles out of town, was an old Root Beer Barrel drive-in that had been converted to a truck stop. It was called the Big Wheel. An old lady named Granny owned the place and she peeked out of the window from time to time at all those kids. She needed someone on the graveyard shift, eleven at night until seven in the morning. She paid sixty-five cents an hour, and I could start that night.

I raced home and called the teenager down the street that baby-sat for people. I bargained with her to come and sleep on my sofa for a dollar a night. She could arrive with her pajamas on and the kids would already be asleep. This seemed like a good arrangement to her, so we made a deal.

That night when the little ones and I knelt to say our prayers we all thanked God for finding Mommy a job.

And so I started at the Big Wheel. When I got home in the mornings I woke the baby-sitter up and sent her home with one dollar of my tip money—fully half of what I averaged every night.

As the weeks went by, heating bills added another strain to my meager wage. The tires on the old Chevy had the consistency of penny balloons and began to leak. I had to fill them with air on the way to work and again every morning before I could go home.

One bleak fall morning, I dragged myself to the car to go home and found four tires in the back seat. New tires! There was no note, nothing, just those beautiful brand new tires. Had angels taken up residence in Indiana? I wondered.

I made a deal with the owner of the local service station. In exchange for his mounting the new tires, I would clean up his office. I remember it took me a lot longer to scrub his floor than it did for him to do the tires.

I was now working six nights instead of five and it still wasn't enough. Christmas was coming and I knew there would be no money for toys for the kids. I found a can of red paint and started repairing and painting some old toys. Then I hid them in the basement so there would be something for Santa to deliver on Christmas morning. Clothes were a worry too. I was sewing patches on top of patches on the boys' pants and soon they would be too far gone to repair.

On Christmas Eve the usual customers were drinking coffee in the Big Wheel. These were the truckers, Les, Frank, and Jim, and a state trooper named Joe. A few musicians were hanging around after a gig at the Legion and were dropping nickels in the pinball machine. The regulars all just sat around and talked through the wee hours of the morning and then left to get home before the sun came up. When it was time for me to go home at seven o'clock on Christmas morning I hurried to the car. I was hoping the kids wouldn't wake up before I managed to get home and get the presents from the basement and place them under the tree. (We had cut down a small cedar tree by the side of the road down by the dump.) It was still dark and I couldn't see much, but there appeared to be some dark shadows in the car—or was that just a trick of the night? Something certainly looked different, but it was hard to tell what. When I reached the car I peered warily into one of the side windows. Then my jaw dropped in amazement. My old battered Chevy was full—full to the top with boxes of all shapes and sizes.

I quickly opened the driver's side door, scrambled inside and kneeled in the front facing the backseat. Reaching back, I pulled off the lid of the top box. Inside was a whole case of little blue jeans, sizes 2–10! I looked inside another box: It was full of shirts to go with the jeans. Then I peeked inside some of the other boxes. There were candy and nuts and bananas. There was an enormous ham for baking, and canned vegetables and pota-toes. There was pudding and Jell-O and cookies, pie filling and flour. There was a whole bag of laundry supplies and cleaning items.

And there were five toy trucks and one beautiful little doll. As I drove back through empty streets as the sun slowly rose on the most amazing Christmas Day of my life, I was sobbing with gratitude. And I will never forget the joy on the faces of my little ones that precious morning.

Yes, there were angels in Indiana that long-ago December. And they all hung out at the Big Wheel truck stop.

MRS. WARREN'S CLASS

COLLEEN TOWNSEND EVANS
FROM *START LOVING*

One of the great joys in life comes from watching a troubled person turn and go in a new—and better—direction. What causes such a thing to happen? A miracle? Sometimes. Forgiveness? Always!

Tom was a charming child, as most rascals are—but he was rebellious, a prankster, a rule breaker, a flaunter of authority. By the time he entered high school, his reputation had preceded him and he filled most of the teachers with dread. He took a special delight in disrupting classes and driving teachers to the limits of their patience. At home, he also was a problem. There were frequent confrontations between parents and child, each one seeking to prove he was more powerful than the other.

So many complaints were filed against Tom that the high school principal decided he would have to expel him—unless a teacher named Mrs. Warren agreed to take him into her class. Mrs. Warren was an exceptionally capable English teacher, but she also was a loving, endlessly patient woman who seemed to have a way with problem students. Yes, Mrs. Warren said, she would find a place for him in her eleven o'clock English Literature class, and also in her home room. She listened calmly as the principal read from a list of Tom's misdemeanors—a long list that had the principal shaking his head as he read. No, Mrs.Warren said, she wouldn't change her mind. She knew what she was getting into—she had heard about the boy.

When Tom was transferred to Mrs. Warren's class, he behaved as he always did upon meeting a new teacher. He slouched in his seat in the last row and glared at her, daring her—by his attitude—to do something about him. At first Mrs. Warren ignored him. Then, as the class began to discuss the reading assignment, Tom whispered a joke to the boy in front of him, making the boy laugh. Mrs.Warren looked up. Then she closed her book, stood and placed another chair at the desk, next to hers.

"Tom, come up here and sit with me for a while," she said—not as a reprimand, but as a friend. It was an invitation she was offering, and her manner was so sweet that Tom couldn't refuse. He sat next to her as she went on with the lesson. "Tom is new to our class and hasn't had time to read the assignment, so if you'll bear with me, I'll read it aloud to him."

With Tom next to her, sharing her book, Mrs. Warren began to read from *A Tale of Two Cities*. She was a fine reader and captured Dickens' sense of drama magnificently. Tom, for all his determination to be an obstruction, found himself following the text, losing himself in the unfolding of a great story, sharing the excitement of it with a woman who really seemed to care about his interest in the book. That evening he startled his parents by sitting down without any prodding to do his home-work—at least the assignment for Mrs. Warren's class.

That was only the beginning… Tom never missed a day of school after that first day in Mrs. Warren's class. Sometimes he cut other classes but never hers. He sat in the front row, participated in discussions, and seemed to enjoy reading aloud when he was called upon to do so. His appetite for reading suddenly became ravenous, and he asked Mrs. Warren to make up a list of books she thought he might enjoy in his free time. After school he stayed in the classroom when the other students went home and had long talks with Mrs. Warren about the things he had read and the ideas they stimulated.

Tom wasn't exactly an angel in other classes, but the effect of his behavior in Mrs. Warren's class began to rub off a little—for which the other teachers were most grateful.

Tom didn't finish high school. In his junior year, after an angry outburst at home, he defiantly joined the Navy. He didn't even say good-bye to Mrs. Warren, who was very sad to see him leave school, because she thought she had failed in her attempt to reach him.

Seven years later, when Mrs. Warren was closing up her desk one afternoon before leaving for home, a young man came to the doorway and stood there, smiling. He was much taller and more muscular now, but Mrs. Warren recognized him within seconds. It was Tom! He rushed to her and hugged her so hard her glasses slid down her nose.

"Where have you been?" she said, adjusting her glasses and looking at him intently. My—he was so clear-eyed, so happy and self-confident!

"In school," he said, laughing.

"But I thought—"

"Sure, you thought I was in the Navy... Well, I was, for a while. I went to school there."

It was a long story he had to tell. Thanks to the Navy he was able to finish high school...and then he went on to college courses. When his enlistment was up, he got a job and continued his education at night. During that time he met a lovely girl. By the time he graduated he was married and had a son. Then he went on to graduate school, also at night.

"Well, what are you doing with your fine education?" Mrs. Warren asked.

"I'm a teacher—I teach English...especially to kids who disrupt other classes."

Tom had never forgotten the feeling of acceptance he had had from that first day in Mrs. Warren's class. More than all the threats, all the arguments and confrontations he had known, her forgiving love got through to him. And now he was passing that love on to other young people. He had learned the give-and-take of forgiveness.

THE OTHER SIDE OF THE CURTAIN

RUTH LEE
FROM *TOUCH 1* MAGAZINE

oolish. That's the way I felt. I didn't know the name of the woman on the other side of the curtain. Couldn't even see her, and still we were having a rather personal conversation.

My mother, in a semiconscious state as a result of a stroke, lay in one hospital bed, and on the other side of the curtain was a stranger—a woman I'd heard the nurse refer to as "Claudine."

The doctor had advised us to stay with Mom and keep her stimulated by talking to her.

From the other side of the curtain, Claudine answered each query I made.

"Can you hear me, Mom?"

"Yes, Dear. I can hear you," Claudine answered.

"I love you, Mom."

"That's nice, Honey. I love you, too," Claudine replied.

A nurse told me Claudine was terminally ill. A brain tumor was claiming her life. She suffered severe depression and cried most of the time. Some days she was irrational.

Before long, I learned there were other days when she regained partial control of her life. On good days, she told me about her son who lived too far away for visits. We talked about his farm, his dogs.

"Hunting dogs," Claudine said. "Beagles. Good rabbit dogs."

During the bad times, Claudine would cradle the telephone in her lap, crying out for contact with old friends.

"Would you dial for me," she'd ask. But the numbers were gone from her mind. She couldn't remember.

Without hesitating, I would punch in the number of the hospital, and say, "Listen. The number is busy right now. You can try later." She would rest, comforted by the buzzing signal.

The floor nurse began to notice my involvement with Claudine. She told me, "I can have her moved if she's becoming a problem."

I shook my head. "She's no trouble. Leave her be."

Even Mom felt I was becoming too involved. Mother was much stronger now and no longer required constant attention, but each day Claudine grew weaker.

"She needs my friendship," I explained, and they could not deny the truth of what I said.

"You'll end up getting hurt," the nurse cautioned. "Why do you think their families stay away?" I knew she referred not just to Claudine, but to all the terminally ill patients in her care.

Then one day the son came to visit. Claudine's boy. His mother had been heavily sedated just prior to his arrival, and all she could do was cling to his hand and cry. The young man wept openly.

I closed the curtain, allowing him privacy.

When visiting hours were over, I kissed Mom's forehead in farewell and, crossing the room, made a decision.

"Bruce?" The young man turned at the sound of his name. "You are Bruce?" I confirmed.

"Yes," he answered. "But how did you know?"

"I know a lot about you. About your farm, your hopes and dreams." Astonishment was written on his face.

I smiled. "I even know about your beagles. One is named Dolly; the other one is Cookie."

"But how...?"

The young man looked at the figure curled into a ball on the bed.

"She's not always like this," I said. "There are moments of happy memories." I knew instinctively what he wanted to hear.

"You will be able to visit with her, Bruce. She'll know you next time you come."

Tears coursed down his face. I held out my arms and he rushed to them.

The time of feeling foolish was gone. Holding and comforting a stranger seemed the natural thing to do.

Reaching out and sharing with others has a way of bringing its own reward.

Laughter is the sun that drives
winter from the human face.

VICTOR HUGO

Friendship

THE HEART OF A FRIEND

I breathed a song into the air,
It fell to earth I know not where…
And the song from beginning to end,
I found again in the heart of a friend.

HENRY WADSWORTH LONGFELLOW

MRS. HILDEBRANDT'S GIFT

ROBERT SMITH
FROM *COUNTRY* MAGAZINE

*I*t's been 30 years since I last saw her, but in memory she's still there every holiday season. I especially feel her presence when I receive my first Christmas card.

I was 12 years old, and Christmas was only 2 days away. The season's first blanket of white magnified the excitement.

I dressed hurriedly, for the snow was waiting. What would I do first—build a snowman, slide down the hill, or just throw the flakes in the air and watch them flutter down?

Our station wagon pulled into the driveway, and Mom called me over to help with the groceries. When we finished carrying in the bags, she said, "Bob, here are Mrs. Hildebrandt's groceries."

No other instructions were necessary. As far back as I could remember, my mom shopped for Mrs. Hildebrandt's food and I delivered it. Our 95-year-old neighbor who lived alone, was crippled from arthritis and could take only a few steps with her cane.

Even though she was old, crippled and didn't play baseball, I liked Mrs. Hildebrandt. I enjoyed talking with her; more accurately, I enjoyed listening to her. She told wonderful stories of her life—about a steepled church in the woods, horse and buggy rides on Sunday afternoon, and her family farm without running water or electricity.

She always gave me a dime for bringing her groceries. It got so that I would refuse only halfheartedly, knowing she would insist. Five minutes later, I'd be across the street in Beyer's candy store.

As I headed over with the bags, I decided this time would be different, though. I *wouldn't* accept any money. This would be my Christmas present to her.

Impatiently, I rang Mrs. Hildebrandt's doorbell. Almost inaudible at first were the slow, weary shuffles of her feet and the slower thump of her cane. The chain on the door rattled and the door creaked open. Two shiny eyes peered from the crack.

"Hello, Mrs. Hildebrandt," I said. "It's me, Bob. I have your groceries."

"Oh, yes, come in, come in," she said cheerfully. "Put the bag on the table." I did so more hurriedly than usual, because I could almost hear the snow calling me back outside.

As we talked, I began to realize how lonely she was. Her husband had died more than twenty years ago, she had no children, and her only living relative was a nephew in Philadelphia who never visited.

Nobody ever called on her at Christmas. There would be no tree, no presents, no stocking.

She offered me a cup of tea, which she did every time I brought the groceries. Well, maybe the snow could wait.

We sat and talked about what Christmas was like when she was a child. We traveled far away and long ago, and an hour passed before I knew it.

"Well, Bob, you must be wanting to play outside in the snow," she said as she reached for her purse.

"No, Mrs. Hildebrandt, I can't take your money this time. You can use it for more important things," I resisted.

She looked at me and smiled. "What more important thing could I use this money for, if not to give it to a friend at Christmas?" she asked, and then placed a whole *quarter* in my hand.

I *tried* to give it back, but she would have none of it.

I hurried out the door and ran over to Beyer's candy store with my fortune. I had no idea what to buy—comic books, chocolate, soda, ice cream. Then I spotted something—a Christmas card with an old country church in the woods on the cover. It was just like the one she'd described.

I handed Mr. Beyer my quarter for the card and borrowed a pen to sign my name.

"For your girlfriend?" he asked. I started to say no, but quickly changed my mind. "Well, yeah, I guess so."

As I walked back across the street with my gift, I was so proud of myself I felt like I had just hit a home run to win the World Series. No, I felt *better* than that!

I rang Mrs. Hildebrandt's doorbell. The almost inaudible sounds of shuffling again reached my ears. The chain rattled and the door creaked open. Two shiny eyes peered from within.

"Hello, Mrs. Hildebrandt," I said as I handed her the card. "Merry Christmas!"

Her hands trembled as she slowly opened the envelope, studied the card and began to cry. "Thank you very much," she said almost in a whisper. "Merry Christmas."

On a cold and windy afternoon a few weeks later, the ambulance arrived next door. My mom said they found her in bed; she had died peacefully in her sleep. Her night table light was still on, illuminating a solitary Christmas card.

THE LOVE SQUAD

VIRELLE KIDDER
FROM *DECISION* MAGAZINE

*O*h, no! Not company!" I groaned the moment that my car rounded the corner and our house came into full view. Usually I'd be thrilled to see four cars lined up in our driveway, but after I spent a week-long vigil at the hospital with an ill child, my house was a colossal mess. Turning off the car engine, I dragged myself to the front door.

"What are you doing home so soon?" my friend Judie called from the kitchen. "We weren't expecting you for another hour! We thought we'd be long gone before you got home." She walked toward me and gave me a hug, then asked softly, "How are you doing?"

Was this my house? Was I dreaming? Everything looked so clean. Where did these flowers come from?

Suddenly more voices, more hugs. Lorraine, smiling and wiping beads of perspiration from her forehead, came up from the family room where she had just finished ironing a mountain of clean clothes. Regina peeked into the kitchen, having finished vacuuming rugs and polishing and dusting furniture in every room in the house. Joan, still upstairs wrestling with the boys' bunk-bed sheets, called down her "hello," having already brought order out of chaos in all four bedrooms.

"When did you guys get here?" was my last coherent sentence. My tears came in great heaving waves. "How come...how come...you did all this?" I cried unashamedly, every ounce of resistant gone.

I had spent the week praying through a health crisis, begging God for a sense of His presence at the hospital. Instead, He laid a mantle of order, beauty and loving care into our home through these four "angels."

"You rest a while, Virelle," Lorraine said firmly. "Here's your dinner for tonight—there are more meals in the freezer." The table was set with flowers and fancy napkins, and a little gift was at my place. A small banquet was arranged, complete with salad and dessert.

"Don't you worry. We're all praying," my friends said. "God has everything under control."

After my friends left, I wandered from room to room, still sobbing from the enormity of their gift of time and work. I found beautiful floral arrangements in every room...and little wrapped gifts on each bed. More tears.

In the living room I found a note under a vase filled with peonies. I was to have come home and found it as their only identity: "The Love Squad was here."

And I *knew* that God had everything under control.

*Friends are lights in winter
the older the friend, the brighter the light.*

ROGER ROSENBLATT

LUTHER'S LUMBER

Joe Edwards

Luther had been home from the war nearly four months, now, and worked at the Carnation Milk plant in Mount Vernon where his wife, Jenny, worked.

This morning he was in the little Miller Café next door to the post office waiting for the mail to be "put up." Sitting across from him in the booth was his old friend, Fred Hill. They were discussing the war which was still going on in the Pacific Theatre. Recruitment posters still lined the walls of the little café.

Fred had not been in the service, because when the war started in 1941, his parents had been in very poor health; his father with a bad heart, and his mother with cancer. He was needed at home to care for them and operate the farm. His parents had since died, and the farm was now his— his and Maggie's.

When Luther, Fred's best friend since childhood had flown over Miller in the B-17, and when the bodies of the Hobbs boys and Billie Martin had been shipped home, and when Perry came home with hooks where his hands should have been, Fred felt guilty. He felt he had not done his part for the war effort, and in his own eyes, he was diminished.

But today, it was Luther who seemed depressed. Fred asked him what was bothering him. "You seem down in the dumps today, Luther," he said. "I can't see what could be botherin' you. You came through the war without a scratch; you got a beautiful wife and a baby on the way; you got a good job. What's the problem?"

"Jenny's mother is in bad shape," said Luther, "We're going to have to take her in, and with the baby coming we don't have the room."

"Can't build a room on?" asked Fred.

"No lumber available," said Luther. "I've tried here. Mount Vernon, Springfield, Joplin, and there won't be any more shipments for the duration. Who knows how long that will be?"

"Tried Will's sawmill?"

"Yeah, but he just saws oak, and it's green. The baby'll be here in August, and we can't wait for the lumber to dry. Besides, you can't build a whole room out of oak, anyway."

"Wouldn't want to," said Fred, "Reckon the mail's up?"

"Probably."

The two young men left the café and went into the post office next door. Buford Patten, the postmaster, had raised the door to the service window, signaling that the mail was in the boxes. Luther and Fred retrieved their mail and left—Luther to work at Mount Vernon, and Fred back to the farm.

That evening, Fred finished the milking and sat on the front porch with Maggie. "Days are getting longer," he said, "Man could get half a day's work done after five o'clock."

"Better put your pa's car up," said Maggie. "Radio says rain tonight."

Fred's father had bought a new 1941 Ford just before his first heart attack, and the car was now Fred's. He had built a new garage for it just before Christmas, and tonight he congratulated himself on getting it built before the lumber ran out. He didn't even know it had until Luther told him this morning.

Fred drove the car into the new garage and latched the door. He walked back around the house to the front porch. Something was nagging at his mind, but he couldn't define it. He shook it off and sat on the porch with Maggie until darkness fell. They could see heat lightning in the west,

STORIES FOR THE HEART

and the wind started to rise. They went in the house to listen to the news of the war on the radio, and shortly went to bed.

The next morning, Fred again drove his pickup into Miller for the mail. The air was fresh and clear now, the rain having washed it clean. The sun was shining, and he felt good. When he reached the café, Luther was there ahead of him.

"Still haven't found any lumber, I guess?"

"No, I asked everybody at work, and nobody knows of any. I don't know what we'll do."

Now the nagging in Fred's mind defined itself. "I found the lumber for you," he said.

"You did? Where?" Luther was delighted.

"Fella I know. He'll let you have it free, you bein' a veteran and all. He doesn't seem to want you to know who he is, so I'll have to haul it in for you. It's good lumber, fir and pine, cut different lengths and got nails in it, but that's no problem. Tell you what, you get your foundation poured, and I'll bring you a pickup load every day and help you build it. We'll have it done before the baby gets here."

"That's a friend for you," Luther said to himself, as he drove to Mount Vernon. That evening he came home with sacks of cement in his pickup.

Luther dug and poured the foundation, and when it was ready for the footings, he told Fred.

"Fine," said Fred. "I'll bring the first load over and be there when you get home from work."

Fred appeared every evening with a load of lumber, and the two men worked until it was too dark to see. Sometimes Maggie came too, and the women sat in the house listening to the radio or talking about babies or Jenny's ailing mother, their sentences punctuated by the sound of the hammers outside.

Over the next few weeks the new room took shape and was finished and roofed. "Where did you get the shingles?" asked Luther.

"Same fella," answered Fred. "He's got all kinds of stuff."

Luther didn't push. Lots of older folks liked to help out the young veterans anonymously. It was common.

It was done! The women fixed the room up inside, and moved Jenny's mother in. The men went back about their business.

At supper one evening, Luther told Jenny he would like to do something nice for Fred and Maggie, since they had been so helpful with the new room.

"I know," said Jenny brightly. "Maggie likes those big wooden lawn chairs like Aunt Birdie has in her lawn. Why not get them a couple of those?"

"Good idea," agreed Luther, and the next Saturday he bought a couple at Callison's hardware and loaded them into his pickup.

When he got out to Fred's farm, there was no one home, Fred and Maggie having gone into Springfield, shopping. *That's okay*, Luther thought, *I'll just put them in the garage in case it rains.*

He drove around the house and into the driveway that led to Fred's new garage.

The garage was gone. Only the foundation remained to show where it had been.

Luther put the chairs on the front porch and drove home, tears in his eyes.

The two men are now in their midseventies and are still the best of friends. They never spoke of the incident.

How could they? There was nothing to say.

TREASURE

PAUL KORTEPETER
FROM *INTERART*

Years ago I found a solitary tea cup at an antique shop with a gorgeous pattern. I fell in love with it on the spot. From then on, I searched high and low for the rest of the set: in china shops, at auctions, flea markets, rummage sales…

Alas, without success. Not even a saucer!

Just as I was beginning to suspect that the cup wasn't part of a set at all, but a one of a kind, never-to-be-found-again treasure, I was served tea on the very same china at the home of a friend!

Well, I stared with wide eyes until my friend said, "Isn't it beautiful? I found it at an estate sale. Unfortunately one of the cups is missing."

With a twinkle in my eye, I knew that my precious cup would soon have a new home.

Count your blessings by smiles, not tears;
Count your age by friends, not years.

AUTHOR UNKNOWN

REPLY TO BOX 222B

BARBARA BAUMGARDNER

*W*as it loneliness, the call of adventure, or just plain insanity that made me answer that newspaper ad? I paced back and forth through my house, telling myself it was a really stupid thing to do. But like a jeweler crafting a priceless, one-of-a-kind brooch, I composed my reply to the tantalizing ad.

For a moment I hesitated. *Am I actually answering a lonely hearts ad?*

I'd always believed that only those who are desperately lonely advertised for a companion or answered the ads of those who did.

That's what I am, I thought, *desperately lonely.*

What would my children think? Would they understand that the bold, black letters just leaped out at my unsuspecting eye? *Christian rancher, 6' tall, 180 pounds, 50+. Hardworking, clean-cut, healthy, good physical condition. Enjoys fishing, camping, cross-country skiing, animals, dining out. Wants to meet sensible and sincere lady, 40–50, attractive, neat, loving, honest, for meaningful relationship. Box 222B.*

Mama mia! What loving, sensible, honest, and *lonely* woman could resist? Well, maybe not sensible.

"Fifty-plus what?" my letter began. "I'm a healthy, hardworking woman who loves to cook, sew, travel, pray, and walk in a desert sunset or barefoot on the beach."

I didn't say I could meet all the requirements in his ad, but I didn't give him any reason to think I couldn't. But could I?

I was already past fifty, questionably attractive, not always neat and very uncertain about pursuing a meaningful relationship. What I really wanted was a friend. Had I been dishonest not to tell him so?

Holding the letter heavenward, I asked God, "If you want me to meet this man, will you bring him to me?" Then I set the stamped envelope on the desk for the following day's mail.

During the next few weeks, I found my hands getting sweaty every time the phone rang. Could it be him? What if he didn't like me? What if he showed disappointment as soon as he set eyes on me? Could I handle that?

One day while dressing before the mirror, I turned from side to side, surveying the ravages of fifty-plus years on this earth. I studied my face, hollow and gaunt, perched atop muscular shoulders and arms. Large, sturdy hands that never knew what to do with themselves. Twenty extra pounds, a thick waist, stalwart thighs above husky calves and large, scrawny feet. I remembered the boy in the fifth grade who told me I was built like a brick outhouse: strong and useful but not much class.

Tears began to flow freely as I slumped to my knees beside my bed. "Oh, God, look at me; I'm a mess. Why did I send that letter? Please forgive me for misleading that man, for communicating the woman I want to be, not the woman I am."

It was Sunday evening a few weeks later when I invited my friend, Jeanette, for waffles after church. As we were leaving the service, she introduced me to a friend from the singles group she sometimes attended. Impulsively, I asked him if he'd like to join us for waffles and he said yes.

We spent the next three hours stuffing ourselves, laughing and talking. Jim was divorced, had several grown children and raised alfalfa for cattle feed. He was a likable man, tall and handsome, considerate, and seemingly ambitious. I felt sad for him as he talked about his loneliness.

Shutting the door behind them after a delightful evening, I began to clear up the clutter. I'd dumped my past few days' mail on the big maple desk in the dining room, and it seemed like a good time to sort it out. I tossed the junk mail in the trash and filed some bills for payment. Then I stared in astonishment. There was the letter! My reply to "Christian Rancher" had never been mailed. All that emotion and self-doubt for nothing.

Then a suspicion crept into my thoughts. Pieces started to fall into place. Jim wore cowboy boots and a western shirt; he was a rancher; he was lonely. Could he and the Christian rancher possibly be one and the same?

I rushed to the phone to call Jeanette. "Do you think he ever put an ad in the newspaper for a woman? Do you suppose he'd call himself a Christian rancher?"

Jeanette roared with laughter. "Yes, everybody at the singles group knows he did that. I guess he's gotten some seventy or eighty answers by now. Some real lulus, too."

I hung up the telephone feeling a trace of excitement, a bit of fool-ishness and a lot of awe at a God who would arrange for a letter that I never mailed to receive an answer. And God and I were the only ones who knew about it.

Several days passed before I picked up the telephone to hear Jim's voice suggesting that we go to the state fair for the day. "I'd love to," I said. *Wow! A real live date with a guy who had seventy or eighty women to choose from!*

A warm toastiness cradled me as I hung up the telephone. Then I raced to the bedroom, my heart pounding with excitement. What would I wear? In front of the mirror once more, I observed a middle-aged woman, still awkward and overweight, with a skinny face and bony feet, but she wasn't afraid anymore. "What you see is what you get," I chuckled.

The next day I stepped out into the sunshine to begin a new friend-ship with a Christian rancher.

What happened that day at the fair? We had fun together. Did we see each other again? Yes. Did we marry? No. But that didn't matter. My self-confidence soared, and I learned something else too: If you're destined to meet a particular person, whether future friend or spouse, it *will* happen, as surely as the sun rises every morning. And it'll happen even if your per-fectly crafted letter sits gathering dust on an old maple desk.

Embracing

We are like angels with just one wing:
We fly only by embracing each other.

AUTHOR UNKNOWN

SAVING THE BEST
FOR LAST

ROCHELLE M. PENNINGTON
FROM *GOD'S MATH*

*S*aving the best for last." The old cliche crossed my mind as we waited for dessert to be served. Undoubtedly, it would be wonderful; worth the wait.

Tonight was our annual ladies Christmas party, and the evening had been a delight. The meal, preceded by a short program, was followed by a gift exchange.

One by one we stood up to open the present which had been placed on the table before us. Small gifts. Simple gifts. Candles, stationery, bubble bath. Polite applause responded to each.

It was not until this orderly process had made a full circle to the last person remaining that anyone noticed that she didn't have a gift to open…and then everyone noticed at once.

Her name was Dorothy, our older—and newest—member. Having joined us nearly a year ago after moving to the community, this was her first Christmas party.

An awkward silence fell upon those gathered as we waited for someone to think of something—and to think of it quick—to save Dorothy from embarrassment. And then someone did. It was Dorothy.

Standing up, she reached for her purse and removed a brown paper grocery sack. Unfolding it, she looked inside the seemingly empty bag, then looked at us.

"Let me tell you about my gift," she said. "I received love and kindness and friendship from you. For these, I am grateful. Thank you."

Dorothy sat down to a roar of applause.

And for the second time, the old cliche crossed my mind. The best, again, had indeed been saved for last.

If instead of a gem, or even a flower,
we should cast the gift of a loving thought
into the heart of a friend—
that would be giving as the angels give.

GEORGE MACDONALD

MY CHILD, MY TEACHER, MY FRIEND

GLORIA GAITHER
FROM *CHRISTIAN HERALD* MAGAZINE

*F*rom the moment I first held you—still drenched in birth—until now as I watch you drive away to the appointments you've made with life, mothering you has been my life's most awesome, fearsome, and joyful adventure. I didn't know that first day what mothering would mean, though I was eager to begin. You seemed so fragile, so small and trusting, depending on me for every life-sustaining need. I thought at first you'd break. "Be sure to support the little head," they told me. But I soon learned you were tougher than you looked, and could out-squeal, out-sleep and out-endure me 10-to-1. In fact, those first three months, I wondered if I'd ever again finish a meal or a night's sleep.

The teaching began immediately. I had studied to be a teacher, but never was there a student as hungry to learn as you. Before you could speak, your eyes asked questions, and your tiny hands reached to touch and learn, taste and see. It wasn't long, though, until your cooing turned inquisitive, with every babbled sentence ending with a question mark. Your first words were: "What's that? What's that?" Soon your questing vocabulary grew, and you were begging, "Teach me something, Mommy. Teach me something."

And I would stop to teach you: numbers, names of things, textures, shapes, sizes, foods, furniture, pets, trees, flowers, stars and clouds. But soon you were teaching me…teaching that when the lesson stopped, the learning kept on going.

You taught me to see the miracles I'd stumbled over every day. You taught me trust and delight and ecstasy. You held a mirror before my attitudes, and role-played all my reactions. You taught me what it meant to live what I verbalized, to believe what I preached, to internalize what I lectured.

You taught me what Jesus meant when he said we must become like children if we are to enter the kingdom of heaven. Through you I understood why he used the metaphor of birth for the truth of conversion. For you, who came to me all wet from birth, baptized the common things with natural freshness, and, with the shower of your laughter, washed away the barnacles of grown-up cynicism and the dust of dull routine. You made things new. You gave me an excuse to be myself again, to skip down forest trails or sled the frozen hillsides clean with snow, to splash through springtime puddles, barefoot glad, and guess at where the shooting stars must go.

You gave me eyes to see the realness of people once again, to look beyond their faces' thin facades. You saw the child inside the aged, the longing and the passion long entrapped by gnarled joints and failing eyesight. You recognized profundity and wisdom in the giggly teen-age baby sitter, beauty in the plain, and creativity in the timid. You showed me that the generation gap is the artificial invention of our culture and bigotry a sick perversion of God's celebration of variety.

I have helped you learn to crawl, toddle, walk, run, swim, dance, ride bikes and drive the car. I have encouraged you to stand tall, walk alone, run from evil, dance for joy, ride out the hard times and drive yourself on when you felt tempted to give up. I have been there waiting when you crossed the road, climbed off the school bus, came in from dates and returned home from college. In fact, now about all I can do for you is *be there,* because gradually you have become your own person—not so much my child, but my friend.

GOD, A DOG, AND ME

DEBORAH HEDSTROM

*D*ogs and I never got on well. They barked; I feared. They slobbered; I shuddered. They wanted petting; I fretted about fleas. So it came as a total surprise when God used one in my life.

It all started when my married daughter came over and blurted out, "Don't say no until you've heard me out."

Having been the mother of four children for more than twenty years, I knew a wheedling plea was on the way. I looked at my daughter who was fidgeting in her chair. "Okay, I'll listen."

Given her chance, the words tumbled out on top of each other. "You know the dog Nathan and I bought? We can't keep it at our apartment. We thought we could because other tenants had dogs, but we got a notice saying dogs must be at least a year old." Pausing only for a brief breath, she cinched her plea with, "We just need a place until we move in a few months. You can leave him in the backyard. We'll bring food over for him and do everything."

I'm not sure why I agreed. Maybe it was the fact my daughter was pregnant. Whatever the reason, "Perry" ended up in my backyard.

At this point, dog lovers might think they know what happened next.

But it didn't. A black, velvet nose and wagging tail at my screen door every day did not win me over. I fed him in the morning, made sure he had water, and once in a while petted him. But I didn't do much more.

After forth-five years of keeping dogs at a distance, I had little doubt my treatment of Perry would change. To deal with the empty house left by grown children, I had started putting my energy into having a perfect looking home. Knowing that "perfection" would never fill the void in my heart, God pushed Perry into my life.

When I'd only had the puppy a couple of weeks, I noticed he'd stopped eating his food. Later I saw he'd been sick in the yard. I called my daughter and her husband, but knew with their jobs and finances, they couldn't help. As we tried to decide what to do, they confessed they'd forgotten to get the dog his puppy shots. I feared the worst but said, "He'll probably get better in a few days."

He didn't. Instead, I woke up one day to a dog so weak he could hardly stand. When he tried, his fluffy malamute tail that normally curled up over his rump, sagged between his back legs. Though he meant nothing to me, his illness tugged at my heart. I found myself remembering my husband's illness and death ten years earlier and I knew I just couldn't let this dog die. Crying, I picked him up and put him in the car.

My tears made the veterinarian think I was deeply attached to the dog. "He has parvovirus," he said. "It attacks the dog's digestive system and often ends in death."

I asked him what I should do but he said that was up to me. Torn by my memories and the awareness that it was my daughter's dog, I agreed to three days of veterinary care.

Three days later Perry came home with me, improving, but his ribs were clearly showing through his sagging skin. He wasn't well enough to put outside, but I was still bothered by thoughts of germs and fleas. Looking at the weak dog, I said, "I have to give you a bath."

I'd never washed an animal in my life and didn't have a clue how to begin, but I did have a shower stall with a sprayer on a long hose. Opening the stall door, I called to Perry. He walked in and submitted to a shampoo, rinse, and towel dry without an ounce of opposition.

Relieved that fleas wouldn't be deposited in my house, I felt better about having the dog inside. But that night I worried that Perry would jump up on my bed. I told him it was off limits. He went to the entrance of my bedroom and lay across it. When I woke up the next morning, Perry was still there, guarding my doorway. I was surprised at how safe I felt. Since my husband's death and my children leaving home, I'd never felt overly fearful, but I was aware of being a woman alone. Perry's presence made me feel less vulnerable.

Though I knew nothing about the care and training of dogs, suddenly I was thrust into the middle of it. When I had a big question, I'd call my son-in-law, but for the most part I just tried to figure things out. I often found myself talking to the dog. "Think you could handle some chicken today?" "Shall we add another block to our walk?" "See this jar of treats. Every time you go potty outside, I'll give you one."

Every few days my daughter and her husband came over, but the arrival of their baby, being unable to move from their apartment, and their alternate-shift jobs kept Perry with me. More and more, he became my companion. He'd lie nearby as I worked at home in the mornings and then eagerly look forward to our afternoon walks.

I felt pleased when my bony puppy filled out into a handsome dog that many people stopped to admire. Though his Alaskan malamute father dominated Perry's looks, his shar-pei mother gave him his gold color and expressive face.

But Perry wasn't the only one who had changed. One day I noticed I no longer raced to wash my hands every time I petted Perry. I played fetch with him and even roughhoused once in a while. I couldn't believe it. I laughed out loud the day I realized I no longer took pride in the unmessed vacuum trails in my carpet. Perry obliterated them as quickly as I made them. My once immaculate house had rubber toys lying around and dog dishes in the kitchen.

By now my daughter and her husband knew Perry was as much or more my dog as theirs. But though they still could not take him, my son-in-law struggled to let go of his dog. I understood but it shook me. Putting Perry on his leash I headed out for a walk. "God, I can't keep falling in love with this dog. It will hurt too much when I've got to give him up. I'm going to put him back in the yard. I have to get used to having an empty house again."

When my words ended, God seemed to whisper, "Will you let fear of pain keep you from the joy I've brought into your life through this dog?"

Perry turned around and looked at me when I started to cry. Regaining control and wiping my eyes with the sleeves of my sweatshirt, I told him, "It's okay. Don't worry. I'm going to keep you as long as the Lord lets me—even if that means some pain in the end."

Four years later, I still have Perry. Given more time, my son-in-law finally realized a large dog just didn't fit in their apartment. One day he told me, "He's your dog, Mom."

I don't know the exact moment I realized that God understood and helped fill the void in my heart left by an empty home. But when I think of how He orchestrated events to get past forty-five years of "Go away, doggie," I appreciate even more the wagging tail that greets me each morning.

One of the most difficult things
to give away is kindness—
it is usually returned.

CORT R. FLINT

Friendship Is a Diamond

Friendship is a diamond
buried in the earth;
a treasure of great worth.
But first it must be mined
then faceted and shined.
It takes pick and shovel and strain,
encompassing time and enduring pain,
until its grace is seen;
a glittering gift of love
that's shared between we three:
First God,
and you,
then me.

SALLY J. KNOWER

THE COMFORT ROOM

MAYO MATHERS
FROM *TODAY'S CHRISTIAN WOMAN* MAGAZINE

*I*s your Comfort Room available next weekend?" The voice of my friend on the telephone sounded weary and faint. "I could sure use a respite."

I smiled, assuring her it was. Hanging up the phone, I walked down the hall to the room she'd inquired about. The Comfort Room developed quite by accident, but there is no doubt in my mind that the people who stay here are no accident at all. God brings them to us when they're most in need of comfort.

I looked around the room, running my hand lightly across the soothing pattern of the wallpaper. Walking over to the antique bed, I stretched out across the quilt with its blue and white wedding ring pattern and luxuriated in the familiar sense of comfort that settled over me like a feathery eiderdown.

My earliest memory of the bed goes back to when I was three years old. My parents had just brought my new baby sister to Grandma's house where I'd been staying. As Mom laid her on the bed, I stood on my tiptoes, eagerly peeking over the high mattress to catch a glimpse of her.

For as long as I can remember, the bed and its accompanying dresser and dressing table occupied what had once been the parlor of my grandparents' large Missouri farmhouse. During those long-ago summers, when all the grandchildren visited, "taking turns" was the order of the day. We took turns on the porch swing, took turns on the bicycle, and even took turns at the chores. But there was no taking turns when it came to sleeping in Grandma's bed. Even on hot, smothery, summer nights she let us all pile in around her at once. Our sweaty little bodies stuck happily together as we listened to Grandma's beloved stories of the "olden days" until one by one, we fell asleep.

Those well-spun tales gave me a strong sense of family identity, pride, and comfort. And I needed plenty of comfort when clouds started building in the summery blue skies that stretched over the corn fields surrounding the farm. How I dreaded the wild, crashing, earsplitting midwestern thunderstorms that resulted from those massive clouds!

Standing at the window, I'd watch the lightning flashes intensify across the sky and count the seconds until I heard the low growl of thunder. Grandma told me that was how to tell how many miles away the storm was.

I hated nighttime storms the most—when I'd have to go upstairs to my bedroom, up even closer to the storm. Sleep was impossible. As the jagged slashes grew more brilliant, the time between the stab of lightning and the crash of thunder grew less and less.

Then suddenly, FLASH! KA-A-A-BOOM! The light and sound came as one! *The storm was here! Right on top of me!* At that point, I'd leap from the bed, and with my sister close behind, we'd slam into our brother in the hallway. The three of us tore down the stairs as one.

Hearing our pounding feet, Grandma would already be scooted over in bed with the covers thrown back for us. We plowed beneath them, scrunching up as close to her as we could. While the thunder shook and rattled the house, she'd jump dramatically and exclaim, "Whew! That one made my whiskers grow!" And from under the pillows where we'd buried our heads, we couldn't help but giggle. In Grandma's bed we were always comforted.

There I found comfort not only from thunderstorms but from lifestorms as well. Hurt feelings, broken hearts, insecurities—all were mended there. When I was lucky enough to have Grandma to myself in her bed—which wasn't often—I'd tell her all my deepest secrets, knowing she took them very seriously.

When my father, her son, died of cancer, I was eight years old. On that last night of his life, instead of spending those moments with him in the hospital, Grandma gathered me into her bed. Curling her body around mine, she infused me with comfort I didn't yet know I needed.

In college, when a broken engagement had crushed my heart and hopes, she comforted me by saying, "The pathway to love never runs smooth, honey, but you'll find your way when it's right." Four years later, her prediction came true.

Shortly after my wedding, Grandma died, bringing an end to the unlimited source of love and comfort that I knew could never be replaced, the kind that only comes from a grandmother. When my aunt called to tell me the beloved bedroom set was mine, I immediately drove to Missouri to pick it up. Although the beautiful pieces had to be placed in storage, I hoped that someday I'd have room for them in our home.

The years melted away with startling speed. Caught up in the happy frenzy of raising our two sons, I rarely thought of the bedroom set stuck away in the attic. There was too much present to think of the past. Before I knew it, our firstborn was packing his belongings to move on to a new phase of life.

The day Tyler left, I went into his empty room and sat down in the middle of the floor while memory after memory scurried up to tap me on the shoulder. His leave-taking had been more wrenching than I had antici-pated. Inside the echoes of the room I tried to come to grips with the door that had just closed on my life.

Quite abruptly, a thought came to mind. I raised my head and looked around my son's room with new eyes. I finally had room for Grandma's bedroom set!

For the next two weeks I worked on the room, lovingly choosing paint, wallpaper, and pictures. Frequent tears splashed into the paint tray as I pondered all the different seasons one passes through in a lifetime. When the painting and papering were done, my husband lugged the bedroom set down from the attic and helped me arrange it in the room. I stopped to consider the completed result and was drawn to the bed where I let my fingers trace around the grooves in the curved footboard of the wonderful old treasure. As I sat quietly, a familiar feeling begged to embrace me—the same feeling I'd had as a child with Grandma beside me in the bed. It was as if she were in the room with me right then comforting me in this new stage of life I was entering.

Right then I christened it the "Comfort Room." From where I sat I prayed, "Lord, I hope everyone who stays in this room feels the comfort I'm feeling now. Bring people to us who need the comfort."

Our first guest in the Comfort Room was a friend who'd just lost her brother and two close friends to death. Next was a couple who were at a transition point in their life, not sure which direction to go. Then a young cousin arrived in need of a temporary home and an out-of-town uncle whose wife was flown to our medical center following a severe heart attack. From the day it was completed, God has seen to it that the Comfort Room is well used.

There is one guest, however, whose arrival I most anticipate. I'm waiting for the day when my son will return and bring with him a grandchild. Then I will be the grandma snuggling up with my grandchild in that old bed. I'll be the one spinning stories of the "olden days." And I'll offer to them what my grandma gave to me—unending comfort, unlimited love.

SOMEONE TO
DIVIDE WITH

FROM *TEA TIME WITH GOD*

At the turn of the century, a man wrote in his diary the story of a young newsboy he met on a street near his home in London. It was well known in the neighborhood that the boy was an orphan. His father had abandoned the family when the boy was a baby, and his mother had died shortly after he began selling newspapers.

All attempts to place the boy in either an institution or a foster home were thwarted, because the boy refused each offer of help and ran away when attempts were made to confine him. "I can take care o' myself jest fine, thank ye!" he would say to kindly old ladies who questioned whether he'd had his porridge that day.

Indeed, he never looked hungry and his persistence at selling papers, load after load, gave the impression he spoke the truth.

But the streets are a lonely place for a child to live, and the man's diary reflects a conversation he had with the child about his living arrangements. As he stopped to buy his paper one day, the man bought a little extra time by fishing around in his pocket for coins and asked the boy where he lived. He replied that he lived in a little cabin in an impoverished district of the city near the river bank. This was something of a surprise to the man.

With more interest, he inquired, "Well, who lives with you?"

The boy answered. "Only Jim. Jim is crippled and can't do no work. He's my pal."

Now clearly astounded that the child appeared to be supporting not only himself but also someone who was unable to contribute any income, the man noted, "You'd be better off without Jim, wouldn't you?"

The answer came with not a little scorn—a sermon in a nutshell: "No, sir, I couldn't spare Jim. I wouldn't have nobody to go home to. An' say, Mister, I wouldn't want to live and work with nobody to divide with, would you?"

Go oft to the house of thy friend,
for weeds choke the unused path.

RALPH WALDO EMERSON

EMPTY PLACES FILLED

CHRIS FABRY

FROM *AT THE CORNER OF MUNDANE AND GRACE*

Life without Jim has been hard. I realized that when we saw him last week. Jim is six years old and tall for his age. He has sandy hair and bright blue eyes, I think.

Before he moved at the end of the last school year, he played with my son Ryan. Ryan is a year and a half younger, but they got along well.

After kindergarten Jim would come over to our place. He and Ryan would play with Jim's cars or set up a McDonald's by our fireplace. They were good for about two hours together. Then they would fight, yell a couple of times, then make up.

I noticed a change in Ryan the first week after Jim moved. He didn't mope or hang his head, but there was something missing. Jim was missing.

A couple of days later the outburst came. Something was thrown, or someone was hit, and there was crying and wailing.

I remember my wife saying, "You miss Jim, don't you, buddy?" Those are the times you thank God for a wife and not a spoon. Ryan nodded and buried his head in her chest. A few minutes later he was back to normal.

The summer went by and talk of Jim subsided. He was out there somewhere. Wisconsin was what they called it, but it was China for all my son knew. A four-hour drive is an eternity when you're four.

But a few weeks ago we heard Jim was coming for a visit. The excitement steadily built.

"When is Jim coming? Is it tomorrow? Can he come over?"

"Next week, bud, next week."

On the night I said, "Jim comes tomorrow," Ryan's eyes widened. He smiled and scrunched beneath the covers and shook with anticipation. It was one of those involuntary reactions that spreads to everyone in the room. I went to bed smiling, remembering my own childhood friend.

His name was Johnny, but we called him Little Johnny, because his older brother was also named John. Little Johnny came to our house, and we dug holes in the earth simply because we could. We stood on an old basketball backboard and pretended the hoop was the hatch to our spacecraft. If you fell off you would be lost forever with only enough oxygen to last five minutes. If your fellow astronaut didn't help you get back on quickly, you would swell up, turn blue, and eventually pop like a balloon. The search-and-rescue missions on that backboard were better than any film I've ever seen.

Somewhere in my elementary years Little Johnny moved.

I never heard from him again. His friendship left an empty hole in my life, with the memories piled up like dirt alongside the edges. I hadn't thought about Little Johnny for a long time, but Jim's return brought the memories back.

In the morning Ryan was up extra early wearing one of my long-forgotten T-shirts that dusts the floor. After a bowl of cereal he was dressed and at the window.

"Remember, buddy," I said, "they're going to call after lunch for you to come over."

Questions persisted before and during lunch. I kept his coat off him as long as I could. We were about an hour away from Jim-down. The baby was asleep. Ryan had eaten lunch and cleaned his room. Barney was finished for the day. We sat and waited.

I got a cover and stretched out on the couch. He came with a couple of books, leaned against my chest, and we read *Hippo Lemonade*. When we got to the scary part, he drifted off. His breathing slowed, his eyes drooped, and soon we were both asleep.

The phone woke us and we both jumped. Jim was on his way. He would pick Ryan up at the corner, and they would walk back together, just like old times. We put our coats on and watched the street for any sign of him. It was a gray day and the street was wet. I heard an old muffler coming and soon a station wagon chugged by our house. When the smoke cleared I saw a blond head and some feet bouncing down the street.

"There he is!" Ryan said.

I crossed with him, and we waited a few inches past the street. Ryan wanted to walk as much sidewalk as he could with his friend. Jim was taller now, his shoulders wider. He cracked chewing gum and his cheeks were red from the cold.

"Hi, Jim," I said enthusiastically. "Boy it's been a long time since we've seen you. How are you doing?"

"Okay," he said softly. He looked at Ryan. "Are you ready?"

"Yeah."

Ryan's turtle tennis shoes scooted along the sidewalk, pushing at the leftover leaves. Hands in pockets. Head straight. No conversation.

They were nearly to the corner when Jim's head turned and he said something. Ryan looked up at him, his hair fluffy in the back, and laughed. They picked up the pace, heads bobbing. I would have given a fair amount of money to hear that conversation. To walk with them and listen to the musings of two friends. But there are some places you cannot go, and there are conversations you cannot hear. I crossed the street alone, and when I turned, they were running.

There are empty places where friends should be. We don't realize it until we find a friend to fill them. The sight of those two rounding the corner was enough to create my own hunger, to make me want to dig a hole or stand on an old backboard again. As I went back to the house, I think I saw the sun peek through the clouds.

Love

ON AN OLD SUN DIAL

Time flies,
Suns rise,
And shadows fall.
Let time go by.
Love is forever over all.

AUTHOR UNKNOWN

THE WALLET

ARNOLD FINE

As I walked home one freezing day, I stumbled on a wallet someone had lost in the street. I picked it up and looked inside to find some identification so I could call the owner. But the wallet contained only three dollars and a crumpled letter that looked as though it had been in there for years.

The envelope was worn and the only thing that was legible on it was the return address. I started to open the letter, hoping to find some clue. Then I saw the dateline—1924. The letter had been written almost sixty years ago.

It was written in a beautiful feminine handwriting on powder blue stationery with a little flower in the left-hand corner. It was a "Dear John" letter that told the recipient, whose name appeared to be Michael, that the writer could not see him anymore because her mother forbade it. Even so, she wrote that she would always love him.

It was signed, Hannah.

It was a beautiful letter, but there was no way except for the name Michael, that the owner could be identified. Maybe if I called information, the operator could find a phone listing for the address on the envelope.

"Operator," I began, "this is an unusual request. I'm trying to find the owner of a wallet that I found. Is there any way you can tell me if there is a phone number for an address that was on an envelope in the wallet?"

She suggested I speak with her supervisor, who hesitated for a moment then said, "Well, there is a phone listing at that address, but I can't give you the number." She said, as a courtesy, she would call that number, explain my story and would ask them if they wanted her to connect me. I waited a few minutes and then she was back on the line. "I have a party who will speak with you."

I asked the woman on the other end of the line if she knew anyone by the name of Hannah. She gasped, "Oh! We bought this house from a family who had a daughter named Hannah. But that was thirty years ago!"

"Would you know where that family could be located now?" I asked.

"I remember that Hannah had to place her mother in a nursing home some years ago," the woman said. "Maybe if you got in touch with them they might be able to track down the daughter."

She gave me the name of the nursing home and I called the number. They told me the old lady had passed away some years ago but they did have a phone number for where they thought the daughter might be living.

I thanked them and phoned. The woman who answered explained that Hannah herself was now living in a nursing home.

This whole thing was stupid, I thought to myself. Why was I making such a big deal over finding the owner of a wallet that had only three dollars and a letter that was almost sixty years old?

Nevertheless, I called the nursing home in which Hannah was supposed to be living and the man who answered the phone told me, "Yes, Hannah is staying with us."

Even though it was already 10 P.M., I asked if I could come by to see her. "Well," he said hesitatingly, "if you want to take a chance, she might be in the day room watching television."

I thanked him and drove over to the nursing home. The night nurse and a guard greeted me at the door. We went up to the third floor of the large building. In the day room, the nurse introduced me to Hannah.

She was a sweet, silver-haired old-timer with a warm smile and a twinkle in her eye. I told her about finding the wallet and showed her the letter. The second she saw the powder blue envelope with that little flower on the left, she took a deep breath and said, "Young man, this letter was the last contact I ever had with Michael."

She looked away for a moment deep in thought and then said softly, "I loved him very much. But I was only sixteen at the time and my mother felt I was too young. Oh, he was so handsome. He looked like Sean Connery, the actor."

"Yes," she continued. "Michael Goldstein was a wonderful person. If you should find him, tell him I think of him often. And," she hesitated for a moment, almost biting her lip, "tell him I still love him. You know," she said smiling as tears began to well up in her eyes, "I never did marry. I guess no one ever matched up to Michael…"

I thanked Hannah and said good-bye. I took the elevator to the first floor and as I stood by the door, the guard there asked, "Was the old lady able to help you?"

I told him she had given me a lead. "At least I have a name, but I think I'll let it go for a while. I spent almost the whole day trying to find the owner of this wallet."

I had taken out the wallet, which was a simple brown leather case with red lacing on the side. When the guard saw it, he said, "Hey, wait a minute! That's Mr. Goldstein's wallet. I'd know it anywhere with that bright red lacing. He's always losing that wallet. I must have found it in the hall at least three times."

"Who's Mr. Goldstein?" I asked as my hand began to shake.

"He's one of the old-timers on the eighth floor. That's Mike Goldstein's wallet for sure. He must have lost it on one of his walks."

I thanked the guard and quickly ran back to the nurse's office. I told her what the guard had said. We went back to the elevator and got on. I prayed that Mr. Goldstein would be up.

On the eighth floor, the floor nurse said, "I think he's still in the day room. He likes to read at night. He's a darling old man."

We went to the only room that had any lights on and there was a man reading a book. The nurse went over to him and asked if he had lost his wallet. Mr. Goldstein looked up with surprise, put his hand in his back pocket and said, "Oh, it is missing!"

"This kind gentleman found a wallet and we wondered if it could be yours?"

I handed Mr. Goldstein the wallet and the second he saw it, he smiled with relief and said, "Yes, that's it! It must have dropped out of my pocket this afternoon. I want to give you a reward."

"No, thank you," I said. "But I have to tell you something. I read the letter in the hope of finding out who owned the wallet."

The smile on his face suddenly disappeared. "You read that letter?"

"Not only did I read it, I think I know where Hannah is."

He suddenly grew pale. "Hannah? You know where she is? How is she? Is she still as pretty as she was? Please, please tell me," he begged.

"She's fine…just as pretty as when you knew her," I said softly.

The old man smiled with anticipation and asked, "Could you tell me where she is? I want to call her tomorrow." He grabbed my hand and said, "You know something, mister, I was so in love with that girl that when that letter came, my life literally ended. I never married. I guess I've always loved her."

"Mr. Goldstein," I said. "Come with me."

We took the elevator down to the third floor. The hallways were darkened and only one or two little night-lights lit our way to the day room where Hannah was sitting alone watching the television. The nurse walked over to her.

"Hannah," she said softly, pointing to Michael, who was waiting with me in the doorway. "Do you know this man?"

She adjusted her glasses, looked for a moment, but didn't say a word. Michael said softly, almost in a whisper, "Hannah, it's Michael. Do you remember me?"

She gasped, "Michael! I don't believe it! Michael! It's you! My Michael!" He walked slowly toward her and they embraced. The nurse and I left with tears streaming down our faces.

"See," I said. "See how the Good Lord works. If it's meant to be, it will be."

About three weeks later I got a call at my office from the nursing home. "Can you break away on Sunday to attend a wedding? Michael and Hannah are going to be married!"

It was a beautiful wedding with all the people at the nursing home dressed up to join in the celebration. Hannah wore a light beige dress and looked beautiful. Michael wore a dark blue suit and stood tall. They made me their best man.

The hospital gave them their own room and if you ever wanted to see a seventy-six-year-old bride and a seventy-nine-year-old groom acting like two teenagers, you had to see this couple.

A perfect ending for a love affair that lasted nearly sixty years.

If I could reinvent the alphabet,
I would put U and I together.

AUTHOR UNKNOWN

THE BUS PASSENGER

AUTHOR UNKNOWN

*T*he passengers on the bus watched sympathetically as the attractive young woman with the white cane made her way carefully up the steps. She paid the driver and, using her hands to feel the location of the seats, walked down the aisle and found a seat he'd told her was empty. Then she settled in, placed her briefcase on her lap, and rested her cane against her leg.

It had been a year since Susan, thirty-four, became blind. Due to a medical misdiagnosis she had been rendered sightless, and she was suddenly thrown into a world of darkness, anger, frustration, and self-pity. Once a fiercely independent woman, Susan now felt condemned by this terrible twist of fate to become a powerless, helpless burden on everyone around her. "How could this have happened to me?" she would plead, her heart knotted with anger.

But no matter how much she cried or ranted or prayed, she knew the painful truth—her sight was never going to return. A cloud of depression hung over Susan's once optimistic spirit. Just getting through each day was an exercise in frustration and exhaustion. And all she had to cling to was her husband, Mark.

Mark was an air force officer and he loved Susan with all of his heart.

When she first lost her sight, he watched her sink into despair and was determined to help his wife gain the strength and confidence she needed to become independent again. Mark's military background had trained him well to deal with sensitive situations, and yet he knew this was the most difficult battle he would ever face.

Finally, Susan felt ready to return to her job, but how would she get there? She used to take the bus, but was now too frightened to get around the city by herself. Mark volunteered to drive her to work each day, even though they worked at opposite ends of the city.

At first, this comforted Susan and fulfilled Mark's need to protect his sightless wife who was so insecure about performing the slightest task. Soon, however, Mark realized that this arrangement wasn't working—it was hectic and costly. Susan is going to have to start taking the bus again, he admitted to himself. But just the thought of mentioning it to her made him cringe. She was still so fragile, so angry. How would she react?

Just as Mark predicted, Susan was horrified at the idea of taking the bus again. "I'm blind!" she responded bitterly. "How am I supposed to know where I'm going? I feel like you're abandoning me."

Mark's heart broke to hear these words, but he knew what had to be done. He promised Susan that each morning and evening he would ride the bus with her, for as long as it took, until she got the hang of it. And that is exactly what happened.

For two solid weeks, Mark, military uniform and all, accompanied Susan to and from work each day. He taught her how to rely on her other senses, specifically her hearing, to determine where she was and how to adapt to her new environment. He helped her befriend the bus drivers who could watch out for her and save her a seat. He made her laugh, even on those not-so-good days when she would trip exiting the bus, or drop her briefcase.

Each morning they made the journey together, and Mark would take a cab back to his office. Although this routine was even more costly and exhausting than the previous one, Mark knew it was only a matter of time before Susan would be able to ride the bus on her own. He believed in her, in the Susan he used to know before she'd lost her sight, who wasn't afraid of any challenge and who would never, ever quit.

Finally, Susan decided that she was ready to try the trip on her own. Monday morning arrived, and before she left, she threw her arms around Mark, her temporary bus riding companion, her husband, and her best friend.

Her eyes filled with tears of gratitude for his loyalty, his patience, his love. She said good-bye, and for the first time, they went their separate ways. Monday, Tuesday, Wednesday, Thursday… Each day on her own went perfectly, and Susan had never felt better. She was doing it! She was going to work all by herself!

On Friday morning, Susan took the bus to work as usual. As she was paying for her fare to exit the bus, the driver said, "Boy, I sure envy you." Susan wasn't certain if the driver was speaking to her or not. After all, who on earth would ever envy a blind woman who had struggled just to find the courage to live for the past year?

Curious, she asked the driver, "Why do you say that you envy me?"

The driver responded, "It must feel so good to be taken care of and protected like you are."

Susan had no idea what the driver was talking about and asked again, "What do you mean?"

The driver answered, "You know, every morning for the past week, a fine looking gentleman in a military uniform has been standing across the corner watching you when you get off the bus. He makes sure you cross the street safely and he watches until you enter your office building. Then he blows you a kiss, gives you a little salute, and walks away. You are one lucky lady."

Tears of happiness poured down Susan's cheeks. For although she couldn't physically see him, she had always felt Mark's presence. She was lucky, so lucky, for he had given her a gift more powerful than sight, a gift she didn't need to see to believe—the gift of love that can bring light where there had been darkness.

LEVI'S VALENTINE

J. STEPHEN LANG
FROM *THE CHRISTIAN READER* MAGAZINE

When Levi Carpenter proposed to Letitia (Letty) McCluskey on New Year's Eve 1919, he said, "Pick a day [for our wedding], and make it one I can always remember."

She chose February 14.

That year, 1920, a foot of snow fell in Fayetteville, Tennessee, on Valentine's Day. Letty said, "Let's put it off a week, to make sure all the guests can arrive." Levi wouldn't hear of it. He was convinced the day was right, snow or no snow. The wedding was hastily moved from the church to the minister's parlor, with five people present.

Because the roads were impassible, all arrangements for flowers, refreshments, and formal wear had been scrapped. Yet, as if by magic, Levi arrived with a bouquet of pink roses for his bride. When prodded, he said he "had connections." Forty-some years later, he confided to me (his great-grandson) that the minister's wife brought them from her own greenhouse.

By the time I came into the world, Levi and his Valentine wife were well past sixty. Living only a few miles away, I saw them almost every weekend. After Valentine's Day, without fail, I knew a huge bouquet of pink roses would be on the mahogany table in the foyer. But that wasn't all.

Somewhere near the vase was Levi's one annual attempt at artistry: a large snowflake intricately cut from paper. Attached to it was a note: "To Letty, my Valentine lady these 44 years." The words never changed from year to year, just the number. Yet true to nature, the snowflakes were always a different design.

At age nine, I discovered a nook in the china cabinet where every anniversary snowflake had been placed, lovingly and dearly, starting with the first one inscribed, "To Letty, my Valentine for a whole year." Levi, a carpenter who was considered "tight-lipped" and unemotional, showed his heart to everyone once a year.

One day Levi sat me down and patiently showed me, step-by-step, how to fold and cut paper snowflakes. But it didn't take long before I became more frustrated than artistic. My efforts resulted in things that looked more like rat's nests than snowflakes. It made me wonder: *Does Great-Granddad really want me to know the secret?*

He seemed to delight in being the only one in the family with an artistic gift. He knew his wealthy brother Claude had taken his wife on a Valentine jaunt to the Caribbean, giving her a pearl necklace on the way. But Claude could only *buy* gifts. Levi could *make* snowflakes. And every one was a reminder of his wedding day, and of the girl he married.

No one ever said to me on February 14, "This is a big day for your great-grandparents." But I knew it was. The only time I recall them kissing was on a Valentine's Day, when my parents and I just happened to arrive at the moment Levi gave Letty her annual snowflake and roses.

When she realized we were watching, Letty's cheeks flushed as she scurried from the room, shrieking, "Levi, you wicked thing!" She wasn't convincing at all.

A few years afterward Levi gave Letty a snowflake on which he had written, "To Letty, my Valentine lady these 56 years." No one was sure if Letty saw this one. She was alive, and conscious, but so heavily medicated that she could only nod faintly when Levi held the snowflake in front of her. He placed it on her bedside table in the nursing home, beside the vase of pink roses.

He turned to Letty and said, "I'll be in tomorrow, early, Letty." Then after a pause, he added, "my love." She nodded faintly again.

Levi took my arm—a rare occurrence—as we left the room. A few feet down the corridor he said, "Boy, go get that snowflake. Them nurses or cleanin' women may throw it out with the garbage."

I retrieved it, knowing Levi intended to take it home to the china cabinet with the others. If Letty ever came home, he would show it to her then.

The following Valentine's Day, Levi and I made our way to the cemetery, bringing a bouquet of pink roses. There was a light dusting of snow, and he brushed it away from the double headstone. He placed the roses in the headstone's vase, hesitated, then put them back in the glass vase he'd brought them in.

"This is foolish, boy," he said. "No point in leavin' these here where no one'll see them."

He let out a deep breath, then said, "She'll see 'em, anyway, wherever they are. We'll come back in April. I'm thinkin' of plantin' a rose bush here, if the church won't mind."

"Pink roses?" I asked.

"Sure, pink's a nice color. Here, go put these flowers back in the car."

I took the vase, trying not to look at his face, knowing that stifling a tear was even harder if he knew I was watching him. I sat in the car, the motor running, holding the vase of roses. Then I saw Levi take something from his coat pocket and tuck it down inside the stone vase. It appeared to be a piece of paper, though I couldn't be sure.

The snow had started to fall in earnest and Levi shuffled back to the car. "Gonna be a big snow this time, I think. Let's get going."

I knew that the one thing he wouldn't discuss was the one thing on his mind. How could the heavy snowfall not remind him of this day 57 years earlier? At 15, I hadn't yet experienced a broken heart, but sitting with my great-granddad, I was near enough to feel it.

The following year I got my driver's license. It was my first time to drive to the family cemetery by myself. There was no snow this Valentine's Day, just a gray, dull chill.

The rose bush Levi and I had planted in April had bloomed beautifully through the summer. It looked rather somber now, as did the entire ceme-tery. The date of Levi's death had been carved on his stone four months earlier.

My parents had placed some silk poinsettias on the grave at Christmas, and they were still there. *Out of season now,* I thought.

As I pulled them from the stone vase, something caught my eye. Barely visible in the pebbles at the bottom of the vase, I saw a corner of white paper. Somehow, after a year of snow and rain and wind, Levi's last paper snowflake was still intact.

I reached for it, thinking I would put it with my great-grandparents' other belongings in my parents' basement.

But the paper wasn't a souvenir for me. It was Levi's anniversary gift. It needed to stay exactly where it was.

Love comforteth like sunshine after rain.

WILLIAM SHAKESPEARE

I LOVE YOU ANYWAY

DR. JOE HARDING

*I*t was Friday morning and a young businessman finally decided to ask his boss for a raise. Before leaving for work, he told his wife what he was about to do. All day long he felt nervous and apprehensive. Finally in the late afternoon he summoned the courage to approach his employer, and to his delight, the boss agreed to the raise.

The elated husband arrived home to a beautiful table set with their best china and lighted candles. Smelling the aroma of a festive meal, he figured that someone from the office had called his wife and tipped her off! Finding her in the kitchen, he eagerly shared the details of his good news. They embraced and danced around the room before sitting down to the wonderful meal his wife had prepared. Next to his plate he found an artistically lettered note that read, "Congratulations, darling! I knew you'd get the raise! This dinner is to show you how much I love you."

Later on his way to the kitchen to help his wife serve dessert, he noticed that a second card had fallen from her pocket. Picking it up off the floor, he read, "Don't worry about not getting the raise! You deserve it anyway! This dinner is to show how much I love you."

Total acceptance! Total love. She stood behind him no matter what—softening the blows, healing the wounds, and believing in him. We can be rejected by many if we're loved by one.

Grow old along with me!
The best is yet to be,
The last of life for which the first was made.

ROBERT BROWNING

CRUMBLING SANDCASTLES

SUE MONK KIDD

FROM *TODAY'S CHRISTIAN WOMAN* MAGAZINE

One mild summer day beside the sea, my husband and I were lying on our beach towels, reading, each locked in our own separate worlds. It had been like that a lot lately. We'd been busy, preoccupied, going in different directions. I'd hoped the leisure of vacation would be different, but so far we'd spent most of it marooned in silence.

I looked up from my book at the ceaseless roll of the waves, feeling restless. I ran my fingers through the sand. "Wanna make a sandcastle?" I asked my husband.

He didn't really, but he humored me. Once we got started, though, he became surprisingly absorbed in the project. We both did. In fact, after a while we were working over that heap of beach sand like it was about to be photographed for Sandcastle digest. Sandy made bridges across the moat, while I crowned the top of the castle with spires. We made balconies and arched windows lined with tiny angel-wing shells. It looked like Camelot.

Neither of us noticed when the tide changed. We never saw the waves slipping up until the first swish of water gnawed a little piece of our castle away. Indignant, we shored it up with sand and patted it down. But as the waves returned with monotonous regularity, our hands grew still and our eyes drifted off toward the horizon. Sandy got on his beach towel. I got on mine. We went back to our silence.

The next time I looked around, the sandcastle we'd labored over was awash in the shifting tide. The bridges were washing away and the spires were starting to lean.

I gave it a soulful look, an inexplicable sadness coming over me. And suddenly in the midst of that ordinary summer, I had a moment of pure, unbidden revelation. There sits my marriage, I thought.

I looked at my husband. The soundlessness between us seemed to reach clear to the sky. It was the hollow silence of a mid-life marriage, a marriage in which the ceaseless noise of everyday living threatens to drown out the music of intimacy.

Dear God, when had the tide shifted? When had mortgages and laundry and orthodontist appointments become more important than those unspeakably long looks we used to exchange? How long since we'd shared our hidden pain or stumbled together upon a joy that was round with wonder and laughter? How had it happened that two people who loved each other could allow such distance to creep in?

I thought of the attentiveness we'd lavished upon our relationship in the beginning, and how, eventually, the endless demands and routines of running a household, raising two children, and juggling two careers had stilled our hands and averted our eyes.

That night, after the children were asleep, my husband found me standing in the shadows on the porch, staring into the night. "You've hardly said two words all evening."

"Sorry," I muttered. "I've just got something on my mind."

"You want to tell me what it is?" he said.

I turned around and looked at him. I took a deep breath. "I'm thinking of us," I said. "I'm thinking that our relationship is being drowned out by the demands of day-to-day living. We've taken our marriage for granted."

"What are you talking about? We have a very committed marriage!" He was indignant.

"Of course we have a committed marriage," I told him. "But sometimes it seems commitment is all we've got. Sometimes we are two strangers existing under one roof, each going separate ways."

He didn't say a word. Now I've done it, I thought. I've rocked the boat to the point of tipping over. I've told my husband our marriage is border-ing on empty commitment. Good grief!

We stared at each other. It was like we were stuck inside some big, dark bubble of pain that wouldn't pop. Tears welled up in my eyes and started down my face. To my amazement, tears started down his face, too.

And suddenly, in what is surely the most endearing moment of my marriage, Sandy took his finger and traced the path of tears on my cheeks, then touched his own wet face, blending our tears together.

Strange how such things can begin to re-create the mystery of relat-edness between two people. Sandy and I walked down the porch steps onto the beach under the blazing stars. Slowly we started to talk. We talked a long time. About the small agonies of being married, about the struggle of it all. We talked about the gnawed and fraying places in our marriage and how they'd happened. We spoke aching words about the unmet needs between us.

We were whirling the darkness that had settled in our relationship. And yes, it was uncomfortable and scary, like bobbing around in the ocean without a boat. But trading chaos and braving pain is often the only way to come upon a new shoreline. For God is in dark water, too.

Finally with the hour late and a sense of deepening and newness growing between us, I said rather dreamily, "It might be nice someday to say our wedding vows to each other again."

"What's wrong with right now?" my husband said. I swallowed. Was there no end to the surprises this man would spring on me tonight?

"B-but what would we say? I mean, I can't remember the vows exactly."

"Why don't we simply say what's in our hearts?"

So out there beneath the light of the stars, with the crash of waves fill-ing the night, we took each other's hand and tried to put words to the music we had begun to recapture between us.

"I promise to listen to you," he said. "To make time for genuine sharing…"

"And I promise to be honest, to work at creating more togetherness between us," I began.

I don't remember all the words; mostly I remember the feelings behind them, the way my voice quivered and his hand tightened over mine. Mostly I thought what we were doing was rebuilding the castle, restoring the bridges, raising the spires.

The next morning we left the children stationed in front of the television with their breakfast cereal and went walking along the ocean edge. The sun poured a golden dial of light across the water that seemed to point us on and on. We talked as we went, a little awed by the events of the night before—knowing in the harsh light of day that saying words is one thing, but living them is another. We couldn't leave our newly spoken vows back there dripping in the moonlight. We had to take them home to the frantic schedules and the broken dryer and the Dorito crumbs under my son's bed.

Miles down the beach we waded knee-high into the surf and stood soaking up the turquoise sky and jade water. We were about to turn back to the condo when it happened. A huge, bottle-nosed dolphin came splashing out of the water a mere twenty yards away, startling us so badly we fell backward into the surf.

Sitting in the water fully clothed...a dolphin diving and surfacing before us in a spinning silver dance, was such an unexpected and exhilarating wonder, the two of us laughed until our insides hurt. I cannot remember a joy ever so plump and full.

At last we picked our delirious selves up and walked in our soggy shorts back up the beach where a few crumbling sandcastles dotted the shore. I took note of each one of them.

And I began to hear a voice deep inside me whispering: "When tomorrow comes and life beats upon your castle walls, remember the power of honest pain and blended tears, Remember the healing of laughter deeply shared. Remember what's important. Hold onto it always."

TITANIC LOVE

JIM PRIEST
FROM *THE DAILY OKLAHOMAN/OKLAHOMA CITY TIMES*

They were the picture of romance as they strolled the deck of the luxury ocean liner.

Arm and arm they walked, heads together, sharing stories and secrets and smiles.

From what people could see, they seemed very much in love. But beneath the surface, where no one could see, there was something else. Something that eyes could not behold, that ears could not hear and that minds could not grasp.

Beneath the surface was a deep and abiding commitment to one another that welded them together stronger and tighter than the rivets holding the unsinkable ship they were aboard.

Their names were Isidor and Ida Strauss.

Immigrants to America, they had scratched and scrapped their way in the new world and made a name for themselves.

With sweat and smarts, they had been able to build a little merchandise store in New York City: they named it Macy's. As they walked the decks of the HMS Titanic that April day in 1912, they were enjoying a much deserved vacation. They were enjoying each other's company. Unknown to them they were enjoying their last day together.

It was April 14, 1912, late in the evening, when the Titanic—the unsinkable ship crossing the Atlantic on her maiden voyage—struck an iceberg and started to sink. Icebergs, of course, only show a small part of themselves, most of the imponderable chunk of ice is below the ocean's surface.

Beneath the surface where no eye could see, no ear could hear, no mind could grasp its depth and size. As the ship began to list and take on water the lives of those on board began to change.

Some fearfully scrambled for safety. Some valiantly helped those in need. Isidor and Ida Strauss walked calmly on the deck, assessing the situation before finally approaching a lifeboat. Mrs. Strauss began to climb into the lifeboat, but changed her mind at the last minute.

She turned to her husband and said, "We have been living together for many years. Where you go, I go."

Members of the crew overheard her and tried to get her to change her mind. She would not listen.

A crew member turned to old Mr. Strauss and said, "I'm sure no one would object to an old gentleman like yourself getting in."

But Mr. Strauss was as stubborn as his wife.

"I will not go before the other men."

So the issue was settled. Neither would go without the other, and neither one would go.

Mrs. Strauss turned to her maid, now safely on board the lifeboat and said, "Here, take my fur coat. I won't be needing it."

Then the old couple walked a few steps to some nearby deck chairs and sat down together to await the inevitable.

Like the iceberg, the Strausses had more beneath the surface than could be seen by a casual observer. True enough, they showed their love for one another, but that was just the part that was visible. Beneath the surface was a solid commitment to one another that nothing, not even the threat of death could shake.

WHERE I BELONG

BOB WELCH
FROM *MOODY* MAGAZINE

*W*ith the freeway ahead of us and home behind, the photographer and I left on a three-day newspaper assignment.

We were bound for the Columbia Gorge, where the Columbia River carves a mile-wide path between Washington and Oregon; where windsurfers come from across the country to dance across waves created by "nuclear winds"; where I would be far from the world of 9-to-5 and deadlines and routines and errands and rushing kids to baseball practices and having to make sure I hadn't left my socks on the bedroom floor.

Frankly, it had not been the perfect farewell. Our family was running on empty. Our '81 car was showing signs of its age. We were all tired, cranky and, spiritually, about a quart low.

My 8-year old son tried to perk us up with his off-key version of a song from the musical *Annie:* The sun will come out tomorrow; bet your bottom dollar that tomorrow there'll be sun....

It didn't work.

I had been busy trying to get ready for the trip; my wife, Sally, had been fretting because my three days of freedom were going to mean, for her, three days of extra responsibility.

"Daddy, are you coming to hear my class sing Thursday night?" Jason, my 8-year-old, asked amid the chaos of my departure.

Bill Cosby would have gotten a funny expression on his face and said, "Well, of course," and everyone would have lived happily ever after.

I didn't feel much like Bill Cosby that morning. "I'm going to be out of town," I said. "Sorry."

Giving Sally a quick kiss, I was on my way. Now, hours later, I was far away from my family—free from the clutter, the runny noses, and the demands on my time.

The photographer and I shared a bit about ourselves as we drove. Roughly my age—mid 30s—he was married but had no children.

He told me how he and his wife had recently taken a trip to the gorge by themselves. My mind did a double take. By themselves? I vaguely remembered what that was like. Taking off when the mood hits. No pleas for horseback rides about the time you're ready to crash for the night. No tornado-swept rooms. No meet-the-teacher nights.

Besides having no children, the photographer had no six-month-old french fries on the floor of his car, no legs of Superman action figures on his dashboard, and no road maps on which most of Idaho had been obliterated by a melted Snickers bar.

For the next couple of days, despite a threat of rain, we explored the gorge: thousand-foot walls of basalt rising on either side of the Columbia; fluorescent-clad sailboarders, like neon gnats, carving wakes in the water.

If the land and water were intriguing, so were the windsurfers. There were thousands, nearly all of them baby boomers, spending their days on the water, their nights on the town, their mornings in bed.

Every fourth car had a board on top. License plates from all over the country dotted the streets. Some of these "boardheads" were follow-the-wind free spirits who lived out of the back of vans; others were well-established yuppies here for a weekend or on vacation.

Seeing this group was like discovering an ancient tribe. While I was busy trying to put on jammed bike chains, my generational brothers were jamming to the rock beat of dance clubs every night. While I was depositing paychecks that were spent on groceries and orthodontia bills and college funds, these people were deciding what color sailboards to buy.

Where had I gone wrong?

On our last night, the cloudy weather continued, which irked the photographer and mirrored the mood that had overcome me. We both needed sunshine, only for different reasons.

As I stared from the motel window at the river below, I felt a sort of emptiness, as if I didn't belong. Not here. Not home. Not anywhere. Just as the winds of the gorge were whipping the river into whitecaps, so were the winds of freedom buffeting my beliefs. God. Marriage. Children. Work. I had anchored my life on such things, and yet now found myself slipping.

Had I made a mistake? Had the boundaries of Scripture become a cage around me? Had I sold out to the rigors of responsibility? Someday, when I was older, would I face the brittle-cold reality of regret, wishing I would have gone with the wind?

I was getting ready for bed when I spotted it—a greeting card in my suitcase, buried beneath some clothes. It was from Sally. The card featured cows—my wife's big on bovines—and simply said, "I'll love you till the cows come home."

I stared at the card for minutes. I repeated the words to myself. I looked at the same handwriting I'd seen on love letters in college, on a marriage certificate, on two birth certificates, on a will. And something inside me melted. My wife's promise bored through my hardened heart, refocusing my blurry perspective. In an instant, I knew exactly where I belonged.

The next day, after a two-hour interview, a six-hour drive, and a three-block sprint, I arrived at my son's school, anxious and out of breath. The singing program had started 20 minutes before; had I missed Jason's song?

I rushed into the cafeteria. It was jammed. Almost frantically, I weaved my way through a crowd of parents clogging the entrance to where I could get a glimpse of the kids on stage. That's when I heard them: 25 first-grade voices trying desperately to hit notes that were five years away.

The sun will come out, tomorrow; bet your bottom dollar that tomorrow there'll be sun...

My eyes searched this collage of kids, looking for Jason.

Finally I spotted him: front row, as usual, squished between a couple of girls whose germs, judging by the look on his face, were crawling over him like picnic ants. He was singing, but with less enthusiasm than when he's been told to clean his room.

Suddenly, his eyes shifted my way, and his face lit up with the kind of smile a father gets to see only in a grade-school program when his eyes meet his child's. He had seen me, a moment that will forever stay frozen in my memory.

Later, through a sea of faces, I caught sight of Sally and my other son. After the program, amid a mass of parent-child humanity, the four of us rendezvoused, nearly oblivious to the commotion surrounding us. I felt no emptiness, only connectedness.

In the days to come, I would resume my part in life as a bike-fixer, nine-to-fiver, Sunday school teacher, and husband—roles that might cause a windsurfer to yawn.

But I decided that for all the temporal freedom of skimming across a river, I'll take the eternal freedom of a faithful God. For all the luxury of a spotless car interior, I'll take the front-row smile of my 8-year-old. And for all the carefree living in the Columbia Gorge, I'll take the responsibility of caring for the woman who has vowed to love me till the cows come home.

A happy marriage is the union of two good forgivers.

ROBERT QUILLEN

THE SPIRIT OF SUNSHINE

AUTHOR UNKNOWN
FROM *LADIES HOME JOURNAL* MAGAZINE

ow's business, Eben?"

The old man was washing at the sink after his day's work.

"Fine, Marthy, fine."

"Does the store look just the same? Land, how I'd like to be there again with the sun shining in so bright! How does it look, Eben?"

"The store's never been the same since you left it, Marthy." A faint flush came into Martha's cheeks. Is a wife ever too old to be moved by her husband's praise!

For years Eben and Martha had kept a tiny notion store, but one day Martha fell sick and was taken to the hospital. That was months ago. She was out now, but she would never be strong again—never more be partner in the happy little store.

I can't help hankering for a sight of the store, thought Martha one afternoon. *If I take it real careful I think I can get down there. 'Tisn't so far.*

It took a long time for her to drag herself downtown, but at last she stood at the head of the little street where the store was. All of a sudden she stopped. Not far from her on the pavement stood Eben. A tray hung from his neck. On this tray were arranged a few cards of collar-buttons, some papers of pins and several bundles of shoe-laces. In a trembling voice he called his wares.

Martha leaned for support against the wall of a building nearby. She looked over the way at the little store. Its windows were filled with fruit. Then she understood. The store had gone to pay her hospital expenses. She turned and hurried away as fast as her weak limbs would carry her.

It will hurt him so to have me find it out! she thought, and the tears trickled down her face.

He's kept it a secret from me, and now I'll keep it a secret from him. He shan't ever know that I know.

That night when Eben came in, chilled and weary, Martha asked cheerily the old question:

"How's business, Eben?"

"Better'n ever, Marthy," was the cheery answer, and Martha prayed God might bless him for his sunshiny spirit and love of her.

In this life we cannot do great things.
We can only do small things with great love.

MOTHER TERESA

NEW BEGINNINGS

PATRICIA WYMAN

FROM *VIRTUE MAGAZINE*

*S*ee you tonight, Lee." This morning, Mark's perfunctory kiss didn't even reach my cheek. Starting toward the door, he turned, "Oh, I may have a meeting tonight. I'll call if I do."

I had not returned his "kiss" nor did I respond to his comment. Oblivious to my lack of response, Mark closed the door behind him.

On impulse, I grabbed my cup of coffee, hurried to the door and reopened it. I watched Mark wind his way around the azalea bushes, losing sight of him when he entered the garage. In the early years of our marriage, this had been a morning tradition. I would stand in the doorway until he backed the car out, tooted the horn and waved good-bye. No wave met my gaze this morning; he no longer expected me to be there.

Returning to the kitchen, I refilled my cup, threw a sweater over my shoulders and went into the back yard to sit on the old glider. Our back yard had always delighted me. I hoped that being there would help me capture memories of happier times.

Although it was only April, the sun warmed my face. The maple trees were beginning to sprout buds, and the morning dew on the yellow wisps of the forsythias reflected the sun's rays.

I looked at the spot where the flowering Japanese cherry tree used to stand. Mark and I had planted it when we moved into the house nearly 20 years ago. As the tree flourished, it came to represent much more than beauty and shade to me. The tree's maturing paralleled the growth of our three children.

The near-hurricane winds had blasted through our region last fall, toppling the tree. When the landscapers dug up the roots, I felt as if my own roots were being torn from me.

Staring at the bare patch that remained, I couldn't help but remember the day I'd learned that we were going to move here.

Married for six years, Mark and I had three small children—Mark Jr., Becca and Emily. All of us were crammed, like an overstuffed suitcase into an incredibly small apartment. I was mashing potatoes for supper when Mark literally bounced into the house.

"Everyone in the den," Mark ordered. "I've got something to tell you." He paced the floor impatiently while waiting for us to get settled. "I've found us a house! It needs all kinds of work, but it's sound—and best of all, it has a huge back yard. No, best of all, we can afford it!"

Sitting in that same back yard on a sunny April morning, I realized all I had left was the house.

The children were off on their own. Even though I held a rewarding job as a nurse for a local pediatrician, I found myself facing hours that I didn't know how to fill, hours when I found myself fighting feelings of desolation and uselessness.

I had always taken my job as a mother seriously. Determined to raise our children in a spiritual home, I had spent vast amounts of time instilling values. I had driven them to practices, games and lessons. I had helped with homework and had filled my days with the 101 other things that children require—the things no one seemed to need anymore. True, Mark's body still lived in our home, but, emotionally, he had moved continents away.

What bothered me most was not knowing when it happened. By the time I recognized his distance, the chasm between us felt too deep and too wide to be crossed.

"Enough of this," I said, and headed for the house. The telephone rang just as I entered the kitchen—Becca's Wednesday morning phone call, right on schedule.

"Mom," she began abruptly, "I know you absolutely despise surprise parties, so I'm not giving you one."

"That's sweet of you to be so thoughtful, Becca. But even if I did like surprise parties, why would you be giving me one?"

"Mother!" In her exasperation she sounded more like my mother than my daughter. "For your 25th anniversary next month."

"Save the big bash for our 50th, honey." *If there is one,* I added silently.

After filling me in on all the amazing things my grandson was doing, Becca said good-bye. As I dressed for work, I continued wondering what hidden ailment was destroying my once-strong marriage.

The thought that I'd refused to dignify with conscious consideration kept poking at me until I said, "No. It can't be someone else. Oh, please, God, please don't let it be someone else."

The next few weeks passed with little change in our relationship. We were painfully polite to one another. Perfunctory kisses became our morning ritual and Mark continued to have periodic, late appointments.

When Mark suggested we go out to dinner one Saturday, I found myself hoping, against all reason, that our "date" would revive something in both our hearts. In anticipation, I pampered myself with a facial, a shampoo, a bubble bath, a manicure and an hour's rest.

I decided on a beige, silk shantung suit that I hadn't been able to fit into in three years. Apparently, my apathy about so many things must have included food.

As he helped me into the car Mark said, "You look...lovely, Lee."

Sadly, the date went downhill from there. After we finished discussing the children and work, our conversation became stilted, awkward.

Over dessert, my hopes rose again when, once more, he said, "You really do look lovely tonight, Lee." But we fell asleep that night in our usual position—back to back—with an ocean of space between us. When I accidentally touched him, I immediately drew away. It seemed indecent—as if I had touched a stranger.

My mind kept whispering, "It's all the fault of that storm," but I knew that whatever was wrong with our marriage couldn't be blamed on a felled tree.

I awoke at six and quietly eased out of the bed. Wrapped in an old, cuddly robe, I took my coffee out into the back yard and sat amid the chirping of sparrows and chickadees.

"It's over," I muttered. "Our marriage is truly over…but I don't want it to be over! I can't let it be over!"

My gaze turned to the spot where the tree had been, and I saw something poking up from the ground. Setting down my cup and wrapping the robe tightly around me, I walked over and knelt down.

Little shoots were pushing their way through the hard earth. I recognized them as lilies of the valley. Perhaps they had been there all along, hiding among the roots of the trees, and I just hadn't noticed. Maybe they had been forced to lie dormant all these years, yielding their space to the overwhelming needs of a growing tree.

Regardless of how they got there, a few little plants stretched toward the sky and the sun.

My thoughts returned to the back yard of my childhood home, filled with lilies of the valley. As my mother stood on our porch admiring them and inhaling their sweet scent, her face would have the same peaceful expression as when she was in church.

"Those little bell-shaped flowers may look delicate," she would say, "but they're as strong as can be. No matter how harsh the winter; they pop right up each spring."

Then, she'd spread her arms as if she could grasp the yard and all it contained. "Can you believe that this abundant growth of beauty started from a few plants? I do believe that they're a message of hope from our Lord."

I went back inside, cooked Mark's favorite breakfast, fixed a tray, and carried it to the bedroom.

Bending down, I gave him a kiss and whispered, "Do you have any idea how much I love you?"

Startled out of a deep sleep, he peered out of heavy lidded eyes and hoarsely asked, "What is it? What's wrong?"

"I'm not sure," I said. "But I'm willing to work on fixing whatever it is. Are you?"

"Lee, there's something that I want to tell you."

"Not now, Mark. Right now, let's plan our trip."

"What trip?" he asked, propping himself on one elbow.

"Our 25th anniversary trip. Where would you like to go?"

"Lee—it isn't what you think—I never…"

"I didn't think you had," I said.

As I stood there with my tousled hair, swaddled in my old robe, Mark took my hand and said, "You're so beautiful."

And the new beginning promised by the lilies took root in my heart.

All, everything that I understand,
I understand only because I love.

LEO TOLSTOY

The Secret

ven the most devoted couple will experience a storm once in a while. A grandmother, celebrating her golden wedding anniversary, once told the secret of her long and happy marriage.

"On my wedding day I decided to make a list of ten of my husband's faults which for the sake of our marriage, I would overlook," she said. "I never did get around to listing them. But whenever my husband did something I didn't like, I would say to myself, 'Lucky for him that's one of the ten.'"

AUTHOR UNKNOWN

THE GOLDEN CRANE

PATRICIA LORENZ

As a teacher of origami (the ancient Japanese art of paper folding) at the LaFarge Lifelong Learning Institute in Milwaukee, Wisconsin, Art Beaudry was asked to represent the school at an exhibit at a large mall in Milwaukee. He decided to take along a couple hundred folded paper cranes to pass out to people who stopped at his booth.

Before that day, however, something strange happened—an inner voice told him to find a piece of gold foil paper and make a gold origami crane. The urging was so strong that Art actually found himself rummaging through his collection of origami papers at home until he found one flat, shiny piece of gold foil. "Why am I doing this?" he asked himself. Art had never worked with the shiny gold paper; it didn't fold as easily or neatly as the crisp multicolored papers. But that little voice kept nudging. Art harrumphed and tried to ignore it. "Why gold foil anyway? Paper is much easier to work with," he grumbled.

The urging continued. "Do it! And you must give it away tomorrow to a special person."

That evening Art very carefully folded and shaped the unforgiving gold foil until it became as graceful and delicate as a real crane about to take flight. He packed the exquisite bird in the box along with about 200 colorful paper cranes he'd made over the previous few weeks.

The next day at the mall, dozens upon dozens of people stopped by Art's booth to ask questions about origami. He demonstrated the art. He folded, unfolded, and refolded. He explained the intricate details, the need for sharp creases.

Then there was a woman standing in front of Art. The special person. Art had never seen her before, and she hadn't said a word as she watched him carefully fold a bright pink piece of paper into a crane with pointed, graceful wings.

Art glanced up at her face, and before he knew what he was doing, his hands were down in the big box that contained the supply of paper cranes. There it was, the delicate gold-foil bird he'd labored over the night before. He retrieved it and carefully placed it in the woman's hand.

"I don't know why, but there's a voice inside me telling me I'm supposed to give you this golden crane. The crane is the ancient symbol of peace," Art said simply.

The woman didn't say a word as she slowly cupped her small hand around the fragile bird as if it were alive. When Art looked up at her face, he saw tears filling her eyes, ready to spill out.

Finally, the woman took a deep breath and said, "My husband died three weeks ago. This is the first time I've been out. Today…" She wiped her eyes with her free hand, still gently cradling the golden crane with the other. She spoke very quietly. "Today is our golden wedding anniversary."

Then this stranger said in a clear voice, "Thank you for this beautiful gift. Now I know that my husband is at peace. Don't you see? That voice you heard, it's the voice of God and this beautiful crane is a gift from Him. It's the most wonderful fiftieth wedding anniversary present I could have received. Thank you for listening to your heart."

And that's how Art learned to listen very carefully when a little voice within him tells him to do something he may not understand at the time.

ROSES FOR ROSE

JAMES KISNER
FROM *SWEET DREAMS AND TENDER TEARS*

Red roses were her favorites, her name was also Rose.
And every year her husband sent them, tied with pretty bows.
The year he died, the roses were delivered to her door.
The card said, "Be my Valentine," like all the years before.

Each year he sent her roses, and the note would always say,
"I love you even more this year, than last year on this day.
My love for you will always grow, with every passing year."
She knew this was the last time that the roses would appear.

She thought, he ordered roses in advance before this day.
Her loving husband did not know, that he would pass away.
He always liked to do things early, way before the time.
Then, if he got too busy, everything would work out fine.

She trimmed the stems, and placed them in a very special vase.
Then, sat the vase beside the portrait of his smiling face.
She would sit for hours, in her husband's favorite chair.
While staring at his picture, and the roses sitting there.

A year went by, and it was hard to live without her mate.
With loneliness and solitude, that had become her fate.
Then, the very hour, as on Valentines before,
The doorbell rang, and there were roses, sitting by her door.

She brought the roses in, and then just looked at them in shock.
Then, went to get the telephone, to call the florist shop.
The owner answered, and she asked him, if he would explain,
Why would someone do this to her, causing her such pain?

"I know your husband passed away, more than a year ago,"
The owner said, "I knew you'd call, and you would want to know.
The flowers you received today, were paid for in advance.
You husband always planned ahead, he left nothing to chance.

"There is a standing order, that I have on file down here,
And he has paid, well in advance, you'll get them every year.
There also is another thing, that I think you should know,
He wrote a special little card…he did this years ago.

"Then, should ever, I find out that he's no longer here,
That's the card…that should be sent, to you the following year."
She thanked him and hung up the phone, her tears now flowing hard.
Her fingers shaking, as she slowly reached to get the card.

Inside the card, she saw that he had written her a note.
Then, as she stared in total silence, this is what he wrote…
"Hello, my love, I know it's been a year since I've been gone,
I hope it hasn't been too hard for you to overcome.

"I know it must be lonely, and the pain is very real.
For if it was the other way, I know how I would feel.
The love we shared made everything so beautiful in life.
I loved you more than words can say, you were the perfect wife.

"You were my friend and lover, you fulfilled my every need.
I know it's only been a year, but please try not to grieve.
I want you to be happy, even when you shed your tears.
That is why the roses will be sent to you for years.

"When you get these roses, think of all the happiness,
That we had together, and how both of us were blessed.
I have always loved you and I know I always will.
But, my love, you must go on, you have some living still.

"Please…try to find happiness, while living out your days.
I know it is not easy, but I hope you find some ways.
The roses will come every year, and they will only stop,
When your door's not answered, when the florist stops to knock.

"He will come five times that day, in case you have gone out.
But after his last visit, he will know without a doubt,
To take the roses to the place, where I've instructed him,
And place the roses where we are, together once again."

LIFE'S FINEST HOUR

EUGENE S. GEISSLER
FROM *THE BEST IS YET TO BE*

Do you remember, Jo, when you first called me "Friend Husband"? It was many, many years ago, early in our marriage. I don't think it struck me as particularly extraordinary at first to be called that name. After all, what else is expected from a husband or wife? But now that I am old and you still say it, it has grown into considerable significance for me.

We have been through a lot together and having survived it all we look forward to continued care for each other. Our tenderness is more precious than ever because of our greater need for each other.

Thirty-five years into our marriage you wrote, "Friend Husband was 20 when I met him—so I have no first-hand knowledge of his early years. The person he was at 28 commanded my immediate interest—there was no strangeness, no tension—and we were friends from our first meeting. And we remain friends together."

Short days ago we quietly celebrated 45 years of marriage. It was indeed one of our finest anniversaries, wasn't it? The next day you took me aside though there was nobody around that could see or hear us. You confided: "Ever since we've been married and then when you were overseas, and all these years since, I've wanted to buy you a gold wedding band. Would you wear it?"

So I sit here with my golden wedding band shining at me. I've had it on less than 45 hours, but it fits and feels like it has been there for 45 years. The next time I left a note for you on the kitchen counter, I delighted in signing it: "Friend Husband w/ the gold ring."

Am I just talking trivia? Or is it perhaps not necessary to say anything? A husband and a wife, friends together for 45 years, might just know what the other is thinking. At the end of such a long period of time, sitting silently together becomes a kind of virtue, a pleasing sound, a language of presence. Would you say that every now and then we are inclined to call it "life's finest hour"?

Five years ago our children decided to re-do our family room into a room for just the two of us. We were caught by surprise, not feeling secure about the offer. You know how people growing older don't like things being changed around. But it was a Christmas present, lovingly signed by our children.

It is a rather long but somewhat narrow room, facing south and front, with a large picture window. On the narrow east end of the room is the library. There you have the wing chair you have always wanted, and there you spend a lot of time reading. Reading is your pastime, much of your entertainment, your therapy and refuge.

My wing chair, matching yours across the room, sits in the corner next to the stove. It's my home base. A couch against the wall opposite the window allows for some good company now and then.

So here we are, daily facing each other across the room—you in the library most of the time, and myself, an up-and-down, in-and-out person, only half as much. But much happens between us here. We say prayers together; we often eat our breakfast and lunch here. We interrupt each other with things to tell, insights to offer, deep thoughts to share, jokes to laugh at, even disagreements to start and stop.

We are aware of our need for each other, our concern for each other, our promises to take care of each other, whichever one is able to do so when that time comes. Sometimes we ask the Lord if we might die close together. Every day we thank God for our being together.

Among the people we seem to pray for more often now are "the old and the infirm," and the other morning we had to add: "among whom we class ourselves." Neither of us is either that old or that infirm to be talking much about it. Still we know it to be coming—the end of those things we have cherished together. To be honest about what lies hidden before us doesn't distract us from those fleeting moments of peace and quiet of soul, which are a foretaste of the good things that wait us in the presence of the Lord.

The way to love someone is to lightly run your finger over that person's soul until you find a crack, and then gently pour your love into that crack.

KEITH MILLER

RUDY'S ANGEL

WILMA HANKINS HLAICZKA

I walked into the grocery store not particularly interested in buying groceries. I wasn't hungry. The pain of losing my husband of thirty-seven years was still too raw. And this grocery store held so many sweet memories.

Rudy often came with me and almost every time he'd pretend to go off and look for something special. I knew what he was up to. I'd always spot him walking down the aisle with the three yellow roses in his hands.

Rudy knew I loved yellow roses. With a heart filled with grief, I only wanted to buy my few items and leave, but even grocery shopping was different since Rudy had passed on.

Shopping for one took time, a little more thought than it had for two. Standing by the meat, I searched for the perfect small steak and remembered how Rudy had loved his steak. Suddenly a woman came beside me. She was blond, slim, and lovely in a soft green pantsuit. I watched as she picked up a large pack of T-bones, dropped them in her basket, hesitated, and then put them back. She turned to go and once again reached for the pack of steaks. She saw me watching her and she smiled.

"My husband loves T-bones, but honestly, at these prices, I don't know."

I swallowed the emotion down my throat and met her pale blue eyes. "My husband passed away eight days ago," I told her.

Glancing at the package in her hands, I fought to control the tremble in my voice. "Buy him the steaks. And cherish every moment you have together." She shook her head, and I saw the emotion in her eyes as she placed the package in her basket and wheeled away.

I turned and pushed my cart across the length of the store to the dairy products. There I stood, trying to decide which size milk I should buy. A quart, I finally decided and moved on to the ice cream section near the front of the store. If nothing else, I could always fix myself an ice cream cone.

I placed the ice cream in my cart and looked down the aisle toward the front. I saw first the green suit, then recognized the pretty lady coming towards me. In her arms she carried a package. On her face was the brightest smile I had ever seen. I would swear a soft halo encircled her blond hair as she kept walking toward me, her eyes holding mine. As she came closer, I saw what she held and tears began misting in my eyes. "These are for you," she said and placed three beautiful long stemmed yellow roses in my arms. "When you go through the line, they will know these are paid for." She leaned over and placed a gentle kiss on my cheek, then smiled again.

I wanted to tell her what she'd done, what the roses meant, but still unable to speak, I watched as she walked away as tears clouded my vision. I looked down at the beautiful roses nestled in the green tissue wrapping and found it almost unreal. How did she know? Suddenly the answer seemed so clear. I wasn't alone.

"Oh, Rudy, you haven't forgotten me, have you?" I whispered, with tears in my eyes. He was still with me, and she was his angel.

Inspiration

Twenty years from now you will be more disappointed
by the things you didn't do than by the ones you did do.
So throw off the bowlines.
Sail away from the safe harbor.
Catch the trade winds in your sails.
Explore.
Dream.
Discover.

MARK TWAIN

OL' ED NEVER FORGOT

MAX LUCADO
FROM *IN THE EYE OF THE STORM*

To the onlookers, some things seem like an empty ritual, when to the person who is informed, they seem more significant than life itself. Take ol' Ed down in Florida. Every Friday evening about the time the sun is the size of a giant orange just about to dip into the water, ol' Ed comes strolling along the beach to find his way to his favorite pier. He's carrying in his bony hand a bucket full of shrimp. The shrimp are not for him. The shrimp are not for the fish. Strangely, the shrimp are for the seagulls. Ed, alone with his thoughts, walks out to the end of the pier with his bucket, not saying a word. But that's where the ritual begins.

Before long the sky becomes a mass of little dots screeching and squawking, making their way to ol' Ed there on the end of the pier. They envelope him with their presence. Their fluttering wings sound like a roar of thunder. Ed stands there and sort of mumbles to them as they're feeding on the shrimp. In fact, he reaches in his bucket and he throws a few up to them. You can almost hear him say, "Thank you. Thank you." Within minutes, the bucket is empty. And Ed stands there, almost as if raptured, in his thoughts of another time and another place. Then, without a word being spoken, he quietly makes his way back home.

Who is ol' Ed anyway? His full name is Eddie Rickenbacker. He was a captain in World War II. He flew a B-17 Flying Fortress. He and seven other men were sent on a mission across the Pacific to locate General MacArthur; however, their plane crashed in the water. Miraculously, they all made it out of the plane into a life raft.

Aboard their life raft, they fought the sun and the sharks. Most of all, they fought hunger, as all eight of these men ate and drank very little, until finally by the eighth day their rations ran out. No food. No water. They needed a miracle for them to survive.

After an afternoon devotional time, the men said a prayer and tried to rest. As Rickenbacker was dozing with his hat over his eyes, something landed on his head. It was a sea gull. That gull meant food…if he could catch it. And he did.

He tore the feathers off and they shared a morsel of it together. Then they used the intestines for fish bait. They were able to survive until they were found and rescued, almost at the end of their lives.

Later, Billy Graham asked Captain Rickenbacker about the story, because he heard that that experience had been used to lead him to a saving knowledge of Jesus Christ. Rickenbacker said to Billy, "I have no explanation except God sent one of His angels to rescue us."

Ol' Ed never forgot. He never stopped saying, "Thank you." Every Friday evening for years until he died, he would go to that old pier with a bucket full of shrimp and a heart full of gratitude for the rescue to say, "Thank you. Thank you. Thank you."

BETTER THAN
A TROPHY

GRACE WITWER HOUSHOLDER

Early in the season my husband told me this would be his
last year coaching baseball.

After ten years he had learned he loved the sport and the kids so
much that he couldn't do it halfway. The 100 percent dedication and many
extra practices were taking an emotional and physical toll. He said it was
time for him to become a spectator again.

Going into the tournament his team of ten- and eleven-year-olds had
the best record in the league. They had gone from 3 to 3 to 10 to 3. It
looked like his players would be bringing home trophies.

But flu struck that night.

In the last inning one of the sick players, the best hitter on the team,
was unable to bat. Tears streaming down his face, he told the coach he
couldn't stand up. He could only lie down. The team would have to bat
out of order and receive its third and final out.

Only I knew how hard it was for my husband to end his coaching
career with a loss.

Three days later this letter from one of the game's umpires appeared
in the local newspaper:

In the post-season tournament of the Youth Baseball Major League, I witnessed a wonderful example of what youth sports are all about. Before the game one team had two players that were feeling sick but still wished to play. The coach granted their wishes and inserted them in the lineup.

In the bottom of the last inning the team was trailing by two runs and had two outs when the next batter was slated to be one of the flu-stricken players. Despite his gutsy play to that point he simple could not fight off his illness anymore. He could not bat. Under strict rules of baseball, which were being played, this resulted in the team batting out of order and committing the third and final out.

The coach could have chosen to fight the rule and try to persuade the other coach to grant his team one more out. But he chose not to. His players could have chosen to look down on their ailing teammate, but they comforted him instead. The fans could have chosen to plead with the officials and prod the coach to action but chose to console their sons.

In an age when winning seems to be the bottom line nobody on the losing side made any excuses or outraged appeals. They accepted their defeat according to the rules of the game.

Baseball can be viewed as a microcosm of real life. Sometimes the breaks go your way; sometimes they don't. You can abide by the rules and face the consequences, or you can break them and possibly cheat someone else. The coach showed that although the rules might not always be in your favor, they are still the rules, and obeying them is better than losing your dignity and compromising the spirit of the game. The children may have cried because their season had ended, but what they accomplished on that evening will forever outlive the tears.*

The day after the letter to the editor, my husband got this letter from one of his ten-year-old players:

Thanks for being my coach. You improved us all. I know it was a bummer to lose because you have won two years in a row. But you never lost your temper, and when you almost did you smiled.

My husband and his team entered the tournament wanting a trophy.

They left with something better.

---

*The name of the umpire writing the letter was Brian Allen.

LOVE AND
THE CABBIE

ART BUCHWALD

I was in New York the other day and rode with a friend in a taxi. When we got out, my friend said to the driver, "Thank you for the ride. You did a superb job of driving."

The taxi driver was stunned for a second. Then he said, "Are you a wise guy or something?"

"No, my dear man, and I'm not putting you on. I admire the way you keep cool in heavy traffic."

"Yeah," the driver said and drove off.

"What was that all about?" I asked.

"I am trying to bring love back to New York," he said. "I believe it's the only thing that can save the city."

"How can one man save New York?"

"It's not one man. I believe I have made that taxi driver's day. Suppose he has twenty fares. He's going to be nice to those twenty fares because someone was nice to him. Those fares in turn will be kinder to their employees or shopkeepers or waiters or even their own families. Eventually the goodwill could spread to at least one thousand people. Now that isn't bad, is it?"

"But you're depending on that taxi driver to pass your goodwill to others."

"I'm not depending on it," my friend said. "I'm aware that the system isn't foolproof so I might deal with ten different people today. If out of ten I can make three happy, then eventually I can indirectly influence the attitudes of three thousand more."

"It sounds good on paper," I admitted, "but I'm not sure it works in practice."

"Nothing is lost if it doesn't. It didn't take any of my time to tell that man he was doing a good job. He neither received a larger tip nor a smaller tip. If it fell on deaf ears, so what? Tomorrow there will be another taxi driver I can try to make happy."

"You're some kind of a nut," I said.

"That shows how cynical you have become. I have made a study of this. The thing that seems to be lacking, besides money of course, for our postal employees, is that no one tells people who work for the post office what a good job they're doing."

"But they're not doing a good job."

"They're not doing a good job because they feel no one cares if they do or not. Why shouldn't someone say a kind word to them?"

We were walking past a structure in the process of being built and passed five workmen eating their lunch. My friend stopped. "That's a magnificent job you men have done. It must be difficult and dangerous work."

The workmen eyed my friend suspiciously.

"When will it be finished?"

"June," a man grunted.

"Ah. That really is impressive. You must all be very proud."

We walked away. I said to him, "I haven't seen anyone like you since *The Man from LaMancha*."

"When those men digest my words, they will feel better for it. Somehow the city will benefit from their happiness."

"But you can't do this all alone!" I protested. "You're just one man."

"The most important thing is not to get discouraged. Making people in the city become kind again is not an easy job, but if I can enlist other people in my campaign…"

"You just winked at a very plain-looking woman," I said.

"Yes, I know," he replied. "And if she's a schoolteacher, her class will be in for a fantastic day."

The grand essentials of happiness are:
Something to do,
Something to love
And something to hope for.

ALLAN K. CHALMERS

*The two most beautiful things in the universe
are the starry heavens above our heads
and the feeling of duty in our hearts.*

BOSSUET

WE COULD HAVE DANCED ALL NIGHT

GUY DOUD

FROM *MOLDER OF DREAMS*

*A*s adviser to our high school student council I worked with the leadership to encourage projects that involved student service. I was impressed with my students' enthusiasm for helping with local canned-food drives and other events to aid charity.

Our "Adopt-a-Grandparent" program had been rewarding for the students who had been involved. They had grown as people by discovering the worth of others. I believe that the true leader is the true servant, and I tried to convey that message to my students. But it never got through to them as clearly as it did the night of the prom.

Tom Rosenberger had given me a call. A friend, and one of the local elementary principals, Tom had heard of an idea at a conference he had attended and called to share the idea with me. I fell in love with it and soon shared it with my student council.

"Mr. President?" I asked.

Mike, the president of the student council, acknowledged me. "Yes, Mr. Doud?"

I started gradually. "I've been thinking of an idea, and I want to bounce it off everyone."

"What's the idea?" asked Mike.

"I think we should host a prom," I said.

"We already have a prom!" answered about thirty students all at once, who seemed to wonder if I had lost my mind. They knew that organizing the prom was the responsibility of the junior class cabinet.

"Oh, I don't mean a prom for eleventh and twelfth graders," I said.

"We're not going to include sophomores!" said one senior boy.

"No. I want to have a prom for senior—" but they didn't let me finish.

"Seniors can already go to the prom," Mike answered, wondering what had gone wrong with his adviser.

"No, for senior citizens. People fifty-five years of age and over. Let's hold a prom for them."

"Why would we want to do that?" asked Mike.

"Let's take the money we've earned this year," I said, "and let's give it back to the community in the form of a gift. That gift will be a prom. We'll invite all senior citizens to come. We'll decorate the gym, hire an orchestra, have corsages for the ladies...." I was beginning to show some real excitement.

"If we spent money doing that, does that mean we wouldn't take our usual spring trip?" asked one girl, putting down the mirror she held in her hand.

"We would spend as much of the money as necessary to make this a most special evening for the senior citizens. The orchestra we hire will play the big band sounds of the twenties and thirties and other dance music. I've already contacted an orchestra, and I've talked with our principal, who thinks it's a great idea. I told him that I thought you guys would think it's a great idea, too." I can be pretty persuasive sometimes.

After much discussion, the council voted to form a committee to plan the senior citizen prom. In the weeks to follow, I watched my students become excited about the prom. Some of the young men in the council decided to order tuxedos so they would look nice as hosts. The girls planned to wear their long dresses to serve as hostesses.

All of Brainerd got excited the week before the prom. Paul Harvey began page two of this national daily broadcast his way: "In Brainerd, Minnesota, the student council is planning a prom...for senior citizens.

That's right! A prom…for senior citizens. The Brainerd students are going to provide an orchestra, corsages, valet parking, free hors d'oeuvres and…they are also going to do the chaperoning!"

I had been somewhat concerned about the lack of advertising. My students had contacted the senior citizen centers in the area and had sent out invitations, but when I heard it announced by Paul Harvey, my fears of poor publicity died.

The night of the prom finally arrived. The students had decorated our gym more beautifully than I had ever seen it. It was like the gym I had seen in my dreams when I had been in high school. The floral department at the vocational school had donated corsages, some of the local banks provided the hors d'oeuvres, the bus company that contracts with the school district provided free transportation to any senior citizen needing it. My students had tried to cover all the bases. We sat back to wait and see how many seniors would attend. The prom was to begin at six-thirty. At four o'clock, they started to come!

One of the first to arrive was an older lady with a cane. She stopped inside the door and looked around.

"Oh," she said, "so this is the new high school."

I didn't remind her that the high school was more than fifteen years old.

"I've never been in here before," she said.

Mark Dinham, one of the main organizers of the prom, grabbed a corsage and asked her if he could pin it on her. She readily agreed.

"The prom doesn't begin until six-thirty," Mark said.

"I'll wait," she said. "I want to get a good seat."

"I hope you'll do some dancing!" I said.

"I'll dance if you dance with me!" she replied as Mark finished pinning her corsage.

He turned a bit red. "Sure, I'll dance with you, but I've got to go home and change clothes," he said.

A few moments later, a couple walked up to the table. "Is this where the prom is being held?" they asked.

"That's right," I said.

I could hardly believe what they had to say: "We're from Oregon, and we're on our way to Wisconsin. We heard it on Paul Harvey yesterday, so we looked up Brainerd on the map and decided to go a little out of our way so we could come to your prom. Are we welcome?"

And people kept coming. By 6:30 when the prom began, more than five hundred senior citizens packed the transformed gymnasium.

But we had developed one major problem. Mike was the first to call it to my attention. I had noticed him dancing with one lady after another. He wasn't able to take a break.

"Mr. Doud," he said, "we have a serious male shortage here."

"What are you going to do about it, Mike?" I asked.

"I know where some of the hockey team is tonight, and I think I could call them and tell them to go home and get their suits on and get over here."

"Good plan," I said.

Soon some of Mike's friends started to arrive. I watched as the lady who had been the first to come walked up to one of the sophomores who had just entered the gym.

"You come dance with me," she said, grabbing his hand before he was sure what had happened.

Mike came up to me. "This is fun. Where did they learn to dance like this?"

Mike and many of my students were amazed that some dances actually had set steps and patterns. I joined in as the senior citizens taught us to waltz and polka. I had never learned to dance, either.

One of the seniors who had dressed up for the occasion had on a beautiful long dress with sequins, and the mirrored ball in the middle of the dance floor reflected light off her dress. We danced. She led.

"If I were about sixty years younger, I'd go after you," she said.

I laughed.

"What grade are you in?" she asked.

I laughed harder. "I'm a teacher here. I'm in charge of these kids."

"Oh," she said, "you're so young and handsome."

I didn't laugh. "And you are very beautiful," I said.

"Oh, come on now...."

The orchestra began to play a song from *My Fair Lady*, and as I followed my partner, I thought of Eliza Doolittle. Henry Higgins saw an elegant woman when everyone else saw a peasant.

"I could have danced all night...." My partner sang along with the music. "That was a good movie," she added, "but I bet it's before your time."

"No, I remember it well." I looked about at my students, every one of them dancing with a senior citizen.

One older man was teaching a sophomore girl how to waltz. I watched her. I was used to seeing her in torn blue jeans. She was beautiful in a long dress.

When the evening finally came to an end, no one wanted to leave.

Mike walked up to me. "That was the most fun I've ever had in high school."

"You mean that was more fun than your junior-senior proms?" I asked.

"No question about it." Mike was definite.

"What made this so much fun?" I asked.

Without thinking for even a moment, Mike answered, "It really feels good to do something for somebody else."

The following Monday, Paul Harvey, who must have spies all about, concluded his broadcast with this story: "Remember last week I told you about how the Brainerd, Minnesota, student council was going to host a prom for senior citizens? Well, they did...and more than five hundred senior citizens showed up. The high school students danced with the seniors, and the chaperons report no major problems.... Oh, there was a little smooching in the corner, but no major problems. Paul Harvey, good day!"

TURN ABOUT

STEVEN J. LAWSON
FROM *ABSOLUTELY SURE*

A soldier who was a Christian made it his practice to conclude every day with Bible reading and prayer. As his fellow soldiers gathered in the barrack and retired for the night, he would kneel by his bunk and offer prayers to the Lord.

The other soldiers saw this and began to mock and harass him. But one night the abuse went beyond verbal assault. As the soldier bowed before His Lord in prayer, one antagonist threw his boot through the dark and hit him in the face. The other soldiers snickered and jeered, hoping for a fight.

But there was no retaliation.

The next morning when the taunting soldier awoke, he was startled to discover something at the foot of his bed. For all to see, there were his boots, returned and polished.

JOHNNY

BARBARA A. GLANZ
FROM *CARE PACKAGES FOR THE WORKPLACE*

*L*ast fall I was asked to speak to 3,000 employees of a large supermarket chain in the Midwest on building customer loyalty and regenerating the spirit in your workplace.

One of the ideas I stressed was the importance of adding a personal "signature" to your work. With all the downsizing, re-engineering, overwhelming technological changes and stress in the workplace, I think it is essential for each of us to find a way we can really feel good about ourselves and our jobs. One of the most powerful ways to do this is to do something that differentiates you from all the other people that do the same thing you do.

I shared the example of a United Airlines pilot who, after everything is under control in the cockpit, goes to the computer and randomly selects several people on board the flight and handwrites them a thank-you note for their business. A graphic artist I work with always encloses a piece of sugarless gum in everything he sends his customers, so you never throw away mail from him!

A Northwest Airlines baggage attendant decided that his personal signature would be to collect all the luggage tags that fall off customers' suitcases, which in the past have been simply tossed in the garbage, and in his free time send them back with a note thanking them for flying Northwest. A senior manager with whom I worked decided that his personal signature would be to attach Kleenex to memos that he knows his employees won't like very much.

After sharing several other examples of how people add their unique spirit to their jobs, I challenged the audience to get their creative juices flowing and to come up with their own creative personal signature.

About three weeks after I had spoken to the supermarket employees, my phone rang late one afternoon. The person on the line told me that his name was Johnny and that he was a bagger in one of the stores. He also told me that he was a person with Down syndrome. He said, "Barbara, I liked what you said!" Then he went on to tell me that when he'd gone home that night, he asked his dad to teach him to use the computer.

He said they set up a program using three columns, and each night now when he goes home, he finds a "thought for the day." He said when he can't find one he likes, he "thinks one up!" Then he types it into the computer, prints out multiple copies, cuts them out, and signs his name on the back of each one. The next day, as he bags customers' groceries—"with flourish"—he puts a thought for the day in each person's groceries, adding his own personal signature in a heartwarming, fun and creative way.

One month later the manager of the store called me. He said, "Barbara, you won't believe what happened today. When I went out on the floor this morning, the line at Johnny's checkout was *three times longer* than any other line! I went ballistic yelling, 'Get more lanes open! Get more people out here,' but the customers said, 'No no! We want to be in Johnny's lane. We want the thought for the day!'"

The manager said one woman approached him and said, "I only used to shop once a week. Now I come here every time I go by because I want the thought for the day!" (Imagine what that does to the bottom line!) He ended by saying, "Who do you think is the most important person in our whole store? Johnny, of course!"

Three months later he called me again. "You and Johnny have transformed our store! Now in the floral department, when they have a broken flower or an unused corsage, they go out on the floor and find an elderly woman or a little girl and pin it on them. One of our meat packers loves Snoopy, so he bought 50,000 Snoopy stickers, and each time he packages a piece of meat, he puts a Snoopy sticker on it. We are having so much fun, and so are our customers!"

That is spirit in the workplace!

Wisdom is oft times nearer when
we stoop than when we soar.

WILLIAM WORDSWORTH

THE AROMA OF CHRISTMAS

BARBARA BAUMGARDNER
FROM *LOOKOUT* MAGAZINE

*S*ometimes I tried to recall the first Christmas. Most of it was a blank. The fragment I could remember included forced laughter, fake smiles, and trying desperately to have a good time.

Christmas had come, right on schedule, only three months after my husband's untimely death. There were no tears or discussion of his absence...only empty festivities. Occasionally I'm glad I don't remember more. "Widow's shock" someone had called it, and they told me I would heal.

Twelve months later that healing was evidenced by the excitement welling up within me as I prepared for a grand and glorious holiday. The kids were coming! Two daughters, a son-in-law and two grandchildren had all agreed to spend Christmas at my home.

I decorated everything I could reach. Glass balls of many colors hung from the leaves of the rubber plant in the entryway and tinsel icicles waved lazily to and fro from branches of the weeping fig tree. Christmas cassettes filled the air with "Joy to the World" and "O Little Town of Bethlehem."

Poinsettias, holly, and mistletoe decorated bedrooms, living room, and over the bathtub. Even the dog diligently guarded the gingerbread boys hanging on the Christmas tree and growled each time the cat walked near.

The aroma of Christmas was the best part because it deliciously replaced the aroma of death that had hung heavily in my home for so long. Spicy snickerdoodles and chewy lemon sugar cookies produced a spirit-lifting, pungent fragrance.

Sticky cinnamon rolls, butter-filled bread twists, and golden brown pumpkin pies found their way out of the busy kitchen of spicy holiday scents and into the freezer to await a celebration of our Savior's birthday and a reunion of family and friends.

The aroma of Christmas was free to soar to the rafters, unhampered this year by an estate to settle, a business to close down, or clothes and tools to dispose of. This year, I could hardly wait to have the family gather for Christmas in my home.

But at 7 A.M. three days before Christmas, the first telephone call came. "Mom, I hope you'll understand. The weather here is below zero, and I've been up all night with freezing, breaking water pipes. There's no way I can leave this mobile home to the elements and come for Christmas. Are you going to be OK with that?"

"Of course!" I knew the weather in Portland had been a record-breaking cold, and Jeri's mobile home was old and not well insulated. Jeri was still single, and to go off and leave could cost her so much in storm-damage repairs. "We'll have Christmas later," I told her. "You take care of that home."

The second call came only twenty minutes later. "Mom, with the wind-chill factor, it's forty-five below. We can't leave the sheep and the water pipes to come home for Christmas. Is there any way you can come here?"

"I don't see how I can get away, honey. That's all right. You and Gregg and the kids have a good Christmas and I'll put your packages on the bus to you."

As I hung up, I felt very, very alone. I lived only one hundred thirty-five miles away from this daughter and my only grandchildren, but I couldn't go there for Christmas because I was committed to some people here in town.

I had invited my brother-in-law, who was a widower, and his eighty-four-year-old mother to come for Christmas dinner, and a young man from the singles group at church had already accepted too. *I sure wouldn't have invited them if I had known my family wasn't going to be here.*

And I had told the old man across the street that I would bring him a plate of dinner at two o'clock on Christmas Day. He was a blunt old codger in his eighties. He always smelled like stale cigars and had brown goo running down his chin, matting his unkempt beard. I hadn't wanted to invite him over, so I offered to bring his dinner to him. "Me and Tish" (his dog) "don't need anything," he had told me. But it soothed my conscience to promise him dinner.

And I had invited a single lady friend with an eight-year-old boy to spend Christmas Eve with me and my family. And now my family wouldn't be here.

"Why, Lord?" I protested aloud. "Why can't I be with my family on Christmas? You knew they weren't going to be able to come; why didn't You stop me from becoming committed to all these others?"

The widow next door had come home from the hospital recently, and her family had left to have Christmas out of town because I had promised to check on her, get her mail and feed the dog. *Boy, am I stuck here!*

I would miss seeing my grandchildren open their beautiful packages and hearing their gleeful cries. And my daughter wanted a food dehydrator so badly. "Lord, You know I got her one; why don't I get to see her open the box and hear her squeal? Lord, it's Christmas!"

Unexpectedly, an awesome humility silenced my complaining heart. Without utterance or movement, the Lord began to answer me: "I know it's Christmas, Barbara; it's *My* birthday. What did you get Me?"

"What do You mean, what did I get You, Lord?"

"Whose birthday is it?" He insisted. "What did you get Me?"

It was at that moment that the expensive gifts around the Christmas tree didn't seem to matter anymore.

"What shall I get You, Lord?" There was only silence. "Could I start by inviting *more* folks to Your birthday party? Perhaps I could take care of my neighbor lady a bit more willingly? I could even invite the old guy from across the street to bring his dog and sit down to the dinner table with us."

My heart began to flutter with anticipation. "There's that man from the gospel mission that I fired last summer while he was trimming my trees because I didn't like his attitude." I began to laugh. "Wouldn't it blow his mind if I'd call and invite him to dinner?

"And the checker from the grocery store who shoveled my driveway out the last time it snowed—he's alone now and will probably eat in a restaurant."

My joy soared! *What a menagerie of misplaced mortals; an ingenious assembly of aristocrats and renegades!*

The list began to grow as I telephoned people who would be alone for Christmas. Soon my table was filled, but not as full as my heart.

The old man across the street could hardly talk, he was so choked with emotion when I invited him to come over and join the crowd for dinner.

"Oh, come all ye faithful," I sang at the top of my lungs. "Come, even if you're not faithful! Y'all come!" And I punched down the last of the bread dough.

I do not remember ever having so much fun preparing Christmas dinner as the day I gave my Christmas to Jesus as a birthday gift. The aroma of the holiday filled my home as I'd planned. And the meaning of Christmas penetrated my heart in a way I'd not anticipated.

Never have I received such a precious gift as when I watched the man from the gospel mission fill his plate five times and I sensed the Lord's nod of approval.

"Alone at Christmas? Never! It's Jesus' birthday, and I'm having a party. You want to come?"

Glory in the Morning

*I*t's 5:30 A.M., and Day knocks at the dark doors of Night. I sit on my porch swing under a dark-green umbrella of maple leaves that hover maternally over the porch roof. And I wait for Sun.

A thin wisp of steam hovers expectantly over the coffee cup I hold. The air vibrates with ecstatic birdsong. Cat curls beside me for her final nap before breakfast. Morning-glories prepare to unfurl the blue trumpets. Then it happens, and I am as awestruck as if I had never seen a sunrise.

Curtains of Night draw back silently, and Sun bursts merrily over the blue haze of distant hills, painting earth in green and brown stripes. It is morning…and it is glorious!

I listen, and hear Sun whistle a song of new opportunity. I hear Nature's first day-song waiting to be sung, and am reminded that "this is the day the Lord has made." And I decide to "rejoice and be glad in it."

LINDA ANDERSEN
FROM *SLICES OF LIFE*

A LITTLE GIRL'S DREAM

JANN MITCHELL
FROM *HOME SWEETER HOME*

he promise was a long time keeping. But then, so was the dream. In the early 1950s in a small southern California town, a little girl hefted yet another load of books onto the tiny library's counter.

The girl was a reader. Her parents had books all over their home, but not always the ones she wanted. She would make her weekly trek to the yellow library with the brown trim, the little one-room building where the children's library actually was just a nook. Frequently, she ventured out of that nook in search of heftier fare.

As the white-haired librarian hand-stamped the due dates in the ten-year-old's choices, the little girl looked longingly at *The New Book* prominently displayed on the counter. She marveled again at the wonder of writing a book and having it honored like that, right there for the world to see.

That particular day, she confessed her goal.

"When I grow up," she said, "I'm going to be a writer. I'm going to write books."

The librarian looked up from her stamping and smiled, not with the condescension so many children receive, but with encouragement.

"When you do write that book," she replied, "bring it into our library

155

STORIES FOR THE HEART

and we'll put it on display, right here on the counter."

The little girl promised she would.

As she grew, so did her dream. She got her first job in ninth grade, writing brief personality profiles, which earned her $1.50 each from the local newspaper. The money paled in comparison with the magic of seeing her words on paper.

A book was a long way off.

She edited her high school newspaper, married, and started a family, but the itch to write burned deep. She got a part-time job covering school news at a weekly newspaper. It kept her brain busy as she balanced babies.

But no book.

She went to work full time for a major daily. Even tried her hand at magazines.

Still no book.

Finally, she believed she had something to say and started a book. She sent it off to two publishers and was rejected. She put it away, sadly. Several years later, the old dream increased in persistence. She got an agent and wrote another book. She pulled the other out of hiding, and soon both were sold.

But the world of book publishing moves slower than that of daily newspaper, and she waited two long years. The day the box arrived on her doorstep with its free author's copies, she ripped it open. Then she cried. She waited so long to hold her dream in her hands. Then she remembered that librarian's invitation, and her promise.

Of course, that particular librarian had died long ago, and the little library had been razed to make way for a larger incarnation.

The woman called and got the name of the head librarian. She wrote a letter, telling her how much her predecessor's words had meant to the girl. She'd be in town for her 30th high school reunion, she wrote, and could she please bring her two books by and give them to the library? It would mean so much to that ten-year-old girl, and seemed a way of honoring all the librarians who had ever encouraged a child.

The librarian called and said, "Come." So she did, clutching a copy of each book.

She found the big new library right across the street from her old high school, just opposite the room where she'd struggled through algebra, mourning the necessity of a subject that writers would surely never use, and nearly on top of the spot where her old house once stood, the neighborhood demolished for a civic center and this looming library.

Inside, the librarian welcomed her warmly. She introduced a reporter from the local newspaper—a descendant of the paper she'd begged a chance to write for long ago.

Then she presented her books to the librarian, who placed them on the counter with a sign of explanation. Tears rolled down the woman's cheeks.

Then she hugged the librarian and left, pausing for a picture outside, which proved that dreams can come true and promises can be kept. Even if it takes 38 years. The ten-year-old girl and the writer she'd become posed by the library sign, right next to the reader-board, which said:

WELCOME BACK, JANN MITCHELL.

One can never consent to creep
when one feels an impulse to soar.

HELEN KELLER

YOU DON'T BRING ME
FLOWERS ANYMORE

AUTHOR UNKNOWN
FROM *MORE OF BITS AND PIECES*

he elderly caretaker of a peaceful, lonely cemetery received a check every month from a woman, an invalid in a hospital in a nearby city. The check was to buy fresh flowers for the grave of her son, who had been killed in an automobile accident a couple of years before.

One day a car drove into the cemetery and stopped in front of the caretaker's ivy-covered administration building. A man was driving the car. In the back seat sat an elderly lady, pale as death, her eyes half-closed.

"The lady is too ill to walk," the driver told the caretaker. "Would you mind coming with us to her son's grave—she has a favor to ask of you. You see, she is dying, and she has asked me, as an old family friend, to bring her out here for one last look at her son's grave."

"Is this Mrs. Wilson?" the caretaker asked.

The man nodded.

"Yes, I know who she is. She's the one who has been sending a check every month to put flowers on her son's grave." The caretaker followed the man to the car and got in beside the woman. She was frail and obviously near death. But there was something else about her face, the caretaker noted—the eyes dark and sullen, hiding some deep, long-lasting hurt.

"I am Mrs. Wilson," she whispered. "Every month for the past two years—"

"Yes, I know. I have attended to it, just as you asked."

"I have come here today," she went on, "because the doctors tell me I have only a few weeks left. I shall not be sorry to go. There is nothing left to live for. But before I die, I wanted to come here for one last look and to make arrangements with you to keep on placing flowers on my son's grave."

She seemed exhausted—the effort to speak sapping her strength. The car made its way down a narrow, gravel road to the grave. When they reached the grave, the woman, with what appeared to be great effort, raised herself slightly and gazed out the window at her son's tombstone. There was no sound during the moments that followed—only the chirping of the birds in the tall, old trees scattered among the graves.

Finally, the caretaker spoke. "You know, Ma'am, I was always sorry you kept sending the money for the flowers."

The woman seemed at first not to hear. Then slowly she turned toward him. "Sorry?" she whispered. "Do you realize what you are saying—my son..."

"Yes, I know," he said gently. "But, you see, I belong to a church group that every week visits hospitals, asylums, prisons. There are live people in those places who need cheering up, and most of them love flowers—they can see them and smell them. That grave—" he said, "over there—there's no one living, no one to see and smell the beauty of the flowers..." he looked away, his voice trailing off.

The woman did not answer, but just kept staring at the grave of her son. After what seemed like hours, she lifted her hand and the man drove them back to the caretaker's building. He got out and without a word they drove off. *I've offended her,* he thought. *I shouldn't have said what I did.*

Some months later, however, he was astonished to have another visit from the woman. This time there was no driver. She was driving the car herself! The caretaker could hardly believe his eyes.

"You were right," she told him, "about the flowers. That's why there have been no more checks. After I got back to the hospital, I couldn't get your words out of my mind. So I started buying flowers for the others in the hospital who didn't have any. It gave me such a feeling of joy to see how much they enjoyed them—and from a total stranger. It made them happy, but more than that, it made *me* happy.

"The doctors don't know," she went on, "what is suddenly making me well, but I do!"

I'm not afraid of storms,
for I'm learning how to sail my ship.

LOUISA MAY ALCOTT

THE CELLIST
OF SARAJEVO

PAUL SULLIVAN

FROM *HOPE* MAGAZINE

s a pianist, I was invited to perform with cellist Eugene Friesen at the International Cello Festival in Manchester, England. Every two years a group of the world's greatest cellists and others devoted to that unassuming instrument—bow makers, collectors, historians—gather for a week of workshops, master classes, seminars, recitals and parties. Each evening the 600 or so participants assemble for a concert.

The opening-night performance at the Royal Northern College of Music consisted of works for unaccompanied cello. There on the stage in the magnificent concert hall was a solitary chair. No piano, no music stand, no conductor's podium. This was to be cello music in its purest, most intense form. The atmosphere was supercharged with anticipation and concentration.

The world-famous cellist Yo-Yo Ma was one of the performers that April night in 1994, and there was a moving story behind the musical composition he would play:

On May 27, 1992, in Sarajevo, one of the few bakeries that still had a supply of flour was making and distributing bread to the starving, war-shattered people. At 4 P.M. a long line stretched into the street. Suddenly, a mortar shell fell directly into the middle of the line, killing 22 people and splattering flesh, blood, bone and rubble.

Not far away lived a 35-year-old musician named Vedran Smailovic. Before the war he had been a cellist with the Sarajevo Opera, a distinguished career to which he patiently longed to return. But when he saw the carnage from the massacre outside his window, he was pushed past his capacity to absorb and endure any more. Anguished, he resolved to do the thing he did best: make music. Public music, daring music, music on a battlefield.

For each of the next 22 days, at 4 P.M., Smailovic put on his full, formal concert attire, took up his cello and walked out of his apartment into the midst of the battle raging around him. Placing a plastic chair beside the crater that the shell had made, he played in memory of the dead Albinoni's Adagio in G minor, one of the most mournful and haunting pieces in the classical repertoire. He played to the abandoned streets, smashed trucks and burning buildings, and to the terrified people who hid in the cellars while the bombs dropped and bullets flew. With masonry exploding around him, he made his unimaginably courageous stand for human dignity, for those lost to war, for civilization, for compassion and for peace. Though the shellings went on, he was never hurt.

After newspapers picked up the story of this extraordinary man, an English composer, David Wilde, was so moved that he, too, decided to make music. He wrote a composition for unaccompanied cello, "The Cellist of Sarajevo," into which he poured his own feelings of outrage, love and brotherhood with Vedran Smailovic.

It was "The Cellist of Sarajevo" that Yo-Yo Ma was to play that evening.

Ma came out on stage, bowed to the audience and sat down quietly on the chair. The music began, stealing out into the hushed hall and creating a shadowy, empty universe, ominous and haunting. Slowly it grew into an agonized, screaming, slashing furor, gripping us all before subsiding at last into a hollow death rattle and, finally, back to silence.

When he had finished, Ma remained bent over his cello, his bow resting on the strings. No one in the hall moved or made a sound for a long time. It was as though we had just witnessed that horrifying massacre ourselves.

Finally, Ma looked out across the audience and stretched out his hand, beckoning someone to come to the stage. An indescribable electric shock swept over us as we realized who it was: Vedran Smailovic, the cellist of Sarajevo!

Smailovic rose from his seat and walked down the aisle as Ma left the stage to meet him. They flung their arms around each other in an exuberant embrace. Everyone in the hall erupted in a chaotic, emotional frenzy—clapping, shouting and cheering.

And in the center of it all stood these two men, hugging and crying unashamedly. Yo-Yo Ma, a suave, elegant prince of classical music, flawless in appearance and performance; and Vedran Smailovic, dressed in a stained and tattered leather motorcycle suit. His wild long hair and huge mustache framed a face that looked old beyond his years, soaked with tears and creased with pain.

We were all stripped down to our starkest, deepest humanity at encountering this man who shook his cello in the face of bombs, death and ruin, defying them all. It was the sword of Joan of Arc—the mightiest weapon of all.

Back in Maine a week later, I sat one evening playing the piano for the residents of a local nursing home. I couldn't help contrasting this concert with the splendors I had witnessed at the festival. Then I was struck by the profound similarities. With his music the cellist of Sarajevo had defied death and despair, and celebrated love and life. And here we were, a chorus of croaking voices accompanied by a shopworn piano, doing the same thing. There were no bombs and bullets, but there was real pain—dimming sight, crushing loneliness, all the scars we accumulate in our lives—and only cherished memories for comfort. Yet still we sang and clapped.

It was then I realized that music is a gift we all share equally. Whether we create it or simply listen, it's a gift that can soothe, inspire and unite us, often when we need it most—and expect it least.

THE BABY BLANKET

WINONA SMITH

*I*t was a spring Saturday, and though many activities clamored for my attention, I had chosen this time to sit and crochet, an activity I enjoyed but had once thought impossible.

Most of the time I don't mind being a "lefty"—I'm quite proud of it, actually. But I admit, it did cause me a few problems three years ago, when I wanted to help out with a project at church.

We were invited to crochet baby blankets, which would be donated to a local Crisis Pregnancy Center at Christmas. I wanted to participate but I knew nothing about how to crochet, and my left-handedness didn't help. I had trouble "thinking backwards."

I suppose where there is a will, there is a way, because a few of the ladies got together and taught me one stitch. That's all I needed. I learned that granny stitch, and before long I had a blanket made. I was so proud of my little accomplishment and it seemed, inexplicably, so important, that I made quite a few more that same year. I even included in each blanket, as a note of encouragement, a poem I had written that read:

Little girls are sweet in their ruffles all pink.
Little boys in overalls look divine.

But no matter which one that the Lord gives to you,
A better "Mom" he never could find.

All of a sudden, my thoughts were interrupted by the ringing of my telephone. I hurried to answer it, and to my surprise and delight, on the other end of the line was Karen Sharp, who had been one of my very best friends ever since elementary school. Karen, her husband, Jim, and their daughter, Kim, had moved away a few years ago. She was calling to say that she was in town for a couple of days and would like to come by. I was thrilled to hear her voice.

At last the doorbell rang. As I flung open the door, we both screamed, as if back in junior high. We hugged each other. Then questions began to fly. Finally, I guided Karen into the kitchen, where I poured a cool glass of tea for both of us and the conversation slowed.

To my delight, Karen seemed to be calm, rested and, most of all, self-assured, which were a few qualities that she had seemed to lose during the last few months before they moved away. I wondered what had caused the positive change.

As we talked and reminisced, Karen began to explain to me the true reasons for her family's move a few years ago. The original reason they had given me was that Jim had a job offer in another city, which they could not afford to pass up. Even though it was Kim's senior year in high school, they still felt it necessary to make the move. Apparently, that had not been the biggest reason.

Karen reached into her purse and pulled out a photograph. When she handed it to me, I saw it was a beautiful little girl—maybe about two or three years old.

"This is my granddaughter, Kayla," Karen said.

I couldn't believe my ears. "You're a *grandmother?*" I asked. "I don't understand."

"You see," Karen went on, "Kim was a few months pregnant when we moved away. We had just found out, and Kim was having a really rough time dealing with it—she even talked about suicide. We were frantic. So we decided to move away, hoping that she would adjust more easily.

When we finally settled in our new home, we hoped that Kim's outlook would begin to improve, but she became more and more depressed. No matter what we said, she felt worthless and like a failure. Then we found a woman named Mrs. Barber, a wonderful pregnancy counselor. She got Kim through some very tough times.

"As the time for delivery came closer, Kim still had not entirely made up her mind about whether to keep the baby or not. Her father and I prayed that she would. We felt prepared to give the baby a loving home—it was, after all, our first grandchild!

"Finally, the day came, and Kim had a six-pound, six-ounce baby girl. Mrs. Barber came to visit her in the hospital. She hugged Kim and told her how proud she was of her. Then she gave Kim a pastel-colored package containing a hand-crocheted baby blanket inside."

At this point, I felt a huge lump come into my throat, and I felt rather limp all over, but I tried not to show my feelings and kept listening to Karen's story.

Karen must have noticed the look on my face. She asked if I was all right. I assured her I was fine and asked her to please continue.

"As I said," she went on, "there was a baby blanket and a little personal note, something about little girls and their ruffles, little boys and their overalls, and a word of encouragement about becoming a new mom.

"We asked who made the blanket, and Mrs. Barber explained that some of the pregnancy centers have people who donate these blankets to new mothers and their babies. Her center was given the surplus from one of the other centers in the state, and she was glad to have one for Kim.

"Kim was so moved by the fact that a total stranger had thought enough to put this much time and effort into a blanket for her baby. She said it made her feel warm all over. She later told her dad and me that the little poem gave her a boost of confidence and helped her to make up her mind to keep little Kayla."

Karen's story had an even happier ending: A year later, Kim was married to a young man who loves both her and Kayla with all his heart. Karen grinned as she told me, then sobered. "My only regret is that I did not feel close enough to our friends here to have been able to lean on you all for support and comfort, instead of turning away.

"We are so thankful for so many things—especially the way everything turned out; but I think the one thing that we are the most thankful for is that kind person who made that little baby blanket for our daughter and her baby. I just wish I could give her a big hug and tell her how much she is loved and appreciated by our family."

I looked again at the photo of the sweet child in my hands. Then I leaned over to Karen and gave her a big hug.

Not a sigh is breathed, no pain felt,
not a grief pierces the soul,
but the throb vibrates to the Father's heart.

AUTHOR UNKNOWN

Family

TRIBUTE

My father never talked to me about how to treat people.
Every act of kindness I have ever shown another person
was because I was trying to imitate him.

PAMELA McGREW

THE NIGHT THE
STARS FELL

ARTHUR GORDON
FROM *A TOUCH OF WONDER*

One summer night in a seaside cottage, a small boy felt himself lifted from bed. Dazed with sleep, he heard his mother murmur about the lateness of the hour, heard his father laugh. Then he was borne in his father's arms, with the swiftness of a dream, down the porch steps, out onto the beach.

Overhead the sky blazed with stars. "Watch!" his father said. And incredibly, as he spoke, one of the stars moved. In a streak of golden fire, it flashed across the astonished heavens. And before the wonder of this could fade, another star leaped from its place, and then another, plunging toward the restless sea. "What is it?" the child whispered. "Shooting stars," his father said. "They come every year on certain nights in August. I thought you'd like to see the show."

That was all: just an unexpected glimpse of something haunting and mysterious and beautiful. But, back in bed, the child stared for a long time into the dark, rapt with the knowledge that all around the quiet house the night was full of the silent music of the falling stars.

Decades have passed, but I remember that night still, because I was the fortunate seven-year-old whose father believed that a new experience was more important for a small boy than an unbroken night's sleep. No doubt in my childhood I had the usual quota of playthings, but these are forgotten now. What I remember is the night the stars fell…

Children will not remember you
for the material things you provided
but for the feeling that you cherished them.

RICHARD I. EVANS

THE JEWELRY BOX

FAITH ANDREWS BEDFORD
FROM *COUNTRY LIVING* MAGAZINE

*T*onight is our anniversary and my husband is taking me out. I look through my closet and pick out a deep green velvet dress with long sleeves and a high neck. It looks wonderful with my mother's seed pearl necklace and my grandmother's tiny pearl earrings.

As I sit at my dressing table, my daughter, Eleanor, perches beside. She loves to watch me get dressed for special occasions. "Mama," she addresses my reflection in the mirror, "may I pick out your jewelry?"

"Of course," I reply.

She opens the drawer where I keep my jewelry box and begins to sift through the contents. There are the macaroni necklaces she made me in kindergarten and the locket my husband gave me when we were engaged. In a little box Eleanor finds my old Girl Scout pin and some badges.

She holds several pairs of earrings up to her small ears, then discards them. She tries on several necklaces, and shakes her head. At last, with a little cry of delight, she pounces on a pair of long, dangly earrings from Ceylon. They are set with flashing mirrors, obviously left over from the seventies. I wore them with bell-bottoms and tunics. In another box she finds two long ropes of beads from the same era.

She drapes the beads around my neck and hands me the earrings. I put them on and give my head a little shake. The earrings glitter brightly.

"Perfect!" She sighs with pleasure. We grin at each other in the mirror.

As Eleanor twirls out of the room to tell her father that I am almost ready, I remember how, when I was Eleanor's age, I used to watch, entranced, as my own Mother prepared for an evening out.

While she pinned up her French twist, I would ask her to tell me where each piece had come from.

In a velvet case lay a beautiful garnet necklace and matching earrings. Mother told me that they belonged to her grandmother who wore them to Boston, where she had seen the famous Sarah Bernhardt perform.

The seed pearl necklace had been given to Mother by her godmother as a wedding present. Like me, she always wore it with the tiny pearl earrings her grandmother left her. Now I have inherited both.

My favorite things in the drawer were the gifts my Father had given her. In a velvet box was a necklace of rhinestones that glittered with the brilliance of real diamonds. Mother told me they were not diamonds at all, but I thought she still looked like a princess.

When Father went on a business trip to Arizona, he brought Mother back a ring with a big square piece of turquoise. It just fit her ring finger; it was too big for my thumb.

For her fortieth birthday, he presented her with some earrings from India. The black enamel had been cut away to reveal silver figures of dancing women bent into impossible positions. My sisters and I tried to imitate them. We couldn't.

The Christmas I was ten I had saved up enough money to buy Mother some earrings at the five and dime: two red plastic bells hung from tiny bows. The edges had been sprinkled with silver glitter. Mother wore them all Christmas day. She shook her head frequently to show us how they actually made a tinkling sound.

A few days later, I came into her room just in time to help zip up her black and white taffeta evening dress.

"Will you pick out some earrings for me, dear?" she asked.

Opening her drawer I sorted through the options. Her dress was pretty,

I thought, but it needed a bit of color. I proudly pulled out the little red plastic bells.

"Just the thing." She said, putting them on. I looked at her and thought no one ever was more beautiful.

My husband's voice pulls me back to the present. "Ready?" he asks.

"Almost," I reply, putting Mother's pearls and Grandmother's earrings back into my jewelry box.

As I come down the stairs, my beads swinging and the brass earrings flashing in the light, I look down and see Eleanor's proud face. "You look beautiful," she sighs.

"Only with your help," I reply as I kiss her good night. She will be asleep by the time I return.

The mother's heart is the child's schoolroom.

HENRY WARD BEECHER

THROUGH A FATHER'S EYES

LONNI COLLINS PRATT
FROM *MOODY* MAGAZINE

I saw the car just before it hit me. I seemed to float. Then darkness smashed my senses.

I came to in an ambulance. Opening my eyes, I could see only shreds of light through my bandaged, swollen eyelids. I didn't know it then, but small particles of gravel and dirt were embedded in my freckled 16-year-old face. As I tried to touch it, someone tenderly pressed my arm down and whispered. "Lie still."

A wailing siren trailed distantly somewhere, and I slipped into unconsciousness. My last thoughts were a desperate prayer: "Dear God, not my face, please...."

Like many teenage girls, I found much of my identity in my appearance. Adolescence revolved around my outside image. Being pretty meant I had lots of dates and a wide circle of friends.

My father doted on me. He had four sons, but only one daughter. I remember one Sunday in particular. As we got out of the car at church, my brothers—a scruffy threesome in corduroy and cowlicks—ran ahead. Mom had stayed home with the sick baby.

I was gathering my small purse, church school papers, and Bible. Dad opened the door. I looked up at him, convinced in my 7-year-old heart that he was more handsome and smelled better than any daddy anywhere.

He extended his hand to me with a twinkle in his eye and said, "A hand, my lady?" Then he swept me up into his arms and told me how pretty I was. "No father has ever loved a little girl more than I love you," he said.

In my child's heart, which didn't really understand a father's love, I thought it was my pretty dress and face he loved.

A few weeks before the accident, I had won first place in a local pageant, making me the festival queen. Dad didn't say much. He just stood beside me with his arm over my shoulders, beaming with pride. Once more, I was his pretty little girl, and I basked in the warmth of his love and acceptance.

About this same time, I made a personal commitment to Christ. In the midst of student council, honor society, pageants and parades, I was beginning a relationship with God.

In the hours immediately after my accident, I drifted in and out of consciousness. Whenever my mind cleared even slightly, I wondered about my face. I was bleeding internally and had a severe concussion, but it never occurred to me that my concern with appearance was disproportionate.

The next morning, although I couldn't open my eyes more than a slit, I asked the nurse for a mirror. "You just concern yourself with getting well, young lady," she said, not looking at my face as she took my blood pressure.

Her refusal to give me a mirror only fueled irrational determination. If she wouldn't give me a mirror, I reasoned, it must be worse than I imagined. My face felt tight and itchy. It burned sometimes and ached other times. I didn't touch it, though, because my doctor told me that might cause infection.

My parents also battled to keep mirrors away. As my body healed internally and strength returned, I became increasingly difficult.

At one point, for the fourth time in less than an hour, I pleaded for a mirror. Five days had passed since the accident.

Angry and beaten down, Dad snapped, "Don't ask again! I said no and that's it!"

I wish I could offer an excuse for what I said. I propped myself on my elbows, and through lips that could barely move, hissed, "You don't love me. Now that I'm not pretty anymore, you just don't love me!"

Dad looked as if someone had knocked the life out of him. He slumped into a chair and put his head in his hands. My mother walked over and put her hand on his shoulder as he tried to control his tears. I collapsed against the pillows.

I didn't ask my parents for a mirror again. Instead, I waited until someone from housekeeping was straightening my room the next morning.

My curtain was drawn as if I were taking a sponge bath. "Could you get me a mirror, please?" I asked. "I must have mislaid mine." After a little searching, she found one and discreetly handed it to me around the curtain.

Nothing could have prepared me for what I saw. An image that resembled a giant scraped knee, oozing and bright pink, looked out at me. My eyes and lips were crusted and swollen. Hardly a patch of skin, ear to ear, had escaped the trauma.

My father arrived a little later with magazines and homework tucked under his arm. He found me staring into the mirror. Prying my fingers one by one from the mirror, he said, "It isn't important. This doesn't change anything that matters. No one will love you less."

Finally he pulled the mirror away and tossed it into a chair. He sat on the edge of my bed, took me in his arms, and held me for a long time.

"I know what you think," he said.

"You couldn't," I mumbled, turning away and staring out the window.

"You're wrong," he said, ignoring my self-pity.

"This will not change anything," he repeated. He put his hand on my arm, running it over an IV line. "The people who love you have seen you at your worst, you know."

"Right. Seen me with rollers or with cold cream, not with my face ripped off!"

"Let's talk about me then," he said. "I love you. Nothing will ever change that because it's you I love, not your outside. I've changed your diapers and watched your skin blister with chicken pox. I've wiped up your bloody noses and held your head while you threw up in the toilet. I've loved you when you weren't pretty."

He hesitated. "Yesterday you were ugly—not because of your skin, but because you behaved ugly. But I'm here today, and I'll be here tomorrow. Fathers don't stop loving their children, no matter what life takes. You will be blessed if life only takes your face."

I turned to my father, feeling it was all words, the right words, spoken out of duty—polite lies.

"Look at me then, Daddy," I said. "Look at me and tell me you love me!"

I will never forget what happened next. As he looked into my battered face, his eyes filled with tears. Slowly, he leaned toward me, and with his eyes open, he gently kissed my scabbed, oozing lips.

It was the kiss that tucked me in every night of my young life, the kiss that warmed each morning.

Many years have passed. All that remains of my accident is a tiny indentation just above one eyebrow. But my father's kiss, and what it taught me about love, will never leave my lips.

The heart of every child beats
to the rhythm of a father's love.

STEVE CURLEY
FROM *STORIES FOR A DAD'S HEART*

FAVORITE CHILD

ERMA BOMBECK
FROM *FOREVER, ERMA*

very mother has a favorite child.
        She cannot help it. She is only human.
I have mine.

That child for whom I feel a special closeness. The one I reach out to in a rare moment, to share a love that no one else could possibly understand.

My favorite child is the one who was too sick to eat the ice cream at his birthday party, had measles at Christmas and wore leg braces to bed because he toed in.

She was the fever in the middle of the night, the asthma attack, the child in my arms at the emergency ward.

My favorite child spent Christmas alone away from the family, was stranded after the game with a gas tank on E, lost the money for his class ring.

My favorite child is the one who screwed up the piano recital, misspelled *committee* in a spelling bee, ran the wrong way with the football and had his bike stolen because he was careless.

My favorite child is the one who fell asleep over an assignment on China that the teacher never bothered to grade, flunked her driver's test five times and told us she could hardly wait to get out of the house.

My favorite child is the one I punished for lying, grounded for insensitivity to other people's feelings and informed he was a royal pain to the entire family.

My favorite child slammed doors in frustration, cried when she didn't think I saw her, withdrew and said she could not talk to me.

My favorite child always needed a haircut, had hair that wouldn't curl, had no date for Saturday night and a car that cost $600 to fix.

My favorite child said dumb things for which there were no excuses. He was selfish, immature, bad-tempered and self-centered. He was vulnerable, lonely, unsure of what he was doing in this world...and quite wonderful.

The one I've loved the most is the one whom I have watched struggle and—because the struggle was his—done nothing.

All mothers have their favorite child. It is always the same one, the one who needs you at the moment for whatever reason—to cling to, to shout at, to hurt, to hug, to flatter, to reverse charges to, to unload on, to use—but mostly, to be there.

Children are a poor man's riches.

ENGLISH PROVERB

A GOOD HEART
TO LEAN ON

AUGUSTUS J. BULLOCK
FROM *THE WALL STREET JOURNAL*

When I was growing up, I was embarrassed to be seen with my father. He was severely crippled and very short, and when we would walk together, his hand on my arm for balance, people would stare. I would inwardly squirm at the unwanted attention. If he ever noticed or was bothered, he never let on.

It was difficult to coordinate our steps—his halting, mine impatient—and because of that, we didn't say much as we went along. But as we started out, he always said, "You set the pace. I will try to adjust to you."

Our usual walk was to or from the subway, which was how he got to work. He went to work sick, and despite nasty weather. He almost never missed a day, and would make it to the office even if others could not. A matter of pride.

When snow or ice was on the ground, it was impossible for him to walk, even with help. At such times my sisters and I would pull him through the streets of Brooklyn, N.Y., on a child's sleigh to the subway entrance. Once there, he would cling to the handrail until he reached the lower steps that the warmer tunnel air kept ice-free. In Manhattan the subway station was the basement of his office building, and he would not have to go outside again until we met him in Brooklyn on his way home.

When I think of it now, I marvel at how much courage it must have taken for a grown man to subject himself to such indignity and stress. And at how he did it—without bitterness or complaint.

He never talked about himself as an object of pity, nor did he show any envy of the more fortunate or able. What he looked for in others was a "good heart," and if he found one, the owner was good enough for him.

Now that I am older, I believe that is a proper standard by which to judge people, even though I still don't know precisely what a "good heart" is. But I know the times I don't have one.

Unable to engage in many activities, my father still tried to participate in some way. When a local sandlot baseball team found itself without a manager, he kept it going. He was a knowledgeable baseball fan and often took me to Ebbets Field to see the Brooklyn Dodgers play. He liked to go to dances and parties, where he could have a good time just sitting and watching.

On one memorable occasion, a fight broke out at a beach party, with everyone punching and shoving. He wasn't content to sit and watch, but he couldn't stand unaided on the soft sand. In frustration he began to shout, "I'll fight anyone who will sit down with me! I'll fight anyone who will sit down with me!"

Nobody did. But the next day people kidded him by saying it was the first time any fighter was urged to take a dive even before the bout began.

I now know he participated in some things vicariously through me, his only son. When I played ball (poorly), he "played" too. When I joined the Navy, he "joined" too. And when I came home on leave, he saw to it that I visited his office. Introducing me, he was really saying, "This is my son, but it is also me, and I could have done this, too, if things had been different." Those words were never said aloud.

He has been gone many years now, but I think of him often. I wonder if he sensed my reluctance to be seen with him during our walks. If he did, I am sorry I never told him how sorry I was, how unworthy I was, how I regretted it. I think of him when I complain about trifles, when I am envious of another's good fortune, when I don't have a "good heart."

At such times I put my hand on his arm to regain my balance, and say, "You set the pace. I will try to adjust to you."

Comfort

*The best place to be when you are sad
is in Grandma's lap.*

AUTHOR UNKNOWN

A MOTHER'S PRAYER

MARGUERITE KELLY
FROM *THE MOTHER'S ALMANAC*

HELP ME give my children the best—not of trappings or toys, but of myself, cherishing them on good days and bad, theirs and mine.

TEACH ME to accept them for who they are, not for what they do; to listen to what they say, if only so they will listen to me; to encourage their goals, not mine; and please, let me laugh with them and be silly.

LET ME give them a home where respect is the cornerstone, integrity the foundation, and there is enough happiness to raise the roof.

MAY I give them courage to be true to themselves; the independence to take care of themselves and the faith to believe in a power much greater than their own.

SEE THAT I discipline my children without demeaning them, demand good manners without forgetting my own and let them know they have limitless love, no matter what they do.

LET ME feed them properly, clothe them adequately and have enough to give them small allowances—not for the work they do but the pleasure they bring—and let me be moderate in all these things, so the joy of getting will help them discover the joy of giving.

SEE THAT their responsibilities are real but not burdensome, that my expectations are high but not overwhelming and that my thanks and praise are thoughtful and given when they're due.

HELP ME teach them that excellence is work's real reward, and not the glory it brings. But when it comes—and it will—let me revel in each honor, however small, without once pretending that it's mine; my children are glories enough.

Above all, let me ground these children so well that I can dare to let them go.

And may they be so blessed.

Most of all the other beautiful things
in life come by twos and threes, by dozens and hundreds.
Plenty of roses, stars, sunsets, rainbows,
brothers and sisters, aunts and cousins,
but only one mother in the whole world.

KATE DOUGLAS WIGGIN

NEW GROUND

MARGARET BECKER
FROM *WITH NEW EYES*

I remember how thick the air felt in my room when I awoke that morning. The month of July in this bedroom was always sticky. For a moment I lay and adjusted to the sounds of the creek, the birds, the cicadas. I thought about how different these sounds were from what I was used to—car horns and the dull whine of rubber on pavement.

At my house in Tennessee, the sounds were of struggle: people rushing from here to there in pursuit of the ever elusive dollar; people hurrying anywhere for a few precious moments of peace. They were sounds of a journey in heated progression.

Here at my parents' retirement home, the sounds were of arrival; of a journey well taken. There were no neighbors shouting to children, no traffic at 8:30 A.M., just the occasional pickup truck on its way to the local store for a paper. I guess that's why the clanking I heard caught my ear. *That's strange,* I thought, glancing at the clock. *It's only nine. What is that?* I listened for a moment. It was a methodical sound whose rhythm I soon recognized. I brushed my curtains aside to see my father.

His reddened face beaded with perspiration, his expression taut with determination, he stood in the middle of the yard pushing a rusty hoe deep into the hard ground. Ten feet around him, in a perfect square, lay dark red, freshly overturned topsoil. It took me a moment to realize what he was doing. The year had been a dry one and the grass, once a carpet of green, now receded into small, disconnected patches of brown stubble. It was not the first time I had seen him turn over topsoil before planting new seed.

He was a diligent worker and I was evidence of it. He had taken a hoe to my life on many occasions, breaking up the fallow ground of my heart, assessing my needs and planting seeds of truth along the way. When I was overwhelmed, he reminded me of my strength. When I was wrong, his correction came swiftly and ended with a hug of assurance: it was forgotten. When I needed his advice, he gave it with respect and caution. He even allowed me a few "weeds" along the way to show me the cost of freedom and the importance of choosing wisely.

As I watched him, my mind slipped back through the years. I remembered curling up in the warmth of his lap where I would hear magnificent stories of kings and princesses from far-off places. I remembered his strong hands playfully whisking me off my feet into his safe embrace. I remembered his inexhaustible patience with my endless questions…the shadow of his body on the dining room table as he checked the answers to my homework…the cool of the evening air fresh on his hand as he lay it on my fevered brow…the gentleness of his step at the yearly father-daughter square dance. I had so many wonderful memories.

As I looked at him that sticky summer morning, it was as if I saw him for the first time: This was my father, an honest man, a kind man, a man who had spent his entire life giving to others.

The tears that brimmed my eyes were a surprise. I wondered what memory had passed my mind and pierced my heart unbeknownst to me. Surely these were all happy memories, nothing to cry over. Nothing that would justify the gnawing in the pit of my stomach.

Looking around my room, my eyes resting on nothing, I searched myself for an answer. Seconds later I looked back out at my father. The warm explosion in my chest felt so unexpected yet so familiar. With stinging clarity the truth revealed itself: How many Saturday mornings had I heard these very same sounds—the dull thud of a shovel, the whir of the lawn mower, the terse clipping of the shears—how many times had I rolled over for another half hour of sleep? How many late Sunday afternoons had I watched my father stiffly lower himself onto the couch, more exhausted from the weekend's chores than he ever was from his normal eight-to-seven workday?

How many times had I told him that I love him? How many times had I assured him that he was an excellent father, generous in the needful things like love and attention—and time? How many opportunities had I let slip by to show him, the way he showed me every day of his life, that I cared?

In that moment I understood the broad scope of love that is the back bone of fatherhood: the constant unnoticeables, the many details that are silently taken care of. I thought about how God, in His fatherly provision, had taken such care in this detail for me—providing this man. Few things have ever made me as thankful as the simple act of breathing did in that moment. I was here, he was here—there was still time.

Hurriedly I slipped out of bed. I put on shorts and sneakers and wiped the tears from my chin. I bowed my head for just a moment. "Thank You, Lord, for the wonderful man You have given me for a father."

I'll never forget the look on his face when I came around the corner with the metal rake in my hand.

"What are you doing up so early, Maggie?" he asked.

"I came out to help you, Dad."

He smiled warmly, with an expression I'd seen only a few times over the years—the kind that hears the unspoken regrets, senses the rawness of the moment, and allows it to pass graciously—the kind that only someone with a parental bond can give. We began to turn over new ground, and with each pull of the ancient rake, I felt a joy and excitement that only comes from reconciling a long overdue debt of love.

THE COSTUME

BILL BUTTERWORTH
FROM *MOODY* MAGAZINE

*P*art of the success that Rhonda and I enjoy in our marriage is in a freedom to explore aspects of life that defy traditional gender roles.

I cook—no big deal.

She fixes leaky faucets—no problem.

I do grocery shopping—so what?

She works well with her table saw, jigsaw, and router—who cares?

This is the stuff that's made our marriage strong.

So I couldn't believe what came from my lips when Jesse came up to me one afternoon last week and said, "Dad, I need a costume for the play I'm in."

"Don't ask me. Go ask your mother."

We both sat there in mild shock.

"Why, Dad?"

"I…I don't know," I stammered. Then I added, "Unless it's because I don't know the first thing about costumes or because I know nothing about sewing or because you've always asked Mama for help with the costumes. Why would you suddenly turn to me for help?"

After a long pause, my son made his reluctant admission. "Mom's not here, and I need it…for tonight."

"Tonight?"

"Yeah…" He forced a laugh. "It kinda snuck up on me."

This is always a toss-up for a parent: Do I lecture him on the peril of procrastination, or do I run to his rescue as the Father of the Year?

After a quick prayer for wisdom, I opted for Father of the Year.

"OK," I began slowly. "What's the first thing we need to do?"

Jesse just sat there for a second and smiled. It was his non-verbal thank-you for helping him out.

"Well, first we need to go to the thrift store to get an old pair of pants that look like burlap."

"Burlap?"

"Yeah…I'm a woodsman in medieval times."

Why couldn't you be Moses—or Dick Tracy—or Bozo? I pondered. *Bathrobes, overcoats, or even clown suits are readily available.*

"All right. Thrift store here we come."

So we drove down and purchased one fine pair of burlap trousers. While we were driving home, Jesse filled me in on the rest of the duties. "Now we gotta make the pants look real old and tattered—you know, holes and jagged cuts on the bottom."

Once home, Jess collected his shirt, boots and hat while I retrieved the sewing kit from Rhonda's side of the master bedroom closet.

Meeting Jesse in the family room, I pulled out a pair of scissors and began to cut up pants and shirt. While I sliced, Jesse and I talked, laughed, and had a great time. It was highly ironic, this male bonding over a sewing kit.

Fortunately, the costume had to look "trashed," as Jesse put it. This was to be no ordinary woodsman. He also doubled as a pauper.

"Your dad's pretty good at rippin' up stuff," I bragged as Jesse tried on his newly old pants.

"Yeah Dad—this is perfect!"

So this is how moms feel when they complete one of their many tasks for their kids! I couldn't contain my pride. During a dress rehearsal, I leaned over to one of the moms and said, "I ripped those pants he's wearing!"

She looked at me kindly, yet quizzically. She couldn't know that I had discovered how to be Father of the Year: be like Mom.

THE REDHEAD AND THE BRUNETTE

JOHN WILLIAM SMITH
FROM *HUGS FOR MOM*

They sat right in front of me on a Southwest flight. Those of you who have flown on Southwest know how close that is—I could smell their perfume. I think they were about the same age and the same build—but all similarity vanished at that point.

The brunette arrived first. She was beautifully, stylishly, immaculately dressed. Everything matched. Her hair was radiant, there were subtle changes of color when she moved her head, and the light shone from any angle with vibrant intensity. Every strand was in place. Her nails were long and manicured, her lipstick and makeup were flawless, and she was breathtakingly beautiful. She carried a very smart-looking, soft-leather briefcase, which must have cost a small fortune, and inside it, she had a powerbook. She was also carrying an exclusive looking shopping bag that had "Macy's" written in large letters on one side.

She had a beautiful smile—a radiant smile that lit up her whole face. She parted her lips slowly, invitingly, and revealed perfect, white, even teeth. It was a deliberate smile—one that she had practiced before the mirror a thousand times. She wore three rings. They weren't the large, gaudy kind, they were the stylish, expensive-looking kind. Two of the rings were on her right hand, and one was on her left. There was no ring on her "ring finger." She placed the shopping bag in an overhead compartment, and sat down in the window seat with her briefcase.

The redhead was carrying a huge diaper bag, a fold-up stroller, and a baby. Her hair was all over her head, not unkempt, but frazzled. Her clothes were modest, they fit loosely on her spare frame, and they had "K-Mart" written all over them. She wore no makeup, and she carried no shopping bag. Her nails were so short that they couldn't be manicured, and she only wore one ring. It was on her "ring finger"—and it wasn't expensive. She smiled at the brunette and asked if she could sit next to her. She had a great smile. It was one of those smiles that just explodes—nobody could ever hope to practice a smile like that. It happened so quickly that you couldn't tell where it started, but before it was over, it had gotten into her eyes, magnified the dimples in her cheeks, wrinkled her nose, lifted her eyebrows, raised her ears, showed the filling in her teeth—and whether you wanted to or not, you found yourself smiling back.

At first, you could tell that the brunette didn't want to be bothered, but the smile did it. She couldn't possibly resist that smile. She smiled back, a little stiffly, and said she would be glad for her to sit next to her. And she said it with so much friendly enthusiasm that I think she surprised herself.

We hadn't seen the baby yet, but as soon as the mother sat down, the baby stuck her head out from under the blanket. She was (I say "she" because she "looked" like a she) about nine months to a year old, I think, and she was the absolute image of her mother—I mean there was no doubt whose baby this was—she even had the same explosive smile.

The redhead was bubbly and excited. I picked up enough of the conversation to know that she had been to see her mother, who had never seen the baby, and she had had a great visit, but she was anxious to get home and see her husband. The brunette was all business. She wasn't unfriendly exactly, but she spoke in clipped, precise tones. She stated her name, her company, her position, the colleges she had attended—told the redhead that her baby was cute—opened her briefcase, took out her powerbook, turned it on, and began scanning some documents in a way that was calculated to let the redhead know that the conversation was over.

But the redhead didn't take the cue.

The redhead was cute, really cute, and she possessed an innate type of enthusiasm and innocence that unsettled the brunette. She chatted easily and naturally about her husband, her house, and her neighbors, and she told the brunette all the plans she had for the baby's room. She was breast-feeding the baby, and it came time to eat. The brunette watched in absolute amazement as the redhead very easily and modestly made arrangements for feeding the baby. While the baby was eating, the mother needed something and asked the brunette if she would mind getting it for her out of the diaper bag. The brunette closed the powerbook, placed it in the leather briefcase, zipped it up, and reached for the diaper bag.

Ten minutes later, the baby was through eating and was ready to play. The mother placed the baby over her shoulder and patted her on the back until she burped. The brunette watched. After the burp, the baby sat on the redhead's lap and cooed, gurgled, grabbed everything in sight, and tried to stuff whatever she grabbed into her mouth. The brunette never took her eyes off of the redhead and the baby.

The baby, smiling at the brunette, was captivated by her dangling, colorful earring and reached for it. The mother grabbed the hand just in time and said, "No! No!" The brunette assured her it was all right, took the earring off, and handed it to the baby—who immediately put it in her mouth. The mother rescued the earring, gently mentioned that it wasn't good to give the baby articles that could be swallowed, and handed the earring back.

"Would you mind if I held her?" I couldn't believe my ears. It was the brunette. ("This ought to be good," I said to myself.)

"My goodness, no. I don't mind at all, but are you sure you want to? She squirms a lot, and she will wrinkle your clothes—and," she added, with a touch of admiration in her voice, "your clothes are so beautiful."

The brunette tentatively held out her hands toward the baby, absolutely convinced, I'm sure, that the baby would reject her. I thought she would too. It was an important moment, a critical moment, and more was riding on it than anybody who was watching could possibly be aware of. The baby looked hesitantly at the extended hands, then looked tentatively at the mother, who smiled reassuringly, then that smile exploded all over the baby's face, and she reached out both of her hands toward the brunette. It was great.

The brunette placed the baby's face right next to hers and held her so tight I thought the baby would cry. She was a little stiff at first, but it didn't take her long to get the hang of it; and before long, she was doing it like an old pro. I couldn't see the brunette's face, but I knew the look of peace and joy that was on it. For the next twenty minutes, this perfectly dressed woman cooed, baby talked, patted, played "patty cake," bounced, and entertained the baby.

After about ten minutes, the baby threw up—I think "spit up" is more accurate. The redhead was horrified and tried to clean it up with a diaper. She apologized all over herself and reached to take the baby back. The brunette—to her credit—was gracious and assured her that she didn't care, and she insisted on keeping the baby.

When the captain announced that we were on our final approach, the redhead took the baby back, and the brunette got out her makeup kit and spent the rest of the time restoring her businesslike, pristine appearance. When we got off the plane, the brunette offered to carry the baby to the baggage claim area, and the redhead said she would be grateful. The redhead put the Macy's shopping bag, the diaper bag, and the leather briefcase in the fold-up stroller, and they chatted on the most intimate terms all the way to baggage claim. I followed closely, determined to see how this was going to play out.

The redhead's husband was waiting for her at baggage claim, and after they had kissed and hugged each other for an inordinately long time, she introduced the brunette, who reluctantly handed the baby to the father. As they waited for their luggage to come, the redhead and her husband stood close together, with their arms around each other—the father holding the baby. Once, the baby reached for the brunette. She started to reach back, but checked herself, and with some effort, deliberately placed her hands at her sides.

The redhead's luggage came first. The husband picked up the bags, and the redhead turned to say goodbye. The brunette and the redhead hugged each other in a genuine, spontaneous display of emotion. Then the brunette picked up the Macy's bag and handed it to the redhead, pleading with her to take it. I couldn't hear all of the conversation, but it was obvious that they were both embarrassed. The brunette won, and the Macy's bag was added to the other luggage. Then the brunette reached out, placed her fingers softly on the cheek of the baby, and whispered some parting affection to her.

Just before they disappeared, she waved goodbye to the baby, whose face was toward her, and the baby made a gesture that might have been interpreted as a farewell wave. When the brunette turned back toward the luggage carousel, there were tears and makeup smudges on both cheeks. She made no attempt to wipe them away. Her luggage came. She got a cart and placed her luggage on it.

She stood a long moment, wiped the tears and smudges with her fingers—making them worse, of course—gathered herself, grabbed the cart handles, and walked determinedly toward the exit.

The redhead, I imagine, went back to her home and the brunette back to her office—both, I feel quite sure—feeling more keenly the value of mothering.

Old Doors

The auction at a quaint old farm
brought many folks that day.
Most items sold for less than half
of what we thought we'd pay.
New owners did not care for old.
So on that day in June,
disinterested, they watched the sale
until the afternoon.
Then as the dusk of evening summoned
farmers to their chores—
the auctioneer began his bid
on beautiful old doors.
The bidding started at a price
below what they appraise.
But every time I gave my bid—
a frail hand would raise.
So back and forth we both would bid
past what I could afford.
Although I wanted those old doors,
I stopped when prices soared.
Then as the sale ended and
I started out to leave,
I met the frail woman with
the doors she did retrieve.
"Why did you pay so much for them?"
Her answer was precise.
"My children's heights are on those doors—
for which there is no price."

CARLA MUIR

AWARD CEREMONY

P. R.

FROM *SONS: A FATHER'S LOVE*

For years I had poked and prodded Gordon, my oldest son, to be a better student, to get higher grades, to get better scores on his exams. I was always a little disappointed in him because he never quite measured up to my standard of excellence. I knew he wasn't stupid, but I wasn't satisfied with his B-average academic performance. It wasn't that I had been such a great student, it's just that I expected better things from him.

When Gordon was a senior in high school, the student body decided to invite parents to an awards assembly so that we could see our kids honored for their various accomplishments. I was rather puzzled by the invitation. Clearly, Gordon was going to be awarded for something, but I couldn't imagine what.

We received a program when we got inside, and I didn't see any possible award that would fit Gordon. I began to feel annoyed. Had they just invited us to fill seats? I would have to sit there and see every straight-A student marching up the aisle, getting applause, while my son sat in the back of the room. Why didn't he try harder? Why was he so mediocre? My attitude grew steadily worse as the ceremony went on.

By the end, I was fuming. But then the principal went to the microphone and made an announcement: "For the first time this year, I am presenting a special award to a young man who has been so exceptional that we could not overlook his accomplishments…"

He called Gordon to the front, and then spent several minutes describing my son's fine character, kindness toward others, trustworthiness, and quiet leadership. "We have never had a student quite like Gordon in our school," he said. "And there may never be another. So we're giving you, Gordon, the first and possibly the last Principal's Cup award for integrity, diligence, and decency. Thank you for what you've brought to our school. No one who has really gotten to know you will ever be quite the same again."

In that moment, I realized that he was talking to me. I had never really gotten to know my son—much less appreciate him for who he was. And I knew that once I did, I—his father—would never be the same again.

To understand your parents' love
you must raise children yourself.

CHINESE PROVERB

DADDY HANDS

Susan Fahncke

I awoke in the night to find my husband, Marty, gently rocking our baby son, Noah. I stood for a moment in the doorway, watching this amazing man with whom I was so blessed to share my life, lovingly stroking Noah's fat pink cheeks in an effort to comfort him. I felt in my heart that something was seriously wrong with Noah. This was one of several nights that Noah had been up, burning with a high fever.

Tears filled my eyes as I watched my beautiful husband move Noah's little cheek up against his own chest, so that Noah could feel the vibrations of his voice. Noah is deaf. Learning to comfort him has brought on a whole new way of thinking for us. We relied on our voices, a soothing lullaby, audio toys, and music to comfort our other children. But with Noah, we need to use touch, his soft blankie, sight, the feel of our voices, and most importantly, the use of sign language to communicate emotions and a sense of comfort to him.

My husband made the sign for "I love you" with his hand and I saw a tear roll down his cheek as he placed Noah's tiny, weak hand on top of his.

We had taken Noah to the doctor more times than I can remember.

It had been a week and a half and Noah's fever remained very high and very dangerous, despite everything the doctor or we had tried. I knew in my soul the way only a mother can know, that Noah was in trouble.

I gently touched my husband's shoulder, and we looked into each other's eyes with the same fear and knowledge that Noah wasn't getting any better. I offered to take over for him, but he shook his head, and once again, I was amazed at this wonderful man who is the father of my children. When many fathers would have gladly handed over the parenting duties for some much needed sleep, my husband stayed stubbornly and resolutely with our child.

When morning finally came, we called the doctor and were told to bring him in again. We already knew that he would probably put Noah in the hospital. So, we made arrangements for the other children, packed bags for all three of us, and tearfully drove to the doctor's office once again. Our hearts filled with dread, we waited in a small room, different from the usual examining room we had become used to. Our doctor finally came in, looked Noah over, and told us the news we expected. Noah had to be admitted to the hospital. Now.

The drive to the hospital in a neighboring town seemed surreal. I couldn't focus on anything, couldn't think, couldn't stop crying. My husband reassured me that he felt in his heart that Noah would be okay. We admitted Noah and were taken to his room right away. It was a torturous night, filled with horrible tests that made my son's tiny little voice echo through the halls as he screamed over and over.

I felt as if I were shattering from the inside out. My husband never wavered in his faith. He comforted me and Noah, and everyone who called to check on Noah. He was a rock.

When the first batch of tests were done, the nurse informed us that a spinal tap would be performed soon. Meningitis was suspected. Marty and I had a prayer together with Noah. Our hands intertwined, we held our son, and the love of my life lifted his voice to the Lord, telling him how grateful we were for this awesome little spirit with whom he had entrusted us. With tears streaming down his face, he humbly asked the Lord to heal our son. My heart filled with comfort and gratitude.

A short time later, the resident doctor came in. He told us that Noah's first results were back, and that he had Influenza A. No spinal tap was needed! Noah would recover and soon be back to his zesty, tornado little self. And Noah was already standing up in the hospital crib, bouncing like he was on a trampoline. My husband's talk with the Lord was already being answered.

Marty and I grinned at each other through our tears, and waited for Noah to be released from the hospital. Finally, in the middle of the night, our own doctor came in and told us that it was fine to take Noah home. We couldn't pack fast enough!

A few days later, I was cooking dinner. Noah was healing, slowly but surely. I felt at peace and knew my husband was the greatest father I could ever want for my children. I peeked around the corner into the living room, and chuckled at the picture I saw. There was my husband, sitting in his "daddy chair," Noah in his lap. They were reading a book, dad taking Noah's teeny hands to help him form the signs for the words in the book. They both looked up and caught me watching them, and my husband and I simultaneously signed "I love you" to each other, then to Noah. And then Noah put his little arm up, trying to shape his chubby hand in his own effort to sign "I love you" to his daddy. I watched with tears in my eyes as my husband carefully helped him form his tiny fingers into the sign with his own gentle hands. Daddy hands.

A MATTER OF PRIDE

TERRY L. PFLEGHAAR
FROM *HOMELIFE* MAGAZINE

*W*ell, she did it! She accomplished the dream of her life, her three-and-a-half-year-old life. She cut her hair!

Her father and I were sitting in our favorite chairs in the living room having a discussion. It was an intense dialogue, at times bordering on becoming a heated debate. On occasion, I would stare out the window and survey our land, a few acres of beautiful winter radiance, a delight to my eyes. My eyes would then return to my man, and I again would join in the conversation.

A hush permeated the room, and we could hear once again the faint sound that had been intermittently peppering our ears for the past few minutes. What was that sound? I cocked my ear. Oh sure, it was the familiar sound of the bathroom cupboard door clicking shut, the cupboard where I kept the garbage can. I turned back to my husband.

There was that sound again! *Wait a minute!* I thought. *I can understand opening it once or twice to throw in a tissue if she were blowing her nose, but what is she doing?*

"Sweetheart," I called. "What are you doing in there?"

She came out to the living room and stood by my chair, a radiant grin

STORIES FOR THE HEART

on her face. At first I didn't see why she was so delighted. All I could see was my good pair of hair-cutting scissors clutched in her left hand.

Her eyes lit up as she fingered her dark locks. "Look at my hair, Mama!"

I looked. I lifted my eyebrows. I closed my eyes and took a deep breath. Holding my breath. I looked again. No, my eyes were not deceiving me. She had cut it!

In my shock, I gently turned her around. She had cut the sides up to her ears, with a few spots close-cropped to the head. Consistent with today's styles, she had permitted a swath of long hair to remain intact, waving down the length of her small back.

Her father and I marched her to the bathroom. There it was, layered in the garbage can. A collection of elegant eight-inch fragments of wavy chocolate-colored hair. I covered my horror-stricken face with my hands. The little darling was chattering, so pleased with herself. After all, she had been wanting it cut since she was two years old! Unfortunately, mother was not so pleased. In my pregnant state of hormonally controlled emotions, I ran to my bedroom, threw myself onto the bed, and cried.

Didn't she know what a priceless treasure she had in that hair? Didn't she realize what she had just lost? It was thick, the envy of her little friends, and admired by mine. "Oh, she's so beautiful! You should model her!" complete strangers would exclaim. Yes, I had to agree, the way those luxurious chestnut locks framed her dark eyes and long, dark eyelashes, she was the portrait of loveliness.

I always encouraged her to thank others for the compliments, afraid she would become prideful. Of course, I didn't consider that perhaps I was the one who was prideful! No, I couldn't be! It wasn't *my* hair.

As I lay on my bed feeling sorry for myself, I could hear her excited prattle in the hall. "Do you like my short hair, Daddy? I love it!" Then it dawned on me. She was happy! I was feeling sorry for me, not her! She had become my own living dolly, my personal creation that I had manipulated and used for my secret glory. She had been pleading for a haircut for a year, and cried almost every time I combed her hair. Nevertheless, I had forced her into the mold I had fashioned for her. I had to suck up my pride, and let her be a person with her own ideas and desires. After all, that was the way God made her!

So I dried my tears, and straightened out my rumpled clothes. Pulling my shoulders back, I walked out into the hall. There was my little darling, her shining brown eyes staring up into mine with expectancy.

"Mama, don't you just love my hair? I cut out all the tanglies!"

I smiled and reached down to pick her up. I kissed her pink cheek and fingered the remains of those soft, long locks that had been the source of my pride. "Yes, honey, I love your hair, and I love you!"

Memories

God gave us memories so that
we might have roses in December.

AUTHOR UNKNOWN

THEIR BEST

Connie Lounsbury
From *Lifewise* magazine

We still talk about that frigid January morning in 1950 when I was 8 years old.

I was brushing my hair, huddled close to the wood stove along with my older brother and three little sisters, trying to keep warm while Mom cooked oatmeal. We heard sounds upstairs like marbles rolling across the floor, so Dad went upstairs to check. Halfway up the stairs he yelled, "The house is on fire!"

We lived way out in the country near Orrock, Minn., with no telephone, so the house and most of our belongings burned to the ground before help arrived. Family photographs, Mom's treadle sewing machine and a few other personal belongs were all they could pull from the house while we girls ran to the neighbors.

Dad had been unemployed that winter, and we had neither money nor insurance with which to replace anything we lost in the fire. After we stayed a few days with relatives, Dad borrowed money to rent an old farmhouse nearby. Mom set up housekeeping with furniture, bedding and kitchen utensils relatives and friends donated.

We didn't have much before the fire, but I hadn't felt our poverty before. Now I stood in someone else's too-large dress, in a colorless, bare-windowed house, looking at a paint-spattered table, mismatched chairs, worn towels and a spatula with a broken handle, and I couldn't keep from crying. We had become paupers who didn't deserve better. While we were extremely grateful for everything we were given, it was a difficult, dreary time for us.

Then a neighbor came with a gift. She handed my mother a set of brand-new, beautifully hand-embroidered pillowcases. The sight of the pure white cotton cases, folded to display the bright, hand-stitched pink, lavender and green floral design, almost took my breath away. I could hardly believe she meant for us to keep them. Others had given us what they least wanted themselves, but this neighbor gave us the best she had!

We hadn't lived in that community very long before the fire, and we soon moved away and lost touch with the neighbors. Now, almost 50 years later, I no longer remember who gave us that gift, but I do remember the sense of self-worth it restored to me. *We must be okay for someone to give us such a beautiful and precious handmade gift.*

It is one of my favorite memories and many times it has been the example that directs my own actions. They gave the best they had.

*Our todays and yesterdays are the blocks
with which to build tomorrow.*

HENRY WADSWORTH LONGFELLOW

A PAIR OF WORN OUT SHOES

THELDA BEVENS

This morning it was his shoes. I was rounding up the garbage and sorting the recycle items, carrying them down to the street and looking around the place for any I had missed. Since the garbage can was only half full (another reminder of how much has changed), I wandered into that place where junk abounds—the garage.

The first item I tossed away was the broken snow shovel, then the hammer claw without a handle, then rusty nails in an old torn paper sack, and two small empty boxes tools had once occupied. And then—there they were. His old shoes. Nike sneakers. Once, a long time ago, white— now red with dirt from our undeveloped, unlandscaped yard. Dotted with splashes of dark paint the color of the trim on our old house. Splotched with blue from painting the porches on our new house. Matted with saw-dust and mud from building steps and handrails in December to please the county inspector. Filthy, ugly, worn-out shoes that I had asked him to throw away a dozen times, but which he kept and wore and cherished. I think he never threw anything away. He was one of those you-never-know-when-you-might-need-it persons. But now he was gone and he didn't need these shoes and I could throw them away right now. Into the garbage. Poof!

Then I looked at them, and saw the years of work—the painting, the remodeling, the building, the repairing, the digging, the sawing, the installing, the creating. So much of what he was and how he lived, and all the things he could do and loved to do were in those old shoes. And now nobody was in those shoes. And no one, I thought, could ever be in those shoes. He walked in them strong and able and confident. How ironic that these ugly old shoes were still here and he who walked in them was gone.

But—the decision was mine; I could throw them away now—if I wanted to. I *should* throw them away. Nothing was stopping me.

I set them carefully on top of the garbage and shut the lid. I waited. But I could not do it. I lifted them out and held them and loved them and cried for the man who had walked in them.

As I hugged those worthless shoes, I tipped them slightly and a tiny stream of what I thought were pebbles flowed downward from the toe of one shoe. The shoes had little rocks in them, I thought, from past digging and gravel spreading. I looked more closely. No. Not rocks at all, but pine nuts deposited by one of the squirrels in our woods—quite a lot of nuts— enough to last a frugal squirrel several days, perhaps a week.

Well—did I think those shoes worthless? Ha! Dar and the squirrels knew better! The shoes' usefulness was never questioned by my husband. And now his view was borne out by nature.

I set the shoes back where I had found them. They were much more needed as a safe place to stash a squirrel's winter food than to adorn a smelly garbage dump. And somehow I am less sad, more reassured by this connection with nature. It pleases me, and I know it would please Dar, to know that a beautiful wild gray creature now walks in his beautiful old shoes.

THE RICH FAMILY

EDDIE OGAN
FROM *VIRTUE* MAGAZINE

I'll never forget Easter 1946. I was 14, my little sister Ocy 12, and my older sister Darlene 16. We lived at home with our mother, and the four of us knew what it was to do without many things.

My dad had died five years before, leaving Mom with seven school kids to raise and no money. By 1946 my older sisters were married and my brothers had left home.

A month before Easter, the pastor of our church announced that a special Easter offering would be taken to help a poor family. He asked everyone to save and give sacrificially.

When we got home, we talked about what we could do. We decided to buy 50 pounds of potatoes and live on them for a month. This would allow us to save $20 of our grocery money for the offering.

Then we thought that if we kept our electric lights turned out as much as possible and didn't listen to the radio, we'd save money on that month's electric bill. Darlene got as many house and yard cleaning jobs as possible, and both of us baby-sat for everyone we could. For 15 cents, we could buy enough cotton loops to make three pot holders to sell for $1. We made $20.00 on pot holders.

That month was one of the best of our lives. Every day we counted the money to see how much we had saved. At night we'd sit in the dark and talk about how the poor family was going to enjoy having the money the church would give them. We had about 80 people in church, so we figured that whatever amount of money we had to give, the offering would surely be 20 times that much. After all, every Sunday the pastor had reminded everyone to save for the sacrificial offering.

The day before Easter, Ocy and I walked to the grocery store and got the manager to give us three crisp $20 bills and one $10 bill for all our change. We ran all the way home to show Mom and Darlene. We had never had so much money before.

That night we were so excited we could hardly sleep. We didn't care that we wouldn't have new clothes for Easter; we had $70 for the sacrificial offering. We could hardly wait to get to church!

On Sunday morning, rain was pouring down. We didn't own an umbrella, and the church was over a mile from our home, but it didn't seem to matter how wet we got. Darlene had cardboard in her shoes to fill the holes. The cardboard came apart and her feet got wet. But we sat in church proudly. I heard some teenagers talking about the Smith girls having on their old dresses. I looked at them in their new clothes, and I felt so rich.

When the sacrificial offering was taken, we were sitting in the second row from the front. Mom put in the $10 bill, and each of us girls put in a $20. As we walked home after church, we sang all the way. At lunch Mom had a surprise for us. She had bought a dozen eggs, and we had boiled Easter eggs with our fried potatoes!

Late that afternoon the minister drove up in his car. Mom went to the door, talked with him for a moment, and then came back with an envelope in her hand. We asked what it was, but she didn't say a word. She opened the envelope, and out fell a bunch of money. There were three crisp $20 bills, one $10 and seventeen $1 bills.

Mom put the money back in the envelope. We didn't talk, we just sat and stared at the floor. We'd gone from feeling like millionaires to feeling like poor white trash.

We kids had had such a happy life that we felt sorry for anyone who didn't have parents like ours and a house full of brothers and sisters and other kids visiting constantly. We thought it was fun to share silverware and see whether we got the fork or the spoon that night. We had two knives, which we passed around to whoever needed them.

I knew we didn't have a lot of things that other people had but I'd never thought we were poor. That Easter Day I found out we were. The minister had brought us the money for the poor family, so we must be poor.

I didn't like being poor. I looked at my dress and worn-out shoes and felt so ashamed that I didn't want to go back to church. Everyone there probably already knew we were poor! I thought about school. I was in the ninth grade and at the top of my class of over 100 students. I wondered if the kids at school knew we were poor. I decided I could quit school since I had finished the eighth grade. That was all the law required at that time.

We sat in silence for a long time. Then it got dark, and we went to bed. All that week, we girls went to school and came home, and no one talked much. Finally on Saturday, Mom asked us what we wanted to do with the money. What did poor people do with money? We didn't know. We'd never known we were poor.

We didn't want to go to church on Sunday, but Mom said we had to. Although it was a sunny day, we didn't talk on the way. Mom started to sing, but no one joined in, and she only sang one verse.

At church we had a missionary speaker. He talked about how churches in Africa made buildings out of sun-dried bricks, but they needed money to buy roofs. He said $100 would put a roof on a church. The minister said, "Can't we all sacrifice to help these poor people?"

We looked at each other and smiled for the first time in a week. Mom reached in her purse and pulled out the envelope. She passed it to Darlene, Darlene gave it to me, and I handed it to Ocy. Ocy put it in the offering.

When the offering was counted, the minister announced that it was a little over $100. The missionary was excited. He hadn't expected such a large offering from our small church. He said, "You must have some rich people in this church."

Suddenly, it struck us! We had given $87 of that "little over $100." We were the richest family in the church! Hadn't the missionary said so?

A PERFECT GIFT

AUTHOR UNKNOWN

*I*t's just a small, white envelope stuck among the branches of our Christmas tree. No name, no identification, no inscription. It has peeked through the branches of our tree at this time of the year for the past ten years or so.

It all began because my husband Mike hated Christmas. Oh, not the true meaning of Christmas, but the commercial aspects of it. You know, the overspending, the frantic running around at the last minute to get a tie for Uncle Harry and the dusting powder for Grandma, the gifts given in desperation because you couldn't think of anything else.

Knowing he felt this way, I decided one year to bypass the usual shirts, sweaters, ties, and so forth. I reached for something special just for Mike. The inspiration came in an unusual way.

Our son Kevin, who was twelve that year, was wrestling at the junior level at the school he attended. Shortly before Christmas, there was a non-league match against a team sponsored by an inner city church. The kids were mostly black.

These youngsters, dressed in sneakers so ragged that shoestrings seemed to be the only thing holding them together, presented a sharp contrast to our boys in their spiffy blue and gold uniforms and sparkling new wrestling shoes.

As the match began, I was alarmed to see that the other team was wrestling without headgear, a kind of light helmet designed to protect a wrestler's ears. It was a luxury the ragtag team obviously couldn't afford. Well, we ended up walloping them.

We took every weight class. And as each of their boys got up from the mat, he swaggered around in his tatters with false bravado, a kind of street pride that couldn't acknowledge defeat.

Mike, seated beside me, shook his head sadly. "I wish just one of them could have won," he said. "They have a lot of potential, but losing like this could take the heart right out of them." Mike loved kids—all kids. He understood kids in competitive situations, having coached Little League football, baseball, and lacrosse. That's when the idea for his present came.

That afternoon, I went to a local sporting goods store and bought an assortment of wrestling headgear and shoes and sent them anonymously to the inner city church. On Christmas Eve, I placed the envelope on the tree, the note inside telling Mike what I had done and this was his gift from me.

His smile was the brightest thing about Christmas that year and in succeeding years. For each Christmas, I followed the tradition—one year sending a group of mentally challenged youngsters to a hockey game, another year a check to a pair of elderly brothers whose home had burned to the ground the week before Christmas—on and on…

The envelope became the highlight of our Christmas. It was always the last thing opened on Christmas morning and our children, ignoring their new toys, would stand with wide-eyed anticipation as their dad lifted the envelope from the tree to reveal its contents.

As the children grew, the toys gave way to more practical presents, but the envelope never lost its allure. Still, the story doesn't end there.

You see, we lost Mike last year due to cancer. When Christmas rolled around, I was still so wrapped in grief that I barely got the tree up. Yet Christmas Eve found me placing an envelope on the tree, and in the morning, it was joined by three more. Each of our children, unbeknownst to the others, had placed an envelope on the tree for their dad.

The tradition has grown and someday will expand even further, with our grandchildren standing around the tree with wide-eyed anticipation, watching as their fathers take down their envelopes.

Mike's spirit, like the spirit of Christmas, will always be with us.

You will find as you look back upon your life,
that the moments that stand out are the
moments when you have done things for others.

HENRY DRUMMOND

WHEN STRANGERS PASSED THROUGH

RUTH LEE
FROM *LIVE* MAGAZINE

At the age of seven, not having a mother caused me to spend a lot of time with my friends. Their mothers wore smiles while correcting my manners, and sewed ruffles where ruffles had no need to be.

I heard their words. I knew what they were doing. They were attempting to fill the "no-mother-emptiness" in my life by treating me like one of their own.

"Girls! Girls! Where are you? Come now, hurry along into the house." We knew what the call from someone's mother signaled.

When we were securely inside we were allowed to watch from behind lace curtained windows as the man in raggedy clothes with a burlap sack thrown over his shoulder shuffled his worn-out shoes down the sidewalk.

Steel tracks carried a steady procession of trains through the small Midwestern town where I grew up. While some of the passengers rode plush seats in deep maroon comfort, others hunkered small in corners of empty box cars.

The Depression was drawing to a close, or so the newspapers said, but in our rural community we had little evidence to support the claim and itinerant men continued to knock on doors asking for food in exchange for chores.

After the stranger had passed, we were allowed to go back to our play, but many times playing was no longer on my mind. I would say good-bye and walk towards home.

More often than not, when I reached our home at the edge of town, the man I had watched through the curtains of lace at my friend's house would be sitting with my father on the back doorstep outside our kitchen. On his lap would be a blue willow plate, heaped full of last night's left-overs.

Once, when I had asked in front of the stranger, "How come that old tramp gets to eat off our best dishes?" my father had reprimanded me with his we'll-talk-about-this-later look.

"Child," he'd explained, "most of the men you see come passing through town are just going through hard times. Many of them are family men, trying to earn a dollar to send on, or maybe trying to get home to those they love."

My father didn't have a degree to frame and hang on the wall, but he was a scholar, a student of human nature. He looked at people in a different way than most folk did, always reaching for a reason that might make an individual act in a certain way. And once he'd found what lay inside, he'd take an even closer look to see what that person could become, if given half a chance.

I'm grown up now, and many things have changed. Our government takes care of the handouts and I guess that's just as well. I still see a lot of people who remind me of those mothers who called us in from play, but I don't see many who remind me of my dad.

THE LITTLE APRON

CHARLENE ANN BAUMBICH
FROM *MAMA SAID THERE'D BE DAYS LIKE THIS*

Each of us possess items with no real earthly value, but the minute we see them, memories flood our minds. I have many such items; I keep them in my view. Some comfort me, some make me laugh. They range from rocks to photos.

Recently I lost one of those items: a pocket knife with a green cover, not more than 2-1/2 inches long. Its blade was shaped like a saber, and it was incredibly sharp. The knife belonged to my grandmother, and I loved using it.

I often imagined what Grandma might have sliced, diced, screwed, slit, or stuck with it. George and I used it just before it disappeared. We were on vacation, sliced a beef salami, and then the knife was gone.

Another of my favorite items is a five-inch diameter rock on a pedestal in our living room. Mom fished it out of the bottom of a lake the last time we caught a fish together.

Several months after Mom's death, I went through her belongings. I sifted through her closet, hanger by hanger. Certain events and outings were triggered by familiar dress clothes, and suddenly, there it was: the apron. It's a pinafore type and ties in the back, with one pocket on the right front. It's probably all cotton, but I don't know for sure. Instantly, I was weeping. I could hardly look at it. The pain was too close, instant, and piercing.

Mom loved to entertain, she loved her home, her duties, and her agenda; but most of all, she loved us. She loved doing for us. And she often wore that apron during the doing. The apron seemed to be a beacon flashing reminders that would nevermore be.

The worn apron now hangs on the wall in my office, a silent reminder of time well spent: peeling potatoes; making her specialty pineapple cream pie with meringue; planting pumpkin seeds in her hand-shoveled mounds of rich black earth; running her Electrolux in a complete panic before company arrived; gifting us with country fried chicken, mashed potatoes, corn on the cob (out of the garden, of course), and the best white chicken gravy laced with crunchies from pan drippings that any human ever put to palate.

The apron also elicits memories of her spunk: how she stood up to a shoe salesman who tried to tell her it was our fault her little girl had blisters on her feet; shooting a fox in our basement; driving a delivery truck to Chicago when she was nine months pregnant to help my father's new business stay afloat; becoming a business woman for the first time, after age fifty; and emptying a punch bowl over the head of a blond bombshell who had flirted once too often with my father....

The apron represents hot tea and cold watermelon. Ironing and wash on the line. Popsicles when we were sick, and Sunday evening popcorn and fresh squeezed lemonade when we were well. It reminds me of the scent of Lilies of the Valley, with which mom slathered herself once a year when Coty released its new batch. It conjures up images of Mom holding her first-born grandson close to her breast and weeping.

And laughter. Endless peals of laughter so quick to pour from her bountiful and overflowing joy-filled spirit.

I thank God for this symbol of motherhood. And, like the knife, should the apron disappear on one of *those* days, although I'll be sad, I know I'll never lose the glorious memories given to me from my "no earthly value," but "all that matters" items.

A thing of beauty is a joy forever;
Its loveliness increases;
It can never pass into nothingness.

<small>KEATS</small>

THE ETCHING

BARBARA BAUMGARDNER

I was barely eighteen when my future husband took me fishing from the banks of the Williamson River in Southern Oregon. We picnicked at Collier Park where he carved my initials deep into the bark of a birch tree. I took a photo for my album.

More than forty years later, I returned to Collier Park, a widow hungry for a hug from the past. The park had been expanded, lawn planted, and modern restrooms installed. Longingly, my eyes searched the numerous carvings chiseled into the bark of the only small grove of white trees on site. I photographed the trees from all sides, hoping one chance shot would show me some remaining record of the leafing out of love in this place.

I found the park host to ask for help. "Would the tree have grown too high for me to identify my initials?"

"Oh no," he replied. "But by now the injured bark would be healed and the carvings significantly stretched out as the tree grew so they'd be pretty difficult to read."

Undaunted by his discouraging words, I stifled a couple of girlish giggles as my search continued for my very own tree-tattoo. How ridiculous I must have looked pointing my camera at all the silent, jagged scars in the tree trunks.

A poem crept into my mind:

Forty-three years ago, my husband to be
carved my initials upon a tree.
Today I return to find his mark
in a lovely place named Collier Park.

A week later when my roll of film was developed and I compared it with the forty-three year old photo, I knew I had found the etching. It was the only double tree trunk in the small grove of now large birches. I laughed. And then I cried. And I remembered.

I suppose now, a generation later, those who play in the park might wonder about the origin of the etchings or perhaps chastise the person who used a sharp pocketknife to record his love for a young girl. However, for me, the deep scars in the tree trunk are a reminder of the scars in my own heart, put there by the sharp blade of death. And like the small grove of large birches, I too have been marvelously healed and stretched.

Enjoy the little things
for one day you may look back
and realize they were the big things.

ROBERT BRAULT

LILACS TO REMEMBER

FAITH ANDREWS BEDFORD
FROM *COUNTRY LIVING* MAGAZINE

The soft spring air is full of the fragrance of the year's first mowing. Neat golden bales dot the meadow, and the fruit trees look as though they've been frosted with vanilla icing. As I stand on my porch and look out across the valley to the mountaintops beyond, I can see that the light green of new leaves has pushed up the slopes and almost reached the peaks. It is time for the first wildflower walk of the season.

My husband and I take our pickup along an old logging trail that winds its way up the mountainside. As we bounce over rocks and displace loose gravel, pale pink mountain laurel branches brush against the windows. The road ends beneath a tangle of wild rhododendron. We lace up our hiking boots and fill our water jugs from a spring that burbles up from beneath a mossy rock.

As we walk, we spot trillium and lady's slippers, false Solomon's seal and dogtooth violets. Sun-warmed pine needles release their pungent fragrance as we maneuver beneath the drooping boughs of the tall trees.

A faint path leads off into a hemlock wood. We have passed it before but never taken it; this time, we decide to explore. Presently, the forest begins to open up and ahead we can see the light of a clearing. In the center rises a stone chimney, a remnant of an abandoned homestead.

I smell the lilacs before I see them. The breeze is suddenly rich and
sweet. Beside the chimney we find an old root cellar ringed with peri-
winkle; blue blossoms pale against shiny green leaves. Next to a broad flat
rock, which must have served as a front step, stands a lilac bush, its thick,
gnarled branches laden with deep purple spires. I draw some to me. The
scent envelops me and, for a moment, I am no longer in a forest clearing
but in my grandmother's garden.

Lilacs were her favorite flower; her yard was ringed with them. But
it was not until I was nine or 10 that I discovered that one of the shrubs
was mine. On a soft spring afternoon much like this one, Grandmother
and I were gathering flowers for her dining room. As I reached up to clip
the white lilac she said, "That's *your* lilac, you know." I turned around in
surprise.

She smiled. "Yes, I planted that in your honor the year you were
born." I regarded the lovely shrub, which was far taller than I was, and felt
very important.

Then Grandmother took my hand and introduced me to all of the
other lilacs in her garden. As we stood beneath the largest one she said, "I
planted this one the year Jimmy was born." ("Jimmy" was my father. It
always startled me to hear anyone call that tall, balding man Jimmy.
Mother called him Jim.)

We moved on to a wine-red lilac. "And this one I planted in memory
of your grandfather the year he died." Her smile faded for a moment, then
she led me toward the front yard. By the gate was a deep-pink lilac just a
bit taller than mine.

"This one I planted the year your parents were married,"
Grandmother said. "It certainly has thrived."

Indeed it had. Several boughs were so heavy with blooms that
Grandmother had to prop them up with forked branches pruned from her
apple tree.

Behind the flower bed were two small lilacs, one light lavender and
one pale pink. "These I planted for your sisters," she said, clipping a sprig
from each and placing them in her basket. "The lavender one is Ellen's; it

is called 'Minuet.' The little pink one is called 'Moonglow'; I planted it three years ago for Beth."

My little sisters were only six and three, but I couldn't wait to tell them that they had their very own lilacs in Grandmother's garden—lilacs with beautiful names.

As we drew close to the terrace, I saw a small lilac bush with just a few tiny blooms. They were the blue of an evening sky and their scent was exotic, almost spicy. I had not seen the bush before. I looked up at Grandmother.

"That one is called 'Nocturne,'" she said, "and I planted it for myself last fall in honor of my retirement from the library." She laughed and added, "I thought I deserved it."

For years, Grandmother had helped the children of our village find the perfect book. Now she would be able to spend her days doing what she loved best: reading and gardening.

For many years, our lilacs, as I came to regard them, filled both her house and ours with fragrant arrangements. At my wedding, I carried a bouquet that Grandmother had fashioned from my lilac bush.

By the time my first child was born, Grandmother could no longer garden. When I told her of Drew's birth she said, "Plant a lilac for him, won't you, dear?" And I promised that I would.

But it was many years before we had a home of our own. Though I planted lilacs for my children, we kept moving and leaving their lilacs behind. By the time we settled down, my firstborn was in high school. I had forgotten about the lilacs.

Now, surrounded once again by the sweet scent of a lilac in bloom, I remember Grandmother and my promise to her. Drew became a father last month; his new daughter, Carter Elisabeth, has his pale hair and blue eyes. I resolve to plant a lilac in honor of her birth and in memory of her great-great grandmother.

As we turn to walk back, I break off a small branch from the lilac bush and tuck it into my hatband. The earthy dampness beneath my feet mingled with the scent of lilac is like a garden after rain.

When I get back home, I shall take down my gardening books and find just the right lilac for my new granddaughter and my grandmother. Perhaps "Vestale," a white one like the one Grandmother planted for me, or maybe "Primrose," an outstanding pale-yellow lilac just the color of Carter's hair.

It must be perfect, this lilac for a first grandchild. It will grow and flourish and then, some spring when she comes to visit, I will pluck for her a bouquet of sweet-scented blossoms from her very own lilac bush. And she will feel very important.

Life is made up, not of great sacrifices or duties,
but of little things in which smiles and kindnesses,
given habitually are what win and preserve the heart.

SIR HUMPHREY DAVY

MY MOTHER'S GLOVES

SHARRON DEAN McCANN
FROM *VIRTUE* MAGAZINE

*T*hey were probably made from a fabric called lisle. I know they were black, white or navy and smelled like cold cream and face powder. Mom wore them all the time but I liked my Mother's gloves best on Sunday mornings during church. I loved the slippery feel of them squished inside my fist. I pulled them on and pretended I was a lady, tucking in the ends where my stubby fingers didn't fill them out.

But once I grew up, Mother's gloves might have been forgotten had I not as a little girl grumbled about all the good things boys got to do. I always wanted to be one of them.

"Boys get to follow in their fathers' footsteps," I muttered. "What do girls ever get to do? Probably just follow in their mothers' gloves."

I put that thought aside, but the idea came back years later as I watched my own children playing dress-up, pretending to be grown. What had I learned with my little hand tucked in Mothers' gloved one?

The tips on Mom's left glove were empty and one gloved finger was hollow halfway down. Long before I was born, when she helped on the hay wagon, her fingertips were cut off in a hayfork accident. To me, they were just her fingers, but she always hated the nubbed ends. She may have worn the gloves to cover her shame. But through them, I learned an awful lot about life.

My first memories were amid Mother's life transitions: She had seen three sons off to war—one never came home—tended an invalid husband, sent her oldest daughter to college, raised a teenage son; and held me, her tag-along baby girl.

When her husband died, she moved us to town, restored old houses—transforming them into homes, then sold them and bought others to fix. She also had a job outside our home, working her way up from a seamstress for a state mental institution to its head housekeeper.

I didn't realize all that I learned from those years until I faced divorce. Crying in the shower one morning, I leaned against the wall with uncontrollable sobs. Thoughts began to tumble out of me. *I can't go on.*

Then: *Yes, I can.* And *How do I know this? Where did I learn how?*

Immediately I knew I'd learned how to survive in hardship by walking, hand in glove, with Mom. We went to church, the market, Grandma's, school events, work parties. And even though Mother had a full-time job, she made time to bake: plump golden loaves of bread, bubbly pies and soft, warm beans filled our kitchen every Saturday. I rarely remember a week that she didn't make extras.

She'd drop these off to the elderly, ill or handicapped. I was taken along to sit quietly listening. The conversations, I've forgotten. But I remember the feather ticks, the sounds of Tigers baseball on the radio, lemonade, cookies, and "how good that was for Mrs. Whoever" and "how little it cost."

Sometime in the summer of 1945 or '46 Mom called me from play to go for a walk and we started around the block with a basketful of food. I thought we were going on a picnic. I badgered Mom with questions: Why were we taking a basket? Who was it for? Where were we going?

At first, she just replied, "To that house down there."

I continued my questions. Finally, she said: "A friend of your brother, Garnett, married a Japanese girl and brought her home to live. No one in town will sell them anything so we are taking them some food." I knew that it was in the war with the Japanese that my brother had been killed.

It took me a lot longer than my Mom to learn forgiveness, but I learned "give-ness" on that short summer walk.

Mom is 92 now. Her gloves lay waiting on the table. Until she was 85, she still drove to church in them, the car always filled with "old ladies who can't drive." And she went to feed her oldest brother every day.

Forty-five years ago, I may have doubted the joy in being female, but now I know for sure: A little girl can hardly go wrong if she grows up to follow in her Mother's gloves.

It is when we forget ourselves
that we do things that will be remembered.

AUTHOR UNKNOWN

PORCH SWING

BRENDA A. CHRISTENSEN

T was six months pregnant with our first child when we bought our house—our very own home.

It was small, but almost storybook perfect. Its early twentieth-century charm didn't hit me the first time we looked at it, as the heat of August aggravated my all-day morning sickness, and the mosquitoes were on the offensive.

My husband liked it immediately. Somehow we were brought back when the real estate company held an open house. After dragging both our families through it, I changed my mind. Suddenly, I saw the hundreds of flowers surrounding the entire yard, including the flower box that was actually the front wall of the front porch.

There was a giant maple tree which must have witnessed every storm our small city had ever encountered and still managed to hold its own. The enormous windows, though stained with years of tobacco smoke and layers of paint, drew me in further, as did the two window seats I had longed for as a young girl, to sit in and dream and wish, or write in my diary. It would be perfect for my little girl.

But the thing that convinced me this was our new home, was the porch swing. It was all I had wanted as we combed the city for a house: No porch for a swing, no deal.

I had such fond memories of sitting on my grandparents' swing. All this place needed was a white picket fence and we were set.

Our baby girl was born and our house seemed to be coming along— it did need some work done—and we spent much of our time outside when the weather began to warm. Walking around the block, playing chase in the grass, and of course, swinging on the porch occupied much of our day. I can't think of the countless times I rocked her to sleep on that swing, and with my second daughter as well.

We learned our ABCs and other charming songs and rhymes, including some we made up. The swing was frequently sticky from the popsicles melting in our hands on a hot summer evening. We played and swung wildly. We watched the traffic go by or the moon drift through the branches of the maple tree as we rocked softly. I sat on that swing and watched my girls play in the yard, jump in the leaves, or run through the sprinkler and smile in delight. I was in heaven.

From the day we bought our little "doll house," as our realtor referred to it, we were planning to sell it. My husband and I worked so hard to make necessary repairs and update the decorations. After five years and two children, we had outgrown our home. The time came to move out into the country where I had always dreamed of raising my children. All I could do was cry the whole day.

We went back to the house one more time to make one final go-round, one last quick meal in the old place, and one last sit on the swing.

I think the last five years of my life in that house flashed before me, sort of like some people say it does before they near death. I cried so hard I could barely see to leave. We all waved good-bye and drove away with tear-stained faces.

It had been over two months and I hadn't driven by, even once, until recently. I really wanted to visit the elderly neighbor lady whom I had befriended.

When I pulled up there was a young woman, about my age when I had my girls, sitting on my porch swing playing with her toddler behind the flowers I had planted earlier this spring. I hollered hello to her as I knocked on the neighbor's door.

I couldn't take my eyes off them. Nor could I hold back the tears that began streaming down my face. My friend wasn't home and I was tempted to go over and introduce myself to the woman but decided not to since I knew I couldn't dry my eyes long enough to so much as say my name.

So I got into my car and pulled away, watching them play on the front porch through my rearview mirror.

I cried in sadness for my loss, and I cried in happiness for their gain. I cried in joy for the fate of my porch swing, making happy memories, as I am sure it did before me, and as I have now seen, it will continue to do without me.

THE BARN

SHARRON DEAN MCCANN

y favorite winter place as a child was the barn at twilight. Not our barn but Uncle Ernie's barn. Uncle Ernie and Aunt Audie, and their collie, Mutty, were neighbors who took care of me. Mutty and I romped through our first seven years of life together.

I always knew when it was time to go to the barn because Mutty would come nuzzle me from whatever I was doing. After pushing and pulling me to the door she waited impatiently while I struggled into leggings, boots, coat, hat, and mittens.

It wasn't far from the house to the barn, but between the two was a fence, a big gate, and a dog gate. We always crawled through the dog gate and stayed together until we got to the barn door. Mutty then scooted through another gate into the barnyard and gently moved through the animals using all her instincts to get them inside.

While she did that I ran through the side door into the main barn floor and up onto the hay mow. Uncle Ernie said the animals came in easier if no one was in their way. I didn't mind hiding because I loved to lay in the dusty hay to look, listen, feel, and smell.

My barn was not a fancy milking parlor. It wasn't scrubbed and clean.

It wasn't a proper red barn with high mows reached by big forks and lifts. The center barn roof was just high enough for a team of horses and a wagon full of hay. The sides sloped down low, to just above Uncle Ernie's head. On one side there were two stalls for the horses, Lady and Tony, and four stanchions for the cows, Bess, Elsie, May, and June. The other sloped side was the sheep barn.

I knew everyone was in the barn when I heard the munching begin. Munching and puffing and lowing. They really did low. Uncle Ernie said it couldn't be called mooing or neighing because the sound was too soft and quiet.

As the stanchions clanked shut, Mutty came to the mow to get me. The barn was steaming with a mixture of cold night air and warming bodies. Uncle Ernie was settled down on his little stool encouraging the big Jersey quartet to give him their cream. While he did the milking, I was suppose to get my chores done.

I ran to the buckets he had fixed for me to give to the animals. I never did much with the manger by the cows because I didn't like cows' faces. Besides, they were already chewing and slurping. The clanging of their stanchions and gurgling water cups was part of the music of the barn.

I dumped the buckets into the sheep mangers quickly and quietly. They were so quiet I thought I should be quiet. The manger was long and narrow and crowded with woolly bodies. Gently they nudged their way in and peacefully munched my little offering to them.

I hurried through pans of milk for the cats and Mutty so that I could have lots of time with the horses. I loved them. Grabbing their bucket of oats I climbed up on the manger in front of Lady and Tony. After I dumped the oats in one end I got more hay and shoved it in their faces. They munched and puffed and didn't seem to mind if I wanted to sit on their manger and rub their noses.

When all the mangers were licked clean, the milking was done, and the lights were out, we were ready to head for the house. Uncle Ernie and I stood in the dark silence and savored the moment. It was a delicious time for me of sound, and sight, and scents.

I grew up and left the barn. I hadn't seen a manger for years when a nurse laid my firstborn son in my arms. He was wrapped in a big sheet that had a tiny hole for his face and bound him like a papoose. I was told not to unwrap him. The big city hospital rules said that wasn't clean or safe for him.

Not clean? The thought shook loose my memories. I remembered a girl named Mary who had laid her firstborn son in a manger. I recalled the mangers in Uncle Ernie's barn. Not white and sterile. If they were ever clean, it was from being scrubbed by the long, thick, rough tongues of Tony, Lady, Bess, Elsie, May, and June. I knew the manger Mary had to use was even rougher than those in my memories.

Not safe? God come to earth as a baby didn't get a blue bassinet in a glass-enclosed nursery, away from the touch, feel, or smell of his mother. He got straw, in a manger, cleaned by animal tongues. Jesus, who came to be the Savior of the world was born in a barn steamy with the warm bodies of animals and filled with the sounds of munching, puffing, and lowing.

I waited until the nurse was gone. Then I unwrapped my firstborn son. I counted his fingers and toes. I held him close to my body and said thank you to that one who long ago slept in a manger, in what is still one of my favorite places, a winter barn.

Life

STEPPING STONES

Dear Lord—
I do not ask to walk smooth paths
Nor bear an easy load.
I pray for strength and fortitude
To climb the rock-strewn road.
Give me such courage that I can scale
The hardest peaks alone,
And transform every stumbling block
Into a stepping-stone.

GAIL BROOK BURKET

A LIGHT IN
THE WINDOW

FAITH ANDREWS BEDFORD
FROM *COUNTRY LIVING* MAGAZINE

*M*oving day was drawing to a close. The van rumbled down the lane leaving us with three hungry children, a frightened cat, and a mountain of boxes to unpack. Our new home seemed vacant and lonely; the nearest neighbor was about a mile down the road. I could see a faint light glimmering through the woods.

Presently I heard the crunch of tires on gravel; a small pickup truck pulled in beside the barn. When I opened the door, I was greeted by a warm smile. Our new neighbor, Marian, had brought us dinner, friendship and advice.

My little red address book, full of all the names and numbers a family needs to function, was of no use in this new place. I peppered Marian with questions. Who was a good vet? Where could I find aged manure for the garden? Was there a good plumber in town?

I learned with dismay that the nearest dentist was 30 miles away. But Marian assured me that the drive was beautiful.

She was right. As we drove down the valley, the hills were ablaze with autumn colors. Sugar maples bordered the old stone walls and yellow willows hung over the stream that meandered alongside the road. In the golden meadows, cows contentedly grazed. We all decided that our favorites were the belted Galloways, whose wide band of white in the middle of their black bodies made one think of Oreo cookies.

By the time we left Dr. Thomasson's office, dusk was beginning to settle. As we passed the edge of town, Drew asked, "Why does each house have a Christmas candle in the window when it isn't even Halloween?"

I remembered that the Syndersville Apple Festival was slated for the coming weekend; we planned to help with the cider pressing. Perhaps this was some sort of tradition, part of the festivities.

That evening, when I called the cat in, she did not come. Kate had been confused ever since the move, meowing forlornly as she wandered through the unfamiliar house. The following morning she was still missing.

Then winter closed in. The children worried about Kate and I tried to reassure them that she had probably found a nice warm barn to stay in for the winter. She was hibernating, I said, like a bear.

Mud season delayed the plowing. Spring chores piled up. Finally, one warm March afternoon as the first daffodils were blooming, the children and I headed back to Syndersville to buy new shoes. Sarah couldn't decide between the red sneakers or the white, and Eleanor took a long time just finding the right pair of party shoes. It was late by the time we left for home. Dusk was beginning to fall.

"Look," said Eleanor as we neared the outskirts of the village, "those houses still have lights in the window."

We saw that four or five houses on the left side of the road and three on the right all had a single candle lit.

I asked Marian if she knew why and she answered, "It's the way it's always been." Then she laughed. "That's a common answer to a lot of questions around here."

The following month, while the children were being seen by Dr. Thomasson, I asked his nurse if she knew the answer to the mystery.

She just shrugged and replied, "That's the way it has always been."

I hid a small smile.

"Excuse me," a voice behind me said. I turned around. An elderly lady in a green print dress motioned to me from a sofa in the waiting room.

"Come sit by me," she said, patting the seat beside her. "I'd be happy to tell you about those candles. I'm Grace Harding and I live in the last house on the left. You know, the little red one?"

"Yes," I said, "I admired your beautiful bank of forsythia on the way into town."

"Forty years ago, when I married Henry and came to Syndersville, the first people to welcome us were the Johnsons, Clem and Anna. They had the farmhouse set back from the road."

I had seen the neat, white frame building set among its barns and outbuildings. It looked sort of like a mother hen surrounded by her chicks.

"They had two sons, Arthur, the elder, a strong helpful boy who took after his father, and James, a quiet sort. He liked to read books. He's a professor over at the state college now." She smiled at Sarah, who was sitting beside me, listening intently. "When we began to have children, their daughter, Mary, used to mind them if we went to the cinema.

"Well, the war came along and Arthur signed up. It nearly tore Anna apart, him being her firstborn and all. But he wouldn't be dissuaded. James stayed home and helped his father run the farm." She sighed. "A lot of the village boys went off to war."

Drawing herself back to her story, she continued, "Arthur wrote home regularly and Anna used to read his letters to all the neighbors. She was very proud of him but worried, nonetheless. Mothers do that."

I nodded in agreement.

"About a year after he'd left, the letters stopped coming. Anna was just frantic. Then a man from the war office came by to tell them that Arthur was missing in action. They didn't know if he had been taken prisoner or…" Her voice trailed off as she looked at Sarah, who was holding my hand tightly.

"That evening, Anna left the porch light on all night. Told Clem that she wouldn't turn it off until Arthur came home. A few days later I noticed that Ella Winter, down the road, had left her light on, too. So had the Moores. At twilight, I turned on a small lamp in my front window. It was the least I could do."

"How long did she have to leave the porch light on?" I asked, half dreading her response.

" util she died," she answered in a soft voice. "After Arthur had been reported missing, I went to pay a visit. When I turned to go, I noticed a big piece of tape over the switch to the porch light. Anna looked at it. 'No one touches that switch,' she said to me. 'Clem tried to turn it off one morning but I stopped him. Told him I didn't care about the electricity.'"

Mrs. Harding looked at Sarah and continued. "A few years later, those little electric Christmas candles came out and the neighbors and I began burning them in our windows. We left them on for Arthur." She paused and then added, "And for all the others."

"The farmhouse still has its porch light on, doesn't it?" asked Sarah.

"Yes, dear," Mrs. Harding replied. "James lives in his parents' house now. The tape is still over the switch."

"Do you think that Arthur might come back someday?" asked Sarah quietly, her face full of worry.

"He might," Mrs. Harding said quietly.

"But he'd be very old, wouldn't he?" said Sarah.

That evening after supper, I heard noises in the attic and felt the cool draft that always means someone has left the door at the top of the stairs open.

"Who's up there?" I called.

"Just me," Sarah's muffled voice responded.

She came down the stairs with one of our window candles in her hand.

"I know it isn't Christmas yet, but I really want to put this in my window," she said, with a look that was at once hopeful and resolute.

"For Arthur?" I asked.

"Well, sort of," Sarah said. "But mostly for Kate. Maybe she's lost and just needs a light to guide her home."

I could not say no.

After I tucked her in, I stood in the doorway and looked at the candle.

Two weeks later, Kate returned followed by three kittens. Where she'd been, we'll never know. We were just glad to have her back.

"Can we leave the light on?" asked Sarah when we settled Kate into her basket. I nodded. For Arthur. And for all the others.

CREATURE COMFORT

BILL HOLTON

FROM *PETLIFE* MAGAZINE

In his 45 years as proprietor of Cooke's Funeral Home in Nitro, West Virginia, Fred Cooke has comforted thousands of bereaved parents, children and spouses. But four years ago when his wife died of cancer, Cooke needed comforting himself. His daughter suggested he get a dog, thinking it would help him feel less alone, and Cooke adopted a rambunctious golden retriever pup and named her Abigail.

At the time, Cooke was living in an apartment above the funeral home. "Most days I'd take Abigail downstairs with me and let her play in my office while I worked," he says. But then one day Abigail got out and went looking for new friends to play with.

Cooke discovered Abigail in the chapel, curled at the feet of a woman seated in a chair near her husband's casket. Cooke apologized profusely for the intrusion, and made as if to lead Abigail away.

"Does she have to go?" the grieving widow asked him. "It's such a comfort, having her here."

Soon, Abigail was sneaking out of Cooke's office regularly and heading straight for one of the funeral home's visitation rooms. "She seems to sense who is most distraught, and that's the person she'll go to first," says Fred. "She'll sit at their feet, perfectly still, and gaze up at them with those

245

compassionate brown eyes of hers, and within minutes they've stopped crying and started stroking her fur."

Off-duty, you won't find a more playful pup than Abigail. She loves to romp and chase sticks and mooch treats from Cooke's dinner plate. "But the moment she steps into that chapel she turns into a completely different dog," says Cooke. "She's quiet and respectful. I think she must have a sixth sense of how to behave."

Abigail's only misstep happened back when she was still a puppy, and even that turned out well. "She ate somebody's carnations," Cooke explains simply.

Cooke rushed out to replace the flowers, but the family wouldn't let him bring them in. "Aunt Mary was a real dog lover," they told him. "You can't imagine how it would have make her smile to see those chewed-up flowers."

A MAILBOX MERCY

NANCY JO SULLIVAN
FROM *MOMENTS OF GRACE*

*I*t was late afternoon, Valentine's Day. I was mad at my mom. Though it had been weeks since the argument, a silly argument, I still found myself brooding.

"Why should I be the one to apologize?" I told myself as I signed my name to a Valentine I had bought out of obligation.

"No 'I love yous' from me," I said as I smacked a stamp on the red envelope.

Moments later, I drove to the post office. Amid the pink shadows of a February sunset, I steered my van into a line of cars waiting at the drop-in mailbox.

Minutes passed. The post office traffic remained at a standstill. Rolling down my van window, I noticed a rusted station wagon at the front of the car line.

Was the car stalled at the mailbox?

Soon, a well-dressed woman in a red Cavalier became impatient with the wait. She honked at the station wagon, loudly, holding her horn down in anger.

Startled by the horn, an elderly man hobbled from the rusted sedan. Holding a cane to balance his uneven gait, he shuffled to the mailbox,

247

clutching a stack of red-enveloped Valentines.

"I'm sorry," he called out to the woman, his voice soft and trembling.

In an instant, the woman opened her car door and rushed to the old man's side, throwing her arms around his shoulders.

"I'm sorry," I heard her say.

In the last sunlit rays of the day, the man gently patted her on the back, resting one hand on his cane.

As I watched from my windshield, I realized that these two strangers had given me a fresh perspective on a passage I had long since committed to memory: "If you forgive others, your heavenly father will forgive you."

Suddenly, I realized that I had been wasting my time, harboring unforgiveness in my heart, waiting for my mother's apology.

While honking the "horn" of anger, I had placed all the blame for the argument on my mom, refusing to acknowledge the hurtful words I had spoken to her.

I needed to ask for her forgiveness.

I also needed to offer her the same kind of mercy I had just witnessed at the mailbox: the unconditional mercy of God.

As the old man and the well-dressed woman parted, the line of cars began to move in a steady pace toward the mailbox.

With one hand on the steering wheel, I carefully reopened my mother's card.

Now one car away from the drop box, I quickly rewrote a new Valentine's greeting:

"I'm sorry—I love you, Mom."

Front Porch Swing

Gently swinging. Quietly creaking. Back and forth. Back and forth. Here I sit. Here I listen. Listening to the music of the front porch swing.

The weathered wood all laced with stains speaks clearly. It talks of cold snow, warm hugs, and hot summer nights. It tattles of spilled lemonade, it whispers of tipped tea cups, and shares of precious tears. This is a sacred place. A place where conversation and emotion grace the air. A place where dreams are free to dance. A place where finding oneself is possible.

Gently swinging. Quietly creaking. I keep listening to the music of the front porch swing.

I hear it speak of hands. Many hands. Smooth hands. Wrinkled hands. Muddy hands. Gloved hands. Helping hands. Holding hands. Hands in love. It is here I fold my hands, and it is here I talk to God. He holds my hands, and it is here that He talks to me.

Gently swinging. Quietly creaking. Back and forth. Back and forth. Here I sit. Here I listen. Listening to the music of the front porch swing.

KIM ENGSTROM

LAUGHTER AND
LIFE JACKETS

N. C. HAAS

ho is this?" my friend asked, pointing to the snapshot of the little boy looking back from my refrigerator door.

"Oh, he's a child we know," I answered, smiling.

When she had gone, I looked again at the picture and laughed. He was such a captivating little boy, with a brightly impatient look that commanded, *Hurry with that camera! I have adventure to live and treasure to find, giants to capture and pirates to hunt!* Who knew what great heroic plan his imagination had concocted the day that picture was taken! Whatever it was, he was completely prepared to accomplish it in the outrageous outfit he had rigged for himself: a baseball cap, oversized sunglasses, bedroom slippers and—last but not least—a life jacket! How could I help but laugh? His energy bounded from that snapshot as though it were going to vault him right off the refrigerator and into my kitchen!

I could hardly believe he was already three years old, though I remembered his beginnings as though they were yesterday. His father and mother, Scott and Lisa,* were young and unmarried when he was conceived. While Lisa was still making college choices, Scott was already a sophomore thinking ahead to graduate school. Too frightened to share their "secret," they guarded it as long as they could, groping alone for a solution, any way out of their painful predicament.

They knew as soon as their secret was told, they would face the overwhelming reality of crushed dreams and agonizing decisions. They wanted a family, but not this way. They believed children needed the solid foundation of a strong marriage, but didn't know if they could build one together.

They could have ended the pregnancy. Others had. No one would know. It would be so simple to start again as though nothing had changed. But, simple as it seemed, God would know. Whatever the consequences, they chose to give their baby life.

Finally, they braced themselves for what their news might bring. Disappointment and hurt from parents, shock and whispers from church friends—and more paralyzing questions. How would they afford medical care when Lisa had no insurance? How could she raise a child and return to school if she and Scott didn't marry? How would Scott manage the financial responsibilities of pregnancy and parenting?

They moved robotically through the next weeks. Scott left college, unsure if he would ever return. He found work as a waiter, while Lisa trudged from door to door looking for anyone who would hire a young pregnant girl with little experience and no degree.

Their list of options grew more complicated. Should their parents raise the child? Should they consider adoption? Nothing seemed ideal. Meanwhile they continued through their bittersweet moments of pregnancy—the sonogram that showed they had a son, the first sounds of his heartbeat, his first rustling movements.

But, as Lisa grew larger, their deadlines pressed on them with relentless urgency. Staggered by decisions only they could make, they pored over detailed files of hopeful adoptive couples, searching for one to whom they might entrust their child. How could they choose?

Their parents struggled, too, smiling bravely at pictures of other people's grandchildren, stifling tears at baby showers. Worrying first that Scott and Lisa wouldn't marry, then worrying they would. Uncertain how to parent—holding too tight, then forcing themselves to let go. Wondering where they had failed. Always asking God to be present with his love and his will.

Finally one bright summer morning, Scott and Lisa's beautiful son was placed in their arms. Clinging to his soft warmth, they were torn again. But there was no time left; they had to decide. The next days were the most painful of all. While their parents asked God for his perfect will, Scott and Lisa struggled tearfully.

Then, bravely determining what they believed was right for their son, they dressed him, took him to a small church to dedicate him to God, then to the agency to give him to the couple they had chosen to parent him.

The terrible conflict of letting go and holding tight ripped through their hearts. They faced moments of heartache, endless moments of wondering.

Time moved them all back to life's healing routine. All that remained was a chapter of memories and a closet full of ongoing prayers. And occasionally a picture and letter from the agency updating Scott and Lisa.

It was an extra picture they had given me that hung now on my refrigerator and made me laugh each time I saw it. It was much too small to contain this three-year-old package of comical energy bursting with so much busy excitement. He really did look as though, at any moment, he would leap right into my morning, scoop me into his adventure, and dare me to keep up.

Oh yes, I laughed back at his eager face, how I would love it if you did! I would catch you up in my arms and twirl you around and around—life jacket, baseball cap, sunglasses, and all! We would spin and laugh together—at the giants you had conquered and the pirates you had caught. We would spin, spin, and laugh again—at the fading memory of the pain that birthed you, at the wonder of the world before you. We would laugh until we cried in raucous celebration of your life.

And when we had spun ourselves dizzy, I would put you down, kneel in front of you and tell you this: Right now you can't see, but God has built bigger plans into your heart and promises into your soul than you can ever imagine. Your life is his, and your greatest adventure will be to dis-cover him and go with him to find his plans and purposes for you. They are exciting plans, I promise, full of wonderful hope and purpose. Go and capture them. Go and live them. And don't forget your life jacket—Nathaniel, my first grandchild.

*How far you go in life depends on your being tender with the young,
compassionate with the aged, sympathetic with the striving,
tolerant with the weak and the strong—
because someday you will have been all of these.*

GEORGE WASHINGTON CARVER

*Names have been changed.

GROWING OLDER

DALE EVANS ROGERS
FROM *TIME OUT, LADIES!*

*L*ord, thou knowest better than I know myself, that I am growing older, and will someday be old.

Keep me from getting talkative, and particularly from the fatal habit of thinking I must say something on every subject and on every occasion.

Release me from the craving to try and straighten out everybody's affairs.

Keep my mind free from the recital of endless details—give me wings to get to the point.

I ask for grace enough to listen to the tales of others' pains. Help me endure them with patience.

But seal my lips on my own aches and pains. They are increasing, and my love of rehearsing them is becoming sweeter as the years go by.

I dare not ask for improved memory, but for a growing humility and a lessening cocksureness when my memory seems to clash with the memories of others.

Teach me the glorious lesson that occasionally I may be mistaken.

Keep me reasonably sweet. I do not want to be a saint—some of them are so hard to live with—but a sour old woman (or man) is one of the crowning works of the devil.

Make me thoughtful, but not moody; helpful, but not bossy.

With my vast store of wisdom, it seems a pity not to use it; but thou knowest, Lord, I want a few friends at the end.

Give me the ability to see good things in unexpected places, and talents in unexpected people. And give me, Lord, the grace to tell them so.

Some people, no matter how old they get,
never lose their beauty—
they merely move it from their faces
into their hearts.

AUTHOR UNKNOWN

THE FAITH OF
A CHILD

DEBORAH HAMMONS
FROM *VIRTUE* MAGAZINE

hen my sister-in-law, Carla, had her brain tumor, I took care of her boys, Bobby and Pete.

For me, twice as many kids not only meant twice as many sweatshirts to wash and socks to sort, but twice as many problems to carry and things to worry about.

I guess I worried most about Bobby. Our oldest son, Jeremy, was self-sufficient and Andrew and Pete played together and shared Andrew's bed at night, but Bobby was left bouncing from person to person for contact and support. I made a sleeping corner for him on Andrew's floor, piling up thick blankets for padding and making an envelope out of a fuzzy quilt. He fit perfectly there.

Everyone thought the boys would have a hard time with their parents' long absence, but after a while anything becomes normal.

Each night, with our shutters closed to the cold, we went through the routine of making sure everyone was clean, teeth were brushed, pajamas on, clothes put away and homework done. Carla or my brother phoned each night to visit with Bobby and Pete. In the middle of a wrestling match, laughing and hollering, they'd be called to the kitchen, and across the distance, through the pin-size holes of the phone's receiver, hear their mother's voice. The questions—What did you do today? How are you feeling?—from faraway Minnesota, were met by small voices.

Boys, who seconds before had been full of life, shrank to the size of a whisper. The pain and loneliness in their voices astonished me. I wanted to grab the phone and say: "No, this isn't the way it is. They're playing and laughing and sleeping through the night. They're eating and reading and we're all just fine." But for those few moments the boys did speak the truth. They were alone, suspended in that half-life of separation.

Carla's daily radiation treatments at the hospital brutalized her body until she spent every waking moment vomiting. She held herself together for those few minutes on the phone with her boys, so they knew she was all right. She told them she was bald now just like Daddy. But Mom would be home, she promised, not soon, but she would be home.

As soon as the phone was hung up, they turned back to our world with a run and a leap, piling on top of each other in physical assault. Like puppies rolling across the floor, they lived each second for itself.

But if every conscious second can be a prayer, our life was a prayer for those three months.

One evening, Bobby announced he had a project due at school. Perched on a stool at the dinner table, he told us of the annual egg drop, a contest where each student invents a way to protect an egg from breaking when it is dropped from an opening in the school's attic.

We all called out ideas as Bobby watched, eyebrows up, eyes wide.

"What do you think?" my husband asked Bobby.

"I think you could fill a milk carton with water and put the egg in that and it wouldn't break."

Our ideas had to do with things we'd seen others try like Styrofoam carved to hold the egg or parachutes attached to cartons filled with popcorn, the egg nestled inside. None of us had thought of water.

Jeremy asked, "What does an egg do in water? Does it sink?"

"Go see," said my husband.

Everyone left their plates and went to the kitchen to drop an egg in water. Everyone except Bobby. He remained at the table.

"I could use rubber bands to hold the egg in the middle of the water," he said.

"You could put salt in the water," Jeremy suggested.

"It's my project. I'm doing it the way I want," Bobby declared from the dining room.

Everyone in the kitchen stopped. My husband said, "You're right."

The boys returned to the table and finished their dinner.

With the help of Jeremy and his Uncle Steve, Bobby somehow rigged an egg suspended between rubber bands surrounded by water inside a cardboard milk carton. That Saturday, Bobby and Steve went out on the balcony in front of the house while the rest of us watched from the patio below. Bobby's grin was huge as he held the heavy carton high in the air. He was sure his idea would work.

"One, two, three," counted Bobby. "Drop off!"

The carton hit the concrete. It split open and water spread from the bottom. Bobby rushed down the stairs and out the door. He looked at the broken carton and the water as he knelt beside his project. Inside, the egg was whole, intact. Bobby lifted it and examined it closely. A string of clear liquid seeped from it.

"One crack," he said.

"Amazing," Steve said, grinning. "I didn't think it would work."

I don't think any of us did. But the results weren't good enough for Bobby. He stuck with his original idea of protecting the egg, but he wanted no damage whatsoever.

"I need a balloon," he said, "one of those balloons you get for your birthday."

"Helium balloons?" I asked.

Bobby nodded.

"But then you won't need the water," said his brother Pete.

"You need it all," said Bobby.

The day of the big egg drop, I took Bobby, his egg, new milk carton, rubber bands and helium balloon to school. He hadn't tried them all together, but he was certain it would work. I stayed to watch.

Bobby's teacher took her class to the lunchroom where a ladder led to the school's attic. One by one, the students climbed the ladder and dropped their eggs from the opening. Some eggs broke, some made it, some cracked. The kids seemed as excited by the failures as the successes.

Bobby's turn finally came. He put his project in the basket rigged to carry it to the attic, then started to climb the ladder. His fingers couldn't reach around the wooden steps. He readjusted his grip and watched his feet. Cautiously, he moved up to the opening. The night before, he'd decorated his milk carton with blue and red stars. At the top, he held it out from him, arms straight and sure, the balloon waving above.

For a second, I couldn't breathe. The strings were crooked. What if it broke? The carton could slip. I wanted it to float gently, slowly to the floor, but for a second all I could imagine was the carton crashing on its side, the egg smashed. With my whole being, I wanted it to work. It had to work, because Bobby believed it would.

He let go. The carton wobbled, then fell swiftly and it was over. The balloon had not made it waft slowly, but the carton landed erect. Bobby rushed down the ladder and ran to pull off the tape sealing the milk carton. He reached in and held up the egg. It was whole. Not one crack. Bobby laughed in triumph, and the class cheered.

That night, after dinner, the dishes, the picking up, the baths, the teeth brushing, hair combing and book reading, the phone rang.

Bobby ran to pick it up. "Hello?" he answered. "Mom? Guess what. My egg didn't break!"

It's been three years now since the doctors found Carla's tumor, its appearance and disappearance equally rare. She drives back to the hospital every six months for a check-up. We pretend it's routine, but breathe more easily once she returns home.

The boys are growing older, our families' lives more separate. I'm busy hauling Andrew and Jeremy to soccer, scouts, Sunday school.

That winter is a dim memory for Pete and Bobby, a time their mom and dad were gone and they slept at their cousins' house. But for me, it remains the winter Bobby showed us the faith of a child. It was the winter we layered around each other so none of us would break.

Understanding

We do not understand:
Joy…until we face sorrow
Faith…until it is tested
Peace…until faced with conflict
Trust…until we are betrayed
Love…until it is lost
Hope…until confronted with doubts

AUTHOR UNKNOWN

BREAKING UP GRANDMA

FROM *FOR SHE IS THE TREE OF LIFE*

he terrible twos stretched into the threes for me. An only child whose mother was ill and hospitalized a good share of the time, I was watched by various relatives. But I missed my mama dreadfully, and acted accordingly. Apparently the only one who could cope with me was my grandmother in Wisconsin.

Grandma was a big strong Norwegian lady who raised eight children and milked nine cows the day after each child was born.

Once when she came to take care of me in our small home on the east side of St. Paul, I proceeded to make her life miserable. When she tried to take me for a walk, I'd scoot ahead of her at surprising speed, leaving her to chase me on her fifty-eight-year-old legs. When she devised an effective harness, I plunked down on the grass in our front yard and yelled. When she called me to eat lunch, I'd squeeze under my parents' iron bed, pulling down the chenille bedspread, or hid behind the brown overstuffed chair in the corner.

It all came to an end the day Grandma decided to soothe me once more in our old black wooden rocking chair. She had patience and lots of love, so she held me in her arms and sang songs from her childhood by the sea.

I was not impressed. I couldn't get away, and I still didn't like it. I pulled tendrils of gray hair out of her neat bun, poked an inquisitive finger up her nose and jabbed her cheeks. Her blue eyes remained amazingly calm. Finally, I slipped my fingers into her mouth. Instantly the singing stopped, and she wiggled her jaw in a funny way.

My hand came out holding her false teeth!

Shocked, I stared at the ugly things, dropped them and started screaming.

I cried for an hour. In between sobs I would hug her and ask if she hurt. I kept hiccuping, "I'm sorry, I'm sorry." She rocked me contentedly.

My terrible threes ended that day.

You know, people have to be treated nice.

They break into little pieces if you don't.

Yesterday is history.

Tomorrow is a mystery.

But today is a gift.

That's why we call it the Present.

AUTHOR UNKNOWN

THE FOX AND
THE WRITER

PHILIP YANCEY
FROM *CHRISTIANITY TODAY* MAGAZINE

Last spring, three kits were born in a fox den visible across a ravine from my driveway. I watched the early progress through binoculars: the kits nursing, sunning themselves, playing, and frantically diving for cover if a large bird sailed overhead.

Fancying myself a latter-day Saint Francis, I decided to befriend them. I took daily walks in the vicinity of the den, whistling softly and leaving small gifts—a bone, a raw egg, a handful of cat food. Purists frown on such interference with nature, I know, but I figure houses like mine, built in the foxes' territory, have already disrupted the natural order.

The first few weeks the kits scrambled into the den whenever they saw me. As they grew accustomed to my presence, though, they retreated to rocks nearby. They peered at me inquisitively, golden eyes alert, ears twitching to every sound, their unscarred red coats glistening in the sun.

Eventually the three began following me. I felt like the Pied Piper. If I stopped, they stopped and hid behind a rock or bush. If I ran, they ran too. If I sat for a picnic lunch, they surrounded me. Once I tossed an apple core into some bushes and in a flash all three pounced. Quivering, frozen in a hunting posture, they waited, and I realized that they were waiting for it to move, like all their food.

As the Colorado summer progressed, I would stand in my driveway and whistle; on command, the three handsome young foxes came bounding across the ravine. They stalked butterflies in a patch of wildflowers. They gave futile chase to wily squirrels. They stood on their hind legs and lapped water from our birdbath—once jumping back in alarm when a skim of ice reflected their own images.

In order to keep the deer, elk, and rabbits out of flower gardens, we have connected water hoses to sprinklers activated by motion sensors. Walk in front of the sensor, and water sprays out with a loud, startling noise. (Neighborhood kids love to introduce their unsuspecting friends to this technology.) The first time the foxes wandered in front of the motion sensor, setting off the water, they high-tailed it, literally, all the way back to their den. Soon, though, they were playing games with the sensor, dashing in front of it to see if they could set it off without getting wet.

If I threw a tennis ball, one would chase it down and run, with the other two in hot pursuit. Like some dogs, though, they never learned to relinquish the retrieved object.

The three had very different personalities. We named the bravest Mr. Bold, the most fearful Shy Guy, and the third Black Socks because of his distinctive leg markings. If I put out food, I started with one pile, which Mr. Bold immediately gobbled up, then moved a few feet away and put down another pile, which Mr. Bold dashed over to investigate.

By the time I set out a third pile, Shy Guy would cautiously approach the dregs left in the first pile—until Mr. Bold charged over to chase him away. Poor Shy Guy—his personality kept him in a state of perpetual hunger.

In animals as in humans, cleverness can help one surmount personality obstacles. Shy Guy prevailed after I started putting food in a metal dog dish. Foxes track food with their noses, not their eyes, and the three could not seem to distinguish the food from the dish. They would smell the food and bite the dish, which didn't taste at all like cat food or lamb bones. Plus, the sound of the metal dish scraping across gravel startled them. They would stare at the dish and circle it for half an hour, smelling the food but not knowing how to get it.

Shy Guy, however, mastered the dish, assuring that from then on he got a fair portion, I would put down two piles of food and leave some in the dish. The other two might chase him away, but, unable to solve the mystery of the dish, they ultimately left its contents to a grinning Shy Guy.

All summer I had three constant companions. As I weeded the garden, cut the grass, or read the mail in a hammock, they followed my every move. If I ate lunch on our wooden balcony, they would climb the steps to join me.

Mr. Bold, especially, seemed without fear. On fine summer days I tote my laptop computer outdoors and sit on a lounge chair in the shade. Mr. Bold would observe me for a while, then curl up, his white-tipped tail folded across his eyes, and go to sleep.

At such moments I felt a thrilling flashback to Eden, when the barrier of fear had not yet arisen between the species, and a flash-forward to heaven, when the lion shall lie down with the lamb and the fox shall curl up with the writer.

Naturalist John Muir once sighed, "It is a great comfort…that vast multitudes of creatures, great and small and infinite in number, lived and had a good time in God's love before man was created."

It can still happen, John.

TO GOD
FROM BEN

GLENDA BARBRE
FROM *CHRISTIAN READER* MAGAZINE

To help our five-year-old son with the trauma of his pet goldfish's demise, I agreed he could "send the goldfish back to God" any way he wanted. Expecting him to give the goldfish a proper burial in our flower garden, I was surprised to receive a call from our rural area's postmaster.

"Could you come over?" she asked. "I have something to show you." I headed right over.

"A lot is expected of the post office," she said, laughing, "but this is the most amazing delivery we've ever been asked to make!"

On the outside of a business-sized envelope, printed in big blue capital letters I recognized Ben's printing: To GOD FROM BEN. Inside the envelope was a very flat, dead goldfish.

CHOIRS OF ANGELS

CHERYL GOCHNAUER

er first Christmas at the nursing home wasn't so bad—she was making new friends. When the school children came to sing carols, she used her cane to carefully maneuver her way to the lunchroom to hear their vivacious, if slightly flat, music.

She loved watching their shining faces, brilliant reminders of youth and energy. In the days to follow, she would replay the scene to herself, humming the tunes as she prepared to celebrate her Lord's birth.

A few years passed, and her nurse wheeled her into the lunchroom to hear the little angels sing. Like so many others at the home, she looked forward to the children's annual visit. For weeks, she had her nurse hand her the calendar so she could painstakingly mark off the days until their arrival. She was not disappointed; the faces were different and the songs were familiarly off-key, but affection poured from the young people's hearts. She soaked it all in, savoring their smiles long after they had left.

Each year, she asked the nurse to push her closer to the choir as their voices became more and more distant. Then came the program where she would not hear them at all, but she still enjoyed reading their lips, their expressive faces forming the words to carols she sang inside her head.

But as time continued to pass, even the children's faces became dim.

Her eyes failed her, and she was lost in a fuzzy world of indistinct sounds and sight. One day, her nurse shouted in her ear—it sounded dim and muffled, but she could just make out an invitation to the children's Christmas program.

Oh no, she responded. I don't want to go.

I don't want those kids staring at me, she thought. *I can't walk; I can't hear; I can't see. They'll ignore me for the useless old thing I am, just sitting here in a wheelchair. No, I don't want to go.*

Dismayed, she felt herself being wheeled out of her room. She felt like yelling, Take me back! But she remembered the spectacles she had witnessed before her eyes gave out, other old folks like herself making fools of themselves, hollering in the halls. She pulled her shawl around her tighter and helplessly hung her head.

She sensed the expanse of the large lunchroom, felt her wheelchair locked into place. In spite of herself, after a few moments, she began to visualize a choir, a conglomeration of hundreds of children's faces, each singing their songs or carefully playing their instruments.

Sweet voices long stilled filled her head, and she caught a tune in her memory. Softly humming to herself, she smiled as her heart swelled with emotion. Before she could stop it, a tear escaped her sightless eyes. And then, it happened.

A tiny hand slipped into hers and squeezed. With that precious touch, it was as though her Lord Himself had transformed once again into the Christ child. She reached out and swept her fingers gently over the child's face, touching the upturned bow of a smile.

Embracing him, she cried, God bless you! Merry Christmas!

And it was.

TORNADO WARNING

SARAH ELIZABETH FARROW
FROM *VIRTUE* MAGAZINE

When I set aside my career as an advertising copy-writer to be an at-home mother, I felt I had to justify my decision by becoming the best of all possible mothers. I began to live by the motto on my favorite coffee mug: "God can't be every-where—that's why He created mothers." I never questioned its message until a violent summer storm hit.

It was a particularly sultry afternoon, and all four of my boys were flopped in front of the TV watching a video I'd rented to alleviate their summer boredom. "I have a few errands to run," I said. "Come along, and we'll get some ice cream."

My suggestion brought only groans of protest. "It's too hot, Mom. We want to stay home and finish watching the movie." I thought it over for a moment and decided the oldest, who was 12, could supervise his broth-ers for the short time it would take me to go to the bank, the dry clean-ers, and the grocery store.

"Chris is in charge. Be good, and I'll bring home ice cream," I said as I headed for the car. Absorbed in the movie, they hardly acknowledged my leaving.

I'd rather veg out this afternoon, too, I thought, scanning the heavy gray sky. *Maybe we'll get a cooling rain by evening.*

Although I rarely left the boys for even a few minutes, I reassured myself they'd be fine and attributed the uneasy feeling in my stomach to the hot and humid weather.

Big spatters of rain had indeed begun to fall while I was at the bank, and the sky was getting darker. Suspecting a thunderstorm might be coming, I decided to skip the dry cleaners and streamline my grocery shopping to get home before the brunt of it hit. I hurried up and down the aisles and was just finishing up when the storm broke. Thunder rumbled and sheets of wind-driven rain slashed against the store windows. While I waited in the checkout line, I began to fret.

At first my worries were more about the household than the children. Would they think to let the dog in? Did they close the windows? Were they still watching the movie oblivious to the storm? My husband and I have a standing joke that a bomb could go off when the TV is on and our kids wouldn't notice. Today, however, I wasn't laughing.

After I paid for my groceries, I tried to make a run for my car. The windswept rain soaked me in seconds and huge hailstones drove me shivering back into the store. While the storm got worse, I paced and chatted with other stranded shoppers to ease my tension.

Air-raid sirens began to wail, signaling this was more than a standard summer storm and that a tornado warning was in effect. I began to worry about the boys in earnest. They didn't even know where I was, and my attempt to call home was thwarted by downed phone lines. *And I always yell at them when they leave without telling me where they're going,* I thought. Were they frightened? Worried about me? Had they thought to switch from VCR to TV to get the news about the tornado warning? *Some mother I am,* I chastised myself.

In the midst of my rising panic, a single line from the Psalms popped into my mind: *Be still and know that I am God.* I wasn't even sure which Psalm it came from until I had a chance to look it up later (Psalm 46:10), but that line acted on me like a tranquilizer. Somehow deep inside I felt assured the boys and our household would be all right.

When the sirens stopped, I headed for my car. The rain had barely let up. Visibility was poor, the streets were slick, and cars were stalled in deep puddles and drifts of hail; but every time I started to panic, that line would come back into my mind: *Be still and know that I am God.* The main street I normally would have taken home looked like a river, so I headed for higher ground. I had a near miss with another car when its driver failed to see my car, even though I had the headlights on! Finally, I pulled up in front of my house, left the groceries in the car, and ran inside.

Everything was dark and quiet. I was afraid the boys had panicked and left, but where would they have gone? Then I heard the radio in the basement. All four were in the laundry room; the dog and cats were with them. "Wow, Mom!" Chris said. "What a storm!"

"Yeah," the twins chimed in. "We were watching that movie when it got really dark."

The youngest hugged me tight, while Chris continued. "The sky turned a creepy color, and we thought we'd better let Shadow in and start shutting windows. When we switched over to TV and heard there was a tornado warning, we all came down here."

A quick check revealed they'd not only remembered the safest place in the house, but they'd closed all the windows, turned off lights, and even unplugged the computer and the television. *Be still and know that I am God…*

Later, as I mopped up the water that had come through the kitchen window before the children could get it shut, examined my hail-devastated garden, and borrowed a neighbor's phone to report ours out of order, I felt strangely relieved rather than depressed. I'd been cramming my children's heads with instructions and warnings almost from their births. "Stay away from tall trees and water in thunderstorms." "Look both ways before crossing." "Never leave home without telling me where you're going." I'd never really trusted them, however, to follow through on their own. Yet when danger threatened and I was away, they kept their heads and remembered just what to do.

As my boys have grown into young men, the lesson of that storm has stuck with me and helped me to "be still" and know that God is God through many more of life's storms. My job, I learned, is to teach and to be a good example; their job is to learn and to follow through; and God's job is to hold us all in the palm of His hand.

I no longer use the "God can't be everywhere..." mug. I replaced it with one that says, "This is the day the LORD has made; let us rejoice and be glad in it" (Psalm 118:24). Now when I drink my morning coffee I'm reminded to take my focus off me and put it where it belongs—on God the Father! I rejoice that He is God, and that He *can* be everywhere.

SHARING

AUTHOR UNKNOWN
FROM *YOU GOTTA KEEP DANCING*

There isn't much that I can do, but I can share my bread with you, and sometimes share a sorrow, too—

There isn't much that I can do, but I can sit an hour with you, and I can share a joke with you, and sometimes share reverses, too—

There isn't much that I can do, but I can share my flowers with you, and I can share my books with you and sometimes share your burdens, too—

There isn't much that I can do, but I can share my songs with you, and I can share my mirth with you, and sometimes come and laugh with you—

There isn't much that I can do, but I can share my hopes with you, and I can share my fears with you, and sometimes shed some tears with you—

There isn't much that I can do, but I can share my friends with you, and I can share my life with you, and oftentimes share a prayer with you.

Faith

TRUSTING GOD

When I doubt His love, I hold to His wisdom.
When I can't understand His justice, I cling to His mercies.
When I wonder about His faithfulness, I cherish His grace.
When I fear His sovereignty, I bow to His holiness.
And in that my heart can rest.

VERDELL DAVIS
FROM *LET ME GRIEVE, BUT NOT FOREVER*

HEAVEN'S GOLD

RHONDA REESE

FROM *CHRISTIAN READER* MAGAZINE

I could barely get my request out. "Lord," I asked one December afternoon two years ago as loneliness and worry knocked me breathless again, "please show me something special I can do to help Mom."

Dad was gone. When he died one month before the holidays, I felt so drained that I considered skipping Christmas. But my grieving, depressed mother needed support. She and Dad were four days shy of celebrating their 55th wedding anniversary when cancer snatched my father away.

A week passed. Then one afternoon while I listened to a talk radio program about money, the show's host read a fax sent to him by a disgruntled shopper. Seems this tired consumer spent an afternoon tromping through stores, growing more exhausted with every step. She resented the pressure of purchasing gifts for mere acquaintances.

"I stayed in that mall for hours," the woman said. "My head pounded. My feet hurt. My stomach swirled. I developed a rotten attitude and just wished Christmas would hurry up and get over."

That's a familiar feeling, I thought. *I wanted to hurry the holiday away, too.*

"I fought my way through the crowds and finally got ready to pay," the woman continued. "As the line moved forward, I watched babies cry, couples argue, and a toddler throw a terrible tantrum. I felt so disillusioned that I almost walked out of the store.

"But then I noticed two children standing in line ahead of me. The boy looked about nine years old. The girl, maybe five. Neither child wore clothes warm enough for the day. Their hair was uncombed, and well, honestly, both kids smelled awful."

My dad grew up poor. I wondered if anyone had ever felt that way about him.

The lady's saga continued. "The boy clutched some one dollar bills in his skinny hand. Coins poked from between the girl's clenched fingers. As the children approached the cash register, the girl plopped the gaudiest pair of sparkly, gold high-heeled shoes I'd ever seen up onto the counter. When the clerk rang them up, the children looked ready to burst into tears. They didn't have enough money. Suddenly I heard myself offer to pay their shortage."

My mind flashed back to a time I saw Dad give $2.00 to a shaky old man in the grocery store line. We never discussed it, but I'd never forgotten the scene.

The tale teller's voice broke as she told how both kids beamed. "The little boy explained that the shoes were for his mother. Then the girl piped up, 'My mamma has 'kemia. Daddy said she's going to Heaven soon. In Heaven they have gold streets. We're getting Mama shoes to match.'"

In stunned silence I realized God had spoken. He was reminding me where Dad now walked—on streets of gold. Would gold shoes help my heartbroken mother?

Before I finished my thought, the storyteller made one last comment. Something about Christmas being the way God wrapped up a love gift and sent him from Heaven.

The gift of God. A baby Savior. The Savior who made it possible for loved ones to walk on the streets of gold.

At home I found a pair of small doll shoes. After coating them with gold glitter and clear paint, I mounted them onto a mahogany plaque. With a burst of energy, I shuffled through a drawer to find my calligraphy pen and a piece of gold parchment. My hands trembled as I wrote: *Departed to Walk on Streets of Gold.* After gluing the parchment to the wood, I smiled at the finished project.

On Christmas Mom's face brightened when she unwrapped the gold shoes and my handwritten explanation. Even though the season still held sadness, the days brought joy as we talked about Pa plodding down gold pavement. I knew the Lord would guide Mother and me as we began taking steps in a healing direction.

Cast all your cares on God;
that anchor holds.

TENNYSON

AN EMPTY CHAIR

WALTER BURKHARDT
FROM *TELL THE NEXT GENERATION*

This was the experience of an old man who lay dying. When the priest came to anoint him, he noticed an empty chair at the man's bedside and asked him who had just been visiting. The sick man replied, "I place Jesus on that chair and I talk to Him." For years, he told the priest, he had found it extremely difficult to pray until a friend explained that prayer was just a matter of talking with Jesus. The friend suggested that he imagine Jesus sitting in a chair where he could speak with Him and listen to what He said in reply. "I have had no trouble praying ever since."

Some days later, the daughter of this man came to the parish house to inform the priest that her father had just died. She said, "Because he seemed so content, I left him alone for a couple of hours. When I got back to the room, I found him dead. I noticed a strange thing, though; his head was resting not on the bed but on an empty chair that was beside his bed."

SPIRIT RENEWED

BARBARA BAUMGARDNER

FROM *RV COMPANION* MAGAZINE

*I*t was a hard summer. My sister had a stroke; my mom was in and out of the hospital; and I sold my big house, opting for a small one in a gated community where someone else mows the lawn. Caregiving, selling, and moving takes its toll, and I was exhausted: physically, mentally, emotionally and spiritually.

Even through the busy times of that summer, I recognized my simmering hostility toward the circumstances that were keeping me from a fling in my new motor home. I kept telling myself that my attitude was selfish, but I just couldn't shake those feelings.

When a few days finally opened up on my calendar, I e-mailed a friend:

"I'm leaving in the morning for a couple days on the coast. I'm tired. I feel so spiritually drained; God seems very far away. Hopefully, I can use these days to be still and find an answer…somewhere on the beach, or in a sunset, or even in the stillness of my own heart. Please pray for me."

Taking only my dog, Molly, I ran away from my troubles.

Parking the motor home at a beachfront campground near Lincoln City, Oregon, I kicked off my shoes and ran barefoot on the sand. Frolicking child-like with Molly filled me with invigorating feelings of release. I gratefully inhaled the salty air and the cool, earthy smell of wet sand. The seagulls filled the moist air with chattering noises, sometimes swooping and dipping overhead, sometimes standing in a row on a piece of driftwood like wooden soldiers at attention. Captivated by my surroundings, it felt like Molly and I, and those noisy birds, were the only living creatures on the face of the earth.

The next day I sat for hours watching the gray-green mounds of water rise and fall, like heavy breathing entities from the ocean floor. The sky changed colors and hues, as a coastal storm swept through the cove. Rain pelted against the metal shell of my motor home. Yes, yes! This is what I came for. How wonderful to finally reach those moments of sorely needed rest and healing.

Later that evening, I watched a brilliant, fuchsia sunset change to pink, then melon and gray; too soon, it was replaced by a pitch-black wall of nothingness.

The next morning was the 17th anniversary of my husband's death. I marveled at my new experiences and how far I'd come from that devastating, stormy time of my life. And I wondered, "Should I head for home or extend this get-away for one more day?"

Glancing out the front window, I was startled to see a piece of a rainbow hanging over the rock-lined cove. The top of the brilliant streams of color disappeared into puffy clouds, and the bottom seemed to have been snipped across by a giant pair of scissors. Framed in my front windshield, it reminded me of God's promise...the one that said He would never send such a violent storm again.

He had rescued me from the raging waters of new widowhood; why should I doubt that He would not rescue me now? As quickly as that thought came to me, the rainbow disappeared, and with it, my hopelessness and self-pity.

As the sand began to dry, I raced down the beach filled with joy, with Molly at my heels...renewed in mind, body, and spirit. We dug holes in the sand and took turns chasing the ball. God had given me this day, just as He gave me this beach, the sand...and a golden, brown dog who loves me almost as much as He does.

TOMMY

JOHN POWELL
FROM *THE CHALLENGE OF FAITH*

Some twelve years ago, I stood watching my university students file into the classroom for our first session in the Theology of Faith. That was the first day I saw Tommy. My eyes and my mind both blinked.

He was combing his long flaxen hair, which hung six inches below his shoulders. I guess it was just coming into fashion then. I know in my mind that it isn't what's on your head but what's in it that counts; but on that day I was unprepared and my emotions flipped. I immediately filed Tommy under "S" for strange...very strange.

Tommy turned out to be the "atheist in residence" in my Theology of Faith course. He constantly objected to, smirked at, or whined about the possibility of an unconditionally loving Father-God. We lived with each other in relative peace for one semester, although I admit he was for me at times a serious pain in the back pew. When he came up at the end of the course to turn in his final exam, he asked in a slightly cynical tone: "Do you think I'll ever find God?"

I decided instantly on a little shock therapy. "No!" I said very emphatically.

"Oh," he responded, "I thought that was the product you were pushing."

I let him get five steps from the classroom door and then called out: "Tommy! I don't think you'll ever find him, but I am absolutely certain that he will find you!" He shrugged a little and left my class and my life. I felt slightly disappointed at the thought that he had missed my clever line: "He will find you!" At least I thought it was clever.

Later I heard that Tommy had graduated and I was duly grateful. Then a sad report, I heard that Tommy had terminal cancer. Before I could search him out, he came to see me. When he walked into my office, his body was badly wasted, and the long hair had all fallen out as a result of chemotherapy. But his eyes were bright and his voice was firm, for the first time, I believe.

"Tommy, I've thought about you so often. I hear you are sick!" I blurted out.

"Oh, yes, very sick. I have cancer in both lungs. It's a matter of weeks."

"Can you talk about it, Tom?"

"Sure, what would you like to know?"

"What's it like to be only twenty-four and dying?"

"Well, it could be worse."

"Like what?"

"Well, like being fifty and having no values or ideals, like being fifty and thinking that booze, seducing women, and making money are the real 'biggies' in life."

I began to look through my mental file cabinet under "S" where I had filed Tommy as strange. *It seems as though everybody I try to reject by classification God sends back into my life to educate me.*

"But what I really came to see you about," Tom said, "is something you said to me on the last day of class." *He remembered!* He continued, "I asked you if you thought I would ever find God and you said, 'No!' which surprised me. Then you said, 'But he will find you.' I thought about that a lot, even though my search for God was hardly intense at the time." *My "clever" line. He thought about that a lot!* "But when the doctors removed a lump from my groin and told me that it was malignant, then I got serious about locating God. And when the malignancy spread into my vital organs, I really began banging bloody fists against the bronze doors of heaven. But God did not come out. In fact, nothing happened. Did you ever try anything for a long time with great effort and with no success? You get psychologically glutted, fed up with trying. And then you quit. Well, one day I woke up, and instead of throwing a few more futile appeals over that high brick wall to a God who may or may not be there, I just quit. I decided that I didn't really care…about God, about an afterlife, or anything like that.

"I decided to spend what time I had left doing something more profitable. I thought about you and your class and remembered something else you had said: 'The essential sadness is to go through life without loving. But it would be almost equally sad to go through life and leave this world without ever telling those you loved that you loved them.'

"So I began with the hardest one: my Dad. He was reading the newspaper when I approached him."

"Dad?"

"Yes, what?" he asked without lowering the newspaper.

"Dad, I would like to talk with you."

"Well, talk."

"I mean…it's really important." The newspaper came down three slow inches.

"What is it?" he asked.

"Dad, I love you. I just wanted you to know that."

Tom smiled at me and said with obvious satisfaction, as though he felt a warm and secret joy flowing inside of him: "The newspaper fluttered to the floor. Then my father did two things I could never remember him ever doing before. He cried and hugged me. And we talked all night, even though he had to go to work the next morning. It felt so good to be close to my father, to see his tears, to feel his hug, to hear him say that he loved me.

"It was easier with my mother and little brother. They cried with me, too, and we hugged each other, and started saying real nice things to each other. We shared the things we had been keeping secret for so many years.

I was only sorry about one thing; that I had waited so long. Here I was just beginning to open up to all the people I had actually been close to.

"Then, one day I turned around and God was there. He didn't come to me when I pleaded with him. I guess I was like an animal trainer holding out a hoop. C'mon, jump through. C'mon, I'll give you three days…three weeks.' Apparently God does things in his own way at his own hour. But the important thing is that he was there. He found me. You were right. He found me even after I stopped looking for him."

"Tom," I practically gasped, "I think you are saying something very important and much more universal than you realize. To me, at least, you are saying that the surest way to find God is not to make him a private possession, a problem solver, or an instant consolation in time of need, but rather by opening to love. You know, the Apostle John said that. He said God is love, and anyone who lives in love is living with God and God is living in him.

"Tom, could I ask you a favor? You know, when I had you in class you were a real pain. But you can make it all up to me now. Would you come into my present Theology of Faith course and tell them what you have just told me? If I told them the same thing it wouldn't be half as effective as if you were to tell them."

"Oooh…I was ready for you, but I don't know if I'm ready for your class."

"Tom, think about it. If and when you are ready, give me a call."

In a few days Tommy called, said he was ready for the class, that he wanted to do that for God and for me. So we scheduled a date. However, he never made it. He had another appointment, far more important than the one with me and my class. Of course, his life was not really ended by his death, only changed. He made the greatest step from faith into vision. He found a life far more beautiful than the eye of man has ever seen or the ear of man has ever heard or the mind of man has ever imagined.

Before he died, we talked one last time. "I'm not going to make it to your class," he said.

"I know, Tom."

"Will you tell them for me? Will you…tell the whole world for me?"

"I will, Tom. I'll tell them. I'll do my best." So to all of you who have been kind enough to hear this simple statement about love, thank you for listening. And to you, Tommy, somewhere in the sunlit, verdant hills of heaven: "I told them, Tommy…as best I could."

Who is Christ?
He is the Truth to be told.
The Way to be walked.
The Light to be lit.

MOTHER TERESA

Little faith will bring your soul to heaven;
great faith will bring heaven to your soul.

CHARLES H. SPURGEON

GIVING GOD PLEASURE

RUTH BELL GRAHAM
FROM *LEGACY OF A PACK RAT*

randmother's brother, Uncle Eddie McCue, lived on the old pre-Civil War home place, "Belvidere," in the Shenandoah Valley of Virginia.

One day, while working on the farm, he discarded his coat and told his collie dog, Chunk, to watch it.

That night, when Uncle Eddie got back to the house, he missed Chunk. No one had seen him. They called, but there was no response. Distressed, they ate supper, then continued searching. Bedtime came and still no Chunk. The next morning they looked outside hopefully. No sign of the old collie.

Time came for Uncle Eddie to return to the fields to work. There, in a distant field he saw something lying on the ground—his forgotten coat. And beside it lay Chunk, head and ears up, his plumed tail thumping the ground in the eager welcome.

That was years ago.

Tonight, as I sit on the porch, our old German shepherd is lying at my feet. He lifts his great head as a low mutter of thunder rumbles in the distance, and gives a deep warning bark. Then as the storm nears he rises with a lurch and tears into the front yard to meet it. The yard is a brief ledge confined by an old rail fence, beyond which it falls precipitously down a bank and is engulfed by the encroaching woods.

The storm is on us, the great dog furiously doing battle with it. As it passes, he returns to the porch, settling contentedly at my feet convinced he has driven it away.

He is a German guard dog, given to us years ago by concerned friends. He had been carefully trained in search and rescue, attack, and obedience.

Search and rescue in these mountains can come in handy. Previous dogs of ours had been used successfully for that purpose.

I cannot imagine an occasion when we would give the order to attack. But a well-trained dog can sense hostility or spot a weapon (or even what resembles a weapon), in which case it's a wise person who freezes in his tracks.

But it's the obedience training that gives us real joy. To stop, to sit, to lie down, to go away, to search, to stay, to heel. A disobedient dog is not only a headache; he can be a liability. Obedience makes a dog a joy.

Is it less so with God and His children?

There are some I know who have been trained in attack. We will not mention names. You may know a few. But they are skilled at it.

Then there are those trained in search and rescue. (I'd put the Salvation Army in this group.)

And there are those who have been trained in obedience.

I think this, more than anything else, must give the Lord pleasure. Simple obedience. Joyful, eager, unquestioning obedience; to be able to say with the psalmist, *"I delight to do thy will, O my God,"* would be the height of training for the Christian.

For it is this that gives God the greatest pleasure.

HONEY, I'M PROUD
OF YOU

LYDIA E. HARRIS

For twenty-six years I saw my husband, Milt, as quiet and unassuming, so it surprised me when he announced his plan. "I'm going to organize a prayer gathering at work for the National Day of Prayer."

I was proud of his courage to try something new; proud of his bold allegiance to God; and proud of his example for our children.

He chose the time—noon, the place—the flagpole outside his six-story building. He advertised the event, pinning computer-made flyers on the bulletin boards throughout the building. Together we prayed that others would notice the posters and join him to pray.

"Who are the Christians at this large company?" we wondered. "With hundreds of employees, surely there are other Christians who want to participate. Could this be the beginning of a regular prayer time or Bible study?"

The National Day of Prayer arrived. Throughout the morning I prayed, "Lord, please send others to pray with Milt. Don't let him stand there alone. I don't want him to feel discouraged or embarrassed."

As Milt walked through our front door that evening, I greeted him with eager questions. "What happened? How many came?"

"There were three besides me," he replied with a grin.

"That's great! Who were they?"

His answer startled me, "The Father, Son, and Holy Spirit."

I was proud of my husband that day and still am. I admire him for praying alone in a public place while others scurried by. His insight taught me a valuable lesson: We are never alone. The triune God is always with us.

A weary Christian lay awake one night
trying to hold the world together by his worrying.
Then he heard the Lord gently say to him,
"Now you go to sleep, Jim, I'll sit up."

RUTH BELL GRAHAM
FROM *PRODIGALS AND THOSE WHO LOVE THEM*

TURNING POINT

BILL BUTTERWORTH
FROM *WHEN LIFE DOESN'T TURN OUT LIKE YOU PLANNED*

*W*ithout question, a real turning point for me in my spiritual journey came the Sunday of the first Christmas I was single again. What had always been the highlight of the year, December 25, was now an awkward occasion of negotiating 'who had whom' from 'when to when' and how to best handle the minutiae of keeping Christmas special to the kids when inside I was a broken-hearted wreck.

As I walked into the sanctuary that Sunday before Christmas, the room was warmly decorated with wreaths and ribbons and lanterns. The central focus, however, was a life-size manger, placed on the floor in front of the pulpit. Real straw was brimming from the four sides of the manger, and it wonderfully re-created what the Christ-child must have lain in on that cold winter's night.

When Ed stood up to preach that morning, I had already wept quietly several times as we sang a procession of well-known Christmas carols. Each song was pregnant with memories of Christmases past, when everything in the world was so much better.

I wonder what Ed will say this year? I found myself thinking before he began. There are only so many ways you can find meaning in gold, frankincense, and myrrh, for example, and no room at the inn only can go so far in its practical application.

Ed chose to go deeper into Luke's gospel account, later in the life of Christ. He chose as his text a verse from the fourth chapter, when Jesus was actually a grown man. But it was a verse that was especially relevant to the Christmas season.... Isaiah had spoken those words centuries before in prophecy of the coming Messiah.

> *The Spirit of the Lord God is upon me,*
> *Because the* LORD *has anointed me*
> *to bring good news to the afflicted;*
> *He has sent me to bind up the brokenhearted,*
> *To proclaim liberty to captives,*
> *And freedom to prisoners.*
>
> ISAIAH 61:1, NAS

When Ed finished reading Isaiah's words, it was as if there was no longer anyone else in the worship service. I felt as if he were speaking directly to me and me alone. He chose to zero in on a key-phrase—"He sent me to bind up the brokenhearted."

"Is this year a difficult Christmas for you?" Ed asked. "Are you brokenhearted over a circumstance that has left you in great pain?"

Tears were streaming down my cheeks as I knew that this was a message from God for me. All that moisture dripping down onto my lap was silently answering Ed, "Yes...yes...I am brokenhearted."

Meanwhile Ed had moved from his position behind the pulpit to a place in front of it. Standing over the manger, he crouched down and said, "If you're here in deep pain, I want you to do something for me. I invite you to leave your burden here in the manger. For remember, Jesus Christ has come to mend that which is torn inside of you. He has come to bind up your broken heart."

I don't remember much of what happened after that, except that in my soul, I gave Christ all the pain my crisis had created. It wasn't the sort of thing that was accompanied by harps, strings, or chills up the spine, but it was an awesomely moving encounter for me. In many ways, it was like nothing I had ever experienced.

Christmas was bearable, thanks to Him who had come to bind up my broken heart. I was so grateful that I had made this discovery at what could have been the most awful time of the year.

A coincidence is a small miracle
where God chose to remain anonymous...

HEIDI QUADE

WHEN THE LORD SAYS PRAY!

CHERI FULLER
FROM *WHEN FAMILIES PRAY*

*T*he missionary rose from his campsite where he had spent the night enroute to a city for medical supplies. He extinguished his small campfire, pulled on his canvas backpack, and hopped on his bicycle to continue his ride through the African jungle. Every two weeks he made this two-day journey to collect money from a bank and purchase medicine and supplies for the small field hospital where he served. When he completed those errands, he hopped on his bike again for the two-day return trip.

When the missionary arrived in the city, he collected his money and medical supplies and was just about to leave for home when he saw two men fighting in the street. Since one of the fighters was seriously injured, the missionary stopped, treated him for his injuries, and shared the love of Christ with him. Then the missionary began his two-day trek home, stopping in the jungle again to camp overnight.

Two weeks later, as was his custom, the missionary again made the journey to the city. As he ran his various errands, a young man approached him—the same man the missionary had ministered to during his previous trip. "I knew you carried money and medicine with you," the man said, "so my friends and I followed you to your campsite in the jungle after you helped me in the street. We planned to kill you and take all the money and drugs. But just as we were about to move in and attack you, we saw twenty-six armed guards surround and protect you."

"You must be mistaken," said the missionary. "I was all alone when I spent the night in the jungle. There were no guards or anyone else with me."

"But sir, I wasn't the only one who saw the guards. My five companions saw them, too. We counted them! There were twenty-six bodyguards, too many for us to handle. Their presence stopped us from killing you."

Months later, the missionary related this story to the congregation gathered at his home church in Michigan. As he spoke, one of the men listening stood up and interrupted him, wanting to know the exact day the incident in the jungle had occurred. When the missionary identified the specific month and day of the week, the man told him "the rest of the story."

"On the exact night of your incident in Africa, it was morning here in Michigan, and I was on the golf course. I was about to putt when I felt a strong urge to pray for you. The urge was so strong, I left the golf course and called some men of our church right here in this sanctuary to join me in praying for you. Would all you men who prayed with me that day stand up?"

One by one the missionary counted the men. There were twenty-six of them, the exact number of "armed guards" the thwarted attackers had seen guarding him!

YOU'LL FIND
PATIENCE

CLARK COTHERN

· FROM *At the Heart of Every Great Father*

*M*urle ducked his head a bit and fiddled with his ever-present white handkerchief as he responded to the pastor's request. The proposition now on the table wasn't at all what the sixty-five-year-old retiree had in mind.

"Yeah, I know I told you I'd help anywhere I could," Murle admitted, "but…" he left the sentence unfinished, flapping his arms in consternation, unaware that he was waving the hanky like a flag of surrender.

"Pastor, I brought up a couple of *girls*—grown-ups now. I'm not sure I'd know what to do with a bunch of these little fellers."

His eyes had that trapped-animal look. He was obviously searching for a way out of the cage in which he suddenly found himself.

Pastor Jim, however, wasn't about to let his friend off the hook. "All you have to do," he said, "is treat those boys like you were treated by your dad when he took you fishing. C'mon, Murle. Whatd'ya say?"

"There's not enough room in my boat for very many." Murle wiped his forehead, casting this one last excuse as bait, hoping the pastor would bite.

No sale.

"Just take 'em two at a time," Jim said without hesitation.

"Dang it, you've thought of everything, haven't you?" Murle chuckled in spite of himself.

"Well? Will you do it?"

"Oh shoot, Pastor, I *suppose* so—for what good it might do." And then he threw in, "All except that Sammy kid." Murle felt sure the pastor would understand about him.

Jim flashed a knowing grin. He knew about Sammy.

"You just start taking them two by two, and we'll pray about little Sammy," said the younger man with a twinkle in his eye.

Murle made good on his promise. He began taking the boys out, two at a time. Many of the young fishermen had very little dad influence in their homes. Murle provided a touch of manhood in the lads' lives.

Six weeks after he began filling his Saturdays with bluegill, bass, and boys, Murle stood in the church office, nervously swiping the beads of perspiration on his forehead as he spoke to the pastor. "He just came runnin' up after church this morning."

"Who did, Murle?" asked Jim, watching the hanky dab at the old gent's shiny head.

"That Sammy kid! He said the other boys had all got a chance and could he please have a chance, too?" Up went the handkerchief.

Pastor Jim raised an eyebrow and smiled. "Oh, the fishing trips. And Sammy wants to go, too, huh? Well…what do you think?"

Down went the hanky, crumpled into a ball. Murle shook his head. "I dunno, Pastor. You know this one. He's enough trouble by himself to sink two boats!"

"You pray about it and then do what you think best, Murle." Jim smiled as he gave his friend a couple of solid pats on the shoulder. He turned to walk away.

"Pastor!" Murle called, stuffing the hanky in his back pocket.

"Yes?" Jim stopped in the doorway.

"Okay, okay, I'll take him…but by himself. With him, one's enough!"

"Good, Murle. Good."

*S*aturday morning a screech of tires sent Jim bolt upright in his chair at the church office.

He left his sermon notes and was headed toward the parking lot when Murle burst through the door at the end of the long hallway, huffing and puffing. All the way down the hall, he kept muttering, "He did it. He *did* it!"

"Who did what, Murle?" Jim knew his friend was flustered because he'd left his pickup truck so fast he had forgotten his handkerchief.

"Little Sammy. He DID it. I can't believe it." The old man was pacing back and forth, rubbing his hands up and down the sides of his jeans.

"Murle, take a couple of nitros and calm down. What did he do? You haven't even gotten out of the parking lot yet."

"I know, I *know*. The little minnow just blurted out and asked me *how does a kid get saved?* You know—as in eternal life!"

"And...what did you say?"

"Well, I told him you have to tell Jesus you're a good-for-nothin' sinner and ask forgiveness for your sins and ask Jesus to come into your life and be the Boss."

"That's fine, Murle. You told him the right thing. But I don't understand—why did you slam on the brakes?"

"Well, the little rug rat got right down on his knees on the floorboard of my truck and started confessin' every bad thing he's ever done since he can remember! He's still at it out there!" Murle waved his hand vaguely toward the parking lot.

Pastor Jim laughed as he walked Murle out to the parking lot, where, together, they knelt with little Sammy and gave thanks to God that he had found a family. The little lad without much dad influence had just become the Father's child. And all because Murle gave a sacrificial gift of time to a young boy.

*L*ittle Sammy grew up to become a sportswriter for a prominent Florida newspaper. Years after his parking-lot confession, Sammy wrote a special column for the paper's Father's Day issue.

It was a tribute to a man named Murle.

Later still, after many such fishing trips, Murle entered eternity. At his memorial service, Sammy, now grown and with kids of his own, stood behind a pulpit and read a tribute to his friend.

It was the article he had written years earlier for a certain Father's Day. The title? "Change a little boy's life. Take him fishing."

Murle's life demonstrated that patience has its rewards.

It is the essence of faith to let God be God.

JON SOBRINO

A RESTING PLACE

MAYO MATHERS

FROM *TODAY'S CHRISTIAN WOMAN* MAGAZINE

The headlights of my car were overpowered by the dense black night as I crept along the mountain road. I peered through the rain-splattered windshield, unsure if my tears or the rain were making visibility so difficult.

Oh, God, why did this happen? I cried. I was returning from a visit with my parents and single younger sister who live several hours away. My sister had been severely brain-injured in a drunk driving accident eighteen months ago. Since then, I'd grabbed at every tiny sign of progress, full of irrational hope for her recovery. But on this visit, I was forced to face reality. My sister would never recover. For the rest of her life, she would require constant care.

Grief consumed me as I twisted my way through the mountain pass. Shifting to a lower gear, I heard a loud *thunk*. Startled, I tried to shift into a different gear, but nothing happened. The car slowed to a standstill along the edge of the road.

Swallowing back fear, I locked the car and walked toward a gleam of light tucked back in the towering pine trees. It turned out to be the window of a small cottage. I approached the porch cautiously, hesitant to knock on an unfamiliar door late at night.

In response to my timid rap, the door swung open to reveal a middle-aged man. "Come in!" he welcomed. I hovered near the door, explained about my car, and asked to use his phone. When I dug out my calling card, he objected. "Your call's on me. I get lots of stranded people knocking on my door out here. It's my way of helping."

My phone call to my husband went unanswered, so I asked the man if he knew of a motel nearby. "No motels," he said, "but I have an idea."

Before I knew it, I was handed over to the elderly owner of a nearby fishing lodge who had a room available. She, too, refused to take money from a stranded traveler.

The "room" actually was a cabin with one entire wall of glass overlooking a magnificent rushing river. A plump couch and chair faced a fireplace where a fire was laid, just waiting for me to strike a match.

Sitting there, warmed by the fire and relaxed by the sound of tumbling water, I opened my Bible to Psalm 139. By the third verse, my tears splashed onto the page. "You chart the path ahead of me and tell me where to stop and rest. Every moment you know where I am" (TLB).

As I contemplated the words, God spoke to my heart. *From the beginning, I knew everything that would be in your path. I'll give you the strength to endure your sister's tragedy, and I'll guide you through your sorrow—but tonight, stop and rest with me.*

Before I fell asleep, I called home to leave a message on the answering machine for my husband. "The car broke down on the mountain tonight. Please come and get me—but don't hurry. God and I are resting."

*Those who hope in the L*ORD *will renew their strength.*
They will soar on wings like eagles;
they will run and not grow weary,
they will walk and not be faint.

ISAIAH 40:31

ANGEL AT WORK?

BILLY GRAHAM
FROM *UNTO THE HILLS*

*T*he British express train raced through the night, its powerful headlight piercing the darkness. Queen Victoria was a passenger on the train.

Suddenly the engineer saw a startling sight. Revealed in the beam of the engine's light was a strange figure in a black cloak standing in the middle of the tracks and waving its arms. The engineer grabbed for the brake and brought the train to a grinding halt.

He and his fellow trainmen clambered down to see what had stopped them. But they could find no trace of the strange figure. On a hunch the engineer walked a few yards further up the tracks. Suddenly he stopped and stared into the fog in horror. A bridge had been washed out in the middle and ahead of them it had toppled into a swollen stream. If the engineer had not heeded the ghostly figure, his train would have plummeted down into the stream.

While the bridge and tracks were being repaired, the crew made a more intensive search for the strange flagman. But not until they got to London did they solve the mystery.

At the base of the engine's head lamp the engineer discovered a huge dead moth. He looked at it a moment, then on impulse wet its wings and pasted it to the glass of the lamp.

Climbing back in to his cab, he switched on the light and saw the "flagman" in the beam, seconds before the train was due to reach the washed-out bridge. In the fog, it appeared to be a phantom figure, waving its arms.

When Queen Victoria was told of the strange happening she said, "I'm sure it was no accident. It was God's way of protecting us."

No, the figure the engineer saw in the headlight's beam was not an angel…and yet God, quite possibly through the ministry of His unseen angels, had placed the moth on the headlight lens exactly when and where it was needed. Truly "He will command his angels concerning you to guard you in all your ways" (Psalm 91:11, NIV).

AN ICE CREAM SOLO

BARBARA BAUMGARDNER

I flunked my first night out alone—my first solo movie since I'd become a widow. It wasn't too hard buying the ticket and the popcorn. Even sitting alone in the big theater was all right. I became so engrossed in the movie that it surprised me when the lights came on and I discovered I was all by myself.

On my way to the car, the tears welled up. I didn't have anyone to have an after-the-show ice cream cone with. Suddenly that seemed very, very important.

I stepped through my garage door into the kitchen and burst into tears. Loudly, I wailed to God. "When is it going to end? How much longer, God, until I can learn to enjoy doing things without having a companion?" The waves of loneliness again washed over me and for a few minutes, I gave in to an incoming tide of sorrow.

When I stopped crying, I felt better but I still wanted some ice cream. Feeling a little foolish, I offered an invitation, "Lord, will you have some ice cream with me?"

Feeling even more foolish, I piled two cereal bowls high with rocky road ice cream from my freezer, and through the giggles asked myself, "I'm really doing this, aren't I?"

Outside on my deck, under a million blinking stars, I leisurely consumed the entire contents of both bowls, savoring each bite in the companionship of the Lord. And I was reminded of His promise, *"I will not leave you comfortless: I will come to you."*

In times of affliction
we commonly meet
with the sweetest experience
of the love of God.

JOHN BUNYAN

YOUR ABBA'S ARMS

MAX LUCADO
FROM *THE GREAT HOUSE OF GOD*

*S*ome time back, my daughter Jenna and I spent several days in the old city of Jerusalem. One afternoon, as we were exiting the Jaffa gate, we found ourselves behind an Orthodox Jewish family—a father and his three small girls.

One of the daughters, perhaps four or five years of age, fell a few steps behind and couldn't see her father.

"*Abba!*" she called to him. He stopped and looked. Only then did he realize he was separated from his daughter.

"*Abba!*" she called again. He spotted her and immediately extended his hand. She took it and I took mental notes as they continued. I wanted to see the actions of an *abba*.

He held her hand tightly in his as they descended the ramp. When he stopped at a busy street, she stepped off the curb, so he pulled her back. When the signal changed, he led her and her sisters through the intersection. In the middle of the street, he reached down and swung her up into his arms and continued their journey.

Isn't that what we all need? An abba who will hear when we call? Who will take our hand when we're weak? Who will guide us through the hectic intersections of life? Don't we all need an abba who will swing us up into his arms and carry us home? We all need a father.

There's a God in heaven who wants you to call him your *abba*.

CIRCLE OF FAITH

DICK EASTMAN

FROM *EVERY HOME FOR CHRIST* MAGAZINE

Little ten-year-old Maria lived in a rural village in central Chile. When her mother died, Maria became the "woman of the house," caring for her father who worked the night shift at the local mine. Maria cooked and cleaned and made sure her father's lunch was ready when he left the house for work each evening.

Maria loved her father and was worried by how despondent he had become since her mother's death. Maria went to church on Sundays and tried to get her father to go with her, but he refused. His heart was too empty.

One evening, as Maria was packing her father's lunchbox, she slipped a gospel booklet inside that she had received from a missionary worker who had been distributing them home to home in the area where they lived. Maria prayed that her father would read the booklet and find the comfort she had found in God's great love.

It was 1:10 A.M. when Maria was suddenly awakened by a horrible sound—the emergency whistle at the mine was blaring through the darkness, calling the townspeople to come running with shovels and willing hands to help dig for miners caught in a cave-in.

Maria made her way through the streets to the mine in search of her father. Scores of men were frantically pulling debris away from the collapsed tunnel where eight men were trapped. One of the men was Maria's father.

Emergency crews worked through the night and finally broke through to a small cavern where they found the miners. Sadly, they were too late. All eight men had suffocated.

The rescue workers were devastated, but as they surveyed the scene, they noticed that the men had died, seated in a circle. As the workers looked closer they discovered Maria's father was sitting with a small gospel booklet in his lap opened to the last page where the plan of salvation was clearly explained. On that page, Maria's father had written a special message to his daughter:

> My darling Maria,
>
> When you read this, I will be with your mother in heaven. I read this little book, then I read it several times to the men while we waited to be rescued. Our hope is fading for this life, but not for the next. We did as the book told us and prayed, asking Jesus into our hearts. I love you very much, Maria, and one day soon, we will all be together in heaven.

God not only hears our words,
He listens to our hearts.

AUTHOR UNKNOWN

*Because
We Care*

BECAUSE WE CARE

Please take a moment to read out loud the verses written on the next page. Although there are hundreds of verses in the Bible that tell about God's love and His gift of salvation, We chose these from the book of Romans in the New Testament.

We care about what happens to you now, but I care even more about where you will spend eternity. If you have never asked Jesus Christ to be your Savior, please consider inviting Him into your life now.

Many years ago each of us at different times prayed a simple prayer that went something like this:

Dear Jesus,

> *I believe You are the Son of God and that You gave Your life as a payment for the sins of mankind. I believe You rose from the dead and You are alive today in heaven preparing a place for those who trust in You.*

> *I have not lived my life in a way that honors You. Please forgive me for my sins and come into my life as Savior and Lord. Help me grow in knowledge and obedience to You.*

> *Thank You for forgiving me. Thank You for coming into my life. Thank You for giving me eternal life. Amen.*

If you have sincerely asked Jesus Christ to be your Savior, He will never leave you or forsake you. Nothing—absolutely nothing—will be able to separate you from His love.

God bless you, dear one. We'll look forward to meeting you one day in heaven.

—ALICE AND BARBARA

For all have sinned and fall short of the glory of God.
ROMANS 3:23

For the wages of sin is death, but the gift of God
is eternal life in Christ Jesus our Lord.
ROMANS 6:23

But God demonstrates his own love toward us in this:
While we were still sinners, Christ died for us.
ROMANS 5:8

If you confess with your mouth, "Jesus is Lord," and believe
in your heart that God raised him from the dead, you will be saved.
For it is with your heart that you believe and are justified,
and it is with your mouth that you confess and are saved.
ROMANS 10:9–10

Everyone who calls on the name of the Lord will be saved.
ROMANS 10:13

I am convinced that neither death nor life,
neither angels nor demons,
neither the present nor the future,
nor any powers, neither height nor depth
nor anything else in all creation,
will be able to separate us from the love of God
that is in Christ Jesus our Lord.
ROMANS 8:38–39

Gentle Is a Grandmother's Love

stories compiled by Alice Gray,
illustrated by Paula Vaughan

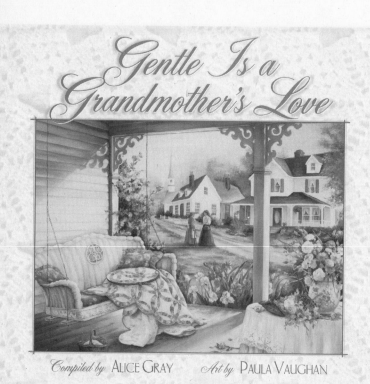

Enjoy the precious influences of a grandmother's love in these
touching stories compiled by Alice Gray. Filled with poignant,
heartwarming moments and enhanced by the lovely artwork of
Paula Vaughan, it will be a treasure you'll return to again and again.

ISBN 1-58860-048-3

Enjoy Reading with Alice Gray from Morning Coffee to Your Afternoon Cup of Tea!

**stories compiled by Alice Gray,
illustrated by Susan Mink Colclough**

Quiet Reflections Journal

Capture your heart's deepest desires and your unspoken dreams in the pages of this exquisite companion journal, sumptuously illustrated by Susan Mink Colclough. Lightly ruled and graced with inspirational quotes and Scripture...a lovely treasure in tandem with *Quiet Moments and a cup of Tea* and *Morning Coffee and Time Alone.*

Quiet Moments and a Cup of Tea

Alice Gray takes you on a quiet journey of faith, hope, and love through stories lavishly illustrated by Susan Mink Colclough. This book will be as cherished as the moments of serenity it offers.

Morning Coffee and Time Alone

Celebrates the morning and anticipates the blessings of each new day as you curl up with Alice Gray's treasure-trove of inspiring stories, Scriptures, and prose. Bringing bright promise of captured moments alone, this book is gracefully illustrated by the hand of Susan Mink Colclough.

ISBN 1-58860-009-2

ISBN 1-58860-008-4

ISBN 1-58860-007-6

The Fragrance of Friendship and A Pleasant Place

stories compiled by Alice Gray,
illustrated by Katia Andreeva

The Fragrance of Friendship

Katia Andreeva captures the lush beauty of fragrant gardens and the sweetness of the beloved bonds of friendship in this charming collection of inspirational quotes and stories. Compiled by Alice Gray, it encompasses the comfort of lifelong friendships and the joy of those found for the first time...a perfect means to express love to dear ones in your life.

ISBN 1-58860-005-X

A Pleasant Place

Alice Gray's compilation of heartwarming stories of goodness and cheer inspire you to spread some sunshine, like ripples in a pond...and be encouraged in the process. Elegantly illustrated in vivid watercolors by the gifted hand of Katia Andreeva.

ISBN 1-58860-006-8

The Stories for the Heart Series

compiled by Alice Gray

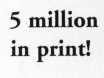

**5 million
in print!**

The Stories for the Heart Series

compiled by Alice Gray

ACKNOWLEDGMENTS

Stories included in this book were collected over a period of twenty years. More than a thousand books, magazines, and other sources were researched for this collection, as well as a review of hundreds of stories sent by friends and readers of the Stories of the Heart collection. A diligent search has been made to trace original ownership, and, when necessary, permission to reprint has been obtained. If I have overlooked giving proper credit to anyone, please accept my apologies. If you will contact Multnomah Publishers, Inc., Post Office Box 1720, Sisters, Oregon 97759, corrections will be made prior to additional printings. Please provide detailed information.

Notes and acknowledgments are listed by story title in the order they appear in each section of the book. For permission to reprint any of the stories, please request permission from the original source listed below. Grateful acknowledgment is made to authors, publishers, and agents who granted permission for reprinting these stories.

ENCOURAGEMENT

"When the Winds Are Strong" by Charles R. Swindoll from the July 1996 Insight for Living ministry letter. Used by permission of Insight for Living, Anaheim, CA 95806.

"The Gift" by Gary B. Swanson. Reprinted from the December 1997 issue of *Focus on the Family* magazine. Used with permission of Joe Wheeler, editor/compiler of *Christmas in My Heart vol. 6* and Review and Herald Publishing. Permission also granted by author, Gary B. Swanson.

"The Red Purse" by Louise Moeri. Reprinted from the July/Aug 1991 issue of *Virtue* magazine. Used with permission of the author who lives in Manteca, CA.

"Ice Cream Party" by Rochelle M. Pennington, freelance writer, newspaper columnist, and contributing author to *Stories for the Heart, Chicken Soup for the Soul,* and *Life's Little Instruction Book.* You may contact her at N1911 Double D Rd., Campbellsport, WI 53010, (920) 533-5880. Used with permission of the author.

"The Bunny and the Eggheads" by Ted Menten. Excerpt reprinted with permission from *Gentle Closings* by Ted Menten, © 1991 by Ted Menten, published by Running Press, Philadelphia and London.

"Molly" by Barbara Baumgardner. Reprinted from the December 17, 1999 Humane Society insert in *The Bulletin* newspaper, Bend, OR. Used by permission of the author.

"We All Need to Be Looked After" by Max Lucado from *In the Grip of Grace*, (© 1996, Word Publishing, Nashville, Tennessee.) All rights reserved.

"Love Letters" by Bob Welch from *Where Roots Grow Deep*, © 1999 by Bob Welch (Harvest House Publishers, Eugene, Oregon 97402). Used by permission.

"God Doesn't Make Nobodies" by Ruth Lee. Reprinted from the March 1998 issue of *Touch 1* magazine. Used by permission of the author. Ruth Lee writes fiction, poetry, and personal essays. Her work has been shared in a variety of publications.

"Overnight Guest" by Hartley F. Dailey from the February 1963 issue of *Sunshine* magazine. Used by permission.

"Unthanked People" by Steve Goodier © 1999. Used by permission of the author. Steve Goodier is the author of a free internet newsletter called *Your Life Support System* at www.lifesupportsystem.com.

"Angels Once in a While" by Barb Irwin who is a freelance writer. Used by permission of the author.

"Mrs. Warren's Class" by Colleen Townsend Evans. Reprinted from START LOVING: THE MIRACLE OF FORGIVING by Colleen Townsend Evans, © 1976 by Colleen Townsend Evans and Laura Hobe. Used by permission from Doubleday, a division of Random House, Inc.

"The Other Side of the Curtain" by Ruth Lee. Reprinted from the March 1998 issue of *Touch 1* magazine. Used with permission of the author. Ruth Lee writes fiction, poetry, and personal essays. Her work has been shared in a variety of publications.

FRIENDSHIP

"Mrs. Hildebrandt's Gift" by Robert Smith. Reprinted from the Feb/Mar 1994 issue of *Country* magazine. Used with permission of the author.

ACKNOWLEDGMENTS

"The Love Squad" by Virelle Kidder © 1999 Virelle Kidder; printed in *Decision* magazine, October 1999; published by the Billy Graham Evangelistic Association. Virelle Kidder is a full time writer, conference speaker, and host of a daily radio show. She is also the author of three books and a contributing writer for *Today's Christian Woman* magazine. Used by permission of the author.

"Luther's Lumber" by Joe Edwards, freelance writer in Springfield, MO. Used by permission.

"Treasure" verse by Paul Kortepeter. Used by permission of InterArt® Holding Corporation, Bloomington, IN.

"Reply to Box 222B" by Barbara Baumgardner. Reprinted from *Chicken Soup for the Single's Soul.* Used by permission of the author. Barbara has written two books, *A Passage Through Grief* and *A Passage Through Divorce,* both published by Broadman and Holman, Nashville, TN.

"Saving the Best for Last" by Rochelle M. Pennington, freelance writer, newspaper columnist, and contributing author to *Stories for the Heart, Chicken Soup for the Soul,* and *Life's Little Instruction Book.* You may contact her at N1911 Double D Rd., Campbellsport, WI 53010, (920)533-5880. Used with permission of the author.

"My Child, My Teacher, My Friend" by Gloria Gaither. Reprinted from the May/June 1990 issue of *Christian Herald* magazine. Used with permission of Gaither Copyright Management, Alexandria, IN.

"God, a Dog, and Me" by Deborah Hedstrom who is the author of 10 books and numerous articles. She lives in Salem, Oregon, and teaches writing at Western Baptist College. Used by permission of the author.

"Friendship Is a Diamond" by Sally J. Knower, © 1985. Used by permission.

"The Comfort Room" by Mayo Mathers. Reprinted from the Nov/Dec. 1997 issue of *Today's Christian Woman.* Used by permission of the author.

"Someone to Divide With" from *Tea Time with God,* © 1996 (Honor Books, Tulsa, OK 74155). Used with permission of the publisher.

"Empty Places Filled" by Chris Fabry. Reprinted from *At the Corner of Mundane and Grace,* © 1999 by Chris Fabry. Used by permission of WaterBrook Press, Colorado Springs, CO. All rights reserved.

LOVE

"The Wallet" by Arnold Fine who is the senior editor of *The Jewish Press*. Used by permission.

"Levi's Valentine" by J. Stephen Lang, reprinted from *Christian Reader,* March/April 2000. Used by permission of the author.

"I Love You Anyway" by Joe A. Harding. Used by permission of the author.

"Crumbling Sandcastles" by Sue Monk Kidd, reprinted from the July/Aug 1989 issue of *Today's Christian Woman*. Used with permission of the author. Sue Monk Kidd has authored six books, including *When the Heart Waits* and *The Dance of the Dissident Daughter* as well as other works of both fiction and nonfiction.

"Titanic Love" by Jim Priest, reprinted from *The Daily Oklahoman/Oklahoma City Times* where he is a newspaper columnist. This story won an outstanding merit award in the 1998 Amy Writing Awards. Used with permission of the author who has published a book, *Family Talk*. He and his wife, Diane, have two children and reside in Oklahoma City, OK.

"Where I Belong" by Bob Welch, reprinted from *Moody* magazine, September 1999. Used with permission of Bob Welch who is the author of *Where Roots Grow Deep* and *A Father for All Seasons,* both published by Harvest House.

"The Spirit of Sunshine" reprinted from *Ladies' Home Journal.*

"New Beginnings" by Patricia Wyman, reprinted from *Virtue* magazine, Mar/April 1997. Used with permission of the author who is retired after working as director of a school for handicapped children. She lives in Leominster, Massachusetts, with her two dogs.

"The Golden Crane" by Patricia Lorenz who is an internationally known inspirational, art-of-living writer. She is the author of *Stuff That Matters for Single Parents* and *A Hug a Day for Single Parents* and has had over 400 articles published in numerous magazines. For speaking engagements contact Associated Speakers, Inc. in Milwaukee, Wisconsin at 800-437-7577 or write to *Lorenz and Friends,* 7457 S. Pennsylvania, Oak Creek, WI 53154. Used by permission.

"Roses for Rose" by James A. Kisner who is the author of *Sweet Dreams and Tender Tears*. He is a modern day poet who writes about life and the joys and tribulations along the way. You can read many of his award winning poems on his Internet pages. For Web site address and book information, e-mail POPPYK1@aol.com.

"Life's Finest Hour" by Eugene S. Geissler, reprinted from *Ave Maria Press* © 1988 which drew the material from Eugene S. Geissler's book, *The Best Is Yet to Be*. Used by permission of the author.

"Rudy's Angel" by Wilma Hankins Hlawiczka, reprinted from *Chicken Soup for the Single Soul*. Used with permission of the author, © 1999.

INSPIRATION

"Ol' Ed Never Forgot" by Max Lucado from *In the Eye of the Storm*, © 1991 Word Publishing, Nashville, Tennessee. All rights reserved.

"Better Than a Trophy" by Grace Witwer Housholder (www.funnyKids.com) is an author, journalist, and mother of four. She lives in Kendsville, Indiana. The umpire in the story is Brian Allen. Used by permission.

"Love and the Cabbie" by Art Buchwald, © 1992. Used by permission of the author.

"We Could Have Danced All Night" by Guy Doud from *Molder of Dreams,* a Focus on the Family book published by Tyndale House, © 1990 by Guy Doud. All rights reserved. International copyright secured. Used by permission.

"Turn About" by Steven J. Lawson from *Absolutely Sure*, © 1999 by Steve Lawson. Used by permission of Multnomah Publishers, Inc.

"Johnny" by Barbara A. Glanz, CSP, from *Care Packages for the Workplace—Dozens of Little Things You Can Do to Regenerate Spirit at Work,* by Barbara A. Glanz, CSP, McGraw-Hill, © 1996. She is also the author of *CARE Packages for the Home,* Andrews McMeel, © 1998. Barbara is an international speaker and uses "Johnny" as one of the signature stories in her presentations. You can reach her at 4047 Howard Avenue, Western Springs, IL 67055; phone 708-246-8594; fax 708-246-5123, e-mail bglanz@baraglanz.com; Web site www.barbaraglanz.com.

"The Aroma of Christmas" by Barbara Baumgardner, reprinted from the December 9, 1984, issue of *Lookout*. Used with permission of the author who lives in Bend, Oregon. Her book, *A Passage Through Grief: An Interactive Journal* is a journaling program for the bereaved.

"Glory in the Morning" by Linda Andersen who is an inspirational author published in 300 articles and is the author of three books. She is the editor of *Stillwater Sampler* newsletter. Linda lives with her husband, Roy, in Hamilton, MI. Used by permission, © 1986.

"A Little Girl's Dream" by Jann Mitchell, *Oregonian* columnist, lecturer, and author of *Home Sweeter Home* and *Love Sweeter Love*. Reach her at 503-221-8516 or jannmitchell@news.oregonian.com.

"You Don't Bring Me Flowers Anymore" from *More of Bits and Pieces*.

"The Cellist of Sarajevo" by Paul Sullivan, pianist and composer, Blue Hill Falls, Maine. Reprinted with permission of the author and the November 1996 *Reader's Digest*.

"The Baby Blanket" by Winona Smith. Used with permission of the author, © 1998

FAMILY

"Tribute" by Pamela McGrew. Used by permission of the author, © 2000.

"The Night the Stars Fell" by Arthur Gordon. Reprinted from *A Touch of Wonder* by Arthur Gordon, Fleming H. Revell, a division of Baker Book House Company, © 1974. Used with permission.

"The Jewelry Box" by Faith Andrews Bedford who writes for numerous magazines, especially *Country Living,* where her column, "Kids in the Country" appears regularly. She is the author of *Frank W. Benson: American Impressionist* and *The Sporting Art of Frank W. Benson*. Used by permission.

"Through a Father's Eyes" by Lonni Collins Pratt, reprinted from *Moody* magazine, September 1992. Used with permission of the author.

"Favorite Child" by Erma Bombeck from *Forever, Erma* © 1996 by the estate of Erma Bombeck, Universal Press Syndicate. All rights reserved. Used by permission.

ACKNOWLEDGMENTS

"A Good Heart to Lean On" by Augustus J. Bullock from *The Wall Street Journal*, June 11, 1997. Used by permission.

"A Mother's Prayer" by Marguerite Kelly from THE MOTHER'S ALMANAC by Marguerite Kelly and Elia Parsons, © 1975 by Marguerite Kelly and Elia Parsons. Used with permission from Doubleday, a division of Random House, Inc.

"New Ground" by Margaret Becker from *With New Eyes*, © 1998 by Margaret Becker, published by Harvest House Publishers, Eugene, OR 97402. Used by permission.

"The Costume" by Bill Butterworth. Reprinted from *Moody* magazine, June 1991. Used by permission of the author.

"The Redhead and the Brunette" by John William Smith from *Hugs for Mom,* © 1997 by Howard Publishing Co., Inc., West Monroe LA, 800-858-4109.

"Old Doors" by Carla Muir. Used by permission.

"Award Ceremony" by P. R. from *Sons: A Father's Love* by Bob Carlisle, © 1999, Word Publishing, Nashville, Tennessee. All rights reserved.

"Daddy Hands" by Susan Fahncke. 1325 North Highway 89, Suite 315F, Farmington, UT 84025. Web site: www.fawnkey.com, e-mail:xox-osooz@fawnkey.com. Used by permission of the author, © 1999.

"A Matter of Pride," by Terry L. Pfleghaar, reprinted from the February 1995 issue of *HomeLife* magazine. Besides writing and parenting, Terry works at her local public library and is attending a university. Anna, now ten years old, is trying to grow her hair out. Used by permission of author.

MEMORIES

"Their Best" by Connie Lounsbury from the Oct/Nov. 1999 issue of *Lifewise* magazine. Connie Lounsbury is a freelance writer who frequently writes for *Guideposts*. She lives in rural Monticello, Minnesota, with her husband David. They have four daughters and nine grandchildren. Used with permission of the author.

"A Pair of Worn Out Shoes" by Thelda Bevens who lives in Bend, Oregon. Used by permission of the author.

"The Rich Family" by Eddie Ogan, reprinted from April/May 1999 issue of *Virtue* magazine. Used with permission of the author.

"When Strangers Passed Through" by Ruth Lee, reprinted from *Gospel Publishing*, January 25, 1998. Used with permission of the author. Ruth Lee's essays, fiction and poetry, have appeared in a variety of publications. She is a seven times first place award winning member of Missouri Writer's Guild.

"The Little Apron" by Charlene Ann Baumbich from *Mama Said There'd Be Days Like This*, © 1995 by Charlene Ann Baumbich. Published by Servant Publications, Box 8617, Ann Arbor, Michigan 48107. Used with permission. Charlene is an author, speaker, and humorist; www.dontmissyourlife.com

"The Etching" by Barbara Baumgardner. Used with permission from the author.

"Lilacs to Remember" by Faith Andrews Bedford who writes for numerous magazines, especially *Country Living*, where her column, "Kids in the Country" appears regularly. She is the author of *Frank W. Benson: American Impressionist* and *The Sporting Art of Frank W. Benson*. Used by permission.

"My Mother's Gloves" by Sharron Dean McCann, reprinted from the Sept/Oct 1992 issue of *Virtue* magazine. Used by permission of author who lives in Grand Marais, MN.

"Porch Swing" by Brenda A. Christensen. Used by permission.

"The Barn" by Sharron Dean McCann. Used by permission.

LIFE

"Stepping Stones" by Gail Brook Burket. Used by permission of the estate of Gail Brook Burket.

"A Light in the Window" by Faith Andrews Bedford who writes for numerous magazines, especially *Country Living*, where her column, "Kids in the Country" appears regularly. She is the author of *Frank W. Benson:*

American Impressionist and *The Sporting Art of Frank W. Benson.* Used by permission.

"Creature Comfort" by Bill Holton, reprinted by courtesy of *PetLife* magazine, published by Magnolia Media Group, Fort Worth, TX.

"A Mailbox Mercy" by Nancy Jo Sullivan from *Moments of Grace,* © 2000 by Nancy Jo Sullivan. Used by permission of Multnomah Publishers, Inc.

"Front Porch Swing" by Kim Engstrom. Used by permission of the author, © 1999.

"Laughter and Life Jackets" by N. C. Haas. The author, writing under the pen name N. C. Haas, is a freelance writer living in Southern California. She can be contacted through WORDable SOLUTIONS, (714)775-6705, or by e-mail at: armhumber@aol.com.

"Growing Older" by Dale Evans Rogers from *Time Out, Ladies!* Fleming H. Revell, a division of Baker Book House Company, © 1966. Used by permission.

"The Faith of a Child" by Deborah Hammons, reprinted from the Sept/Oct 1994 issue of *Virtue* magazine. Used with permission from the author who currently teaches high school English. Deborah has written and produced over seventy TV shows on the extraordinary people of Wyoming.

"Breaking Up Grandma" by Marjorie Maki from *For She Is the Tree of Life* by Valerie Kack-Brice, © 1995 by Valerie Kack-Brice, by permission of Conari Press.

"The Fox and the Writer" by Philip Yancey, reprinted from the September 7, 1998, issue of *Christianity Today.* Used by permission of the author.

"To God from Ben" by Glenda Barbre from *Christian Reader* magazine, September/October 1996. Used by permission of the author.

"Choirs of Angels" by Cheryl Gochnauer who is the author of *So You Want to Be a Stay-at-Home Mom.* She also writes *Homebodies,* a weekly newspaper column and online ministry (www.homebodies.org) for family-focused women.

"Tornado Warning" by Sarah E. Farrow, reprinted from the June/July 1999 issue of *Virtue* magazine. Used by permission of the author who lives with her husband of 32 years in Colorado.

"Sharing," author unknown. Reprinted from *You Gotta Keep Dancin'* by Tim Hansel.

FAITH

"Trusting God" by Verdell Davis from *Let Me Grieve, But Not Forever,* Word Publishing, Nashville, Tennessee. All rights reserved.

"Heaven's Gold" by Rhonda Reese from *Christian Reader* magazine, Nov/Dec 1998. Used by permission of the author.

"An Empty Chair" by Walter Burkhardt from *Tell the Next Generation,* Paulist Press, Ramsey NJ, © 1982. Used by permission.

"Spirit Renewed" by Barbara Baumgardner from *RV Companion* magazine, November/December 1999, P.O. Box 174, Loveland, CO 80539. Used by permission.

"Tommy" by John Powell from *The Challenge of Faith,* Thomas Moore Press, © 1998. Used by permission.

"Giving God Pleasure" by Ruth Bell Graham from *Legacy of a Pack Rat,* Thomas Nelson Publishers, Nashville TN, © 1989. Used by permission of the author.

"Honey, I'm Proud of You" by Lydia E. Harris, MA, who is a freelance writer living in Seattle, Washington, with Milt, her husband of 32 years. She has two adult children and one grandson.

"Turning Point" by Bill Butterworth, from *When Life Doesn't Turn Out Like You Planned,* Thomas Nelson, Nashville TN, © 1995. Used with permission from author.

"When the Lord Says Pray!" by Cheri Fuller from *When Families Pray,* © 1999 by Cheri Fuller. Used by permission of Multnomah Publishers, Inc.

"You'll Find Patience" by Clark Cothern from *At the Heart of Every Great Father,* © 1998 by Clark Cothern. Used by permission of Multnomah Publishers, Inc.

ACKNOWLEDGMENTS

"A Resting Place" by Mayo Mathers reprinted from the Sept/Oct 1995 issue of *Today's Christian Woman*. Used by permission of the author who lives in Bend, Oregon, with her husband, Steve. They are the parents of two sons.

"Angel at Work?" by Billy Graham from *Unto the Hills*, © 1996, Word Publishing, Nashville, Tennessee. All rights reserved.

"An Ice Cream Solo" by Barbara Baumgardner who is a hospice volunteer which laid the foundation for her first book, *A Passage Through Grief: An Interactive Journal*. A year later, *A Passage Through Divorce* was published. She can be contacted by e-mail at barbarab@empnet.com. Used by permission of the author.

"Your Abba's Arms" by Max Lucado from *The Great House of God*, © 1993, Word Publishing, Nashville, Tennessee. All rights reserved.

"Circle of Faith" by Dick Eastman from the August 1999 issue of *Every Home for Christ*, P.O. Box 35930, Colorado Springs, CO 80935-3593.